Breaking through the glass ceiling
Women in management

BREAKING through the
glass ceiling

Women in management

Linda Wirth

INTERNATIONAL LABOUR OFFICE · GENEVA

Wirth, Linda
Breaking through the glass ceiling: Women in management
Geneva, International Labour Office, 2001

Woman manager, woman worker, professional worker, labour market segmentation, career development, equal employment opportunity, equal treatment, sex discrimination, developed country, developing country.
14.04.2

ISBN 92-2-110845-7

ILO Cataloguing-in-Publication Data

Photocomposed in Switzerland   BRI
Printed in Switzerland   SRO

PREFACE

We have made significant progress in advancing gender equality in recent decades. Globally, women's labour force participation has increased. Women around the world have been moving steadily into occupations, professions and managerial jobs previously reserved for men. Their access to education and training continues to improve, providing many with the necessary qualifications to aspire to jobs in senior management. Spurred on by women's movements worldwide, governments, businesses, trade unions and civil society organizations have devoted much thought and energy to overcoming troubling and persistent gender inequalities. Every major United Nations conference repeats our global commitment to achieving gender equality. But many of the results fall short of expectations.

At the ILO, we are especially concerned by the patterns of attitudinal and institutional discrimination that continue to bar women from certain jobs and hinder their career development. Occupational segregation by sex persists — as do social policies based on a traditional model of the family with a male breadwinner. We also see that females occupy few of the positions with the most power. Real obstacles remain, and these are often rooted in the way work and life are organized. In most societies, men still have a disproportionate responsibility for meeting the financial needs of a family while women carry a larger responsibility for caregiving and family well-being. This means that the challenges for women in the world of work often revolve around balancing work and family commitments. Women are still concentrated in the most precarious forms of work throughout the world. They too often experience a "sticky floor" and too rarely break through the "glass ceiling". For women who also experience racial discrimination, the barrier to top jobs is even worse.

There is a growing awareness and mounting evidence that gender equality boosts enterprise productivity, spurs economic growth and improves the welfare of families. Today, the best organizations and firms depend on a balanced mix of so-called "masculine" and "feminine" attributes. An increasing number are adopting measures to attract and retain women so as to benefit from their qualifications and talent in a highly competitive environment. Increasing numbers of women are joining the paid workforce, as well as establishing and managing a growing proportion of businesses in many countries.

This book helps us to better understand the problems women face in rising through the ranks and securing top positions, and offers some useful strategies for shattering the glass ceiling. It builds on a report prepared to guide the discussions at a tripartite ILO meeting for the financial and professional services sector on women and management, held in Geneva in 1997.[1] It contains additional information on women in decision-making and in finance, including the banking sector, and expands on the issue of diversity management and the family. Examples and data have been updated as far as possible.

Chapter 1 examines current gender inequalities in the labour market and in political and social life. It focuses on women's participation in the workforce, occupational segregation, pay differentials and gender time division. Chapter 2 looks at the progress made by women in professional and managerial jobs. It presents statistics relating to their progress at top levels of the public service, in finance and banking, and in politics. Chapter 3 provides data on male and female participation in education and training. It discusses strategies to help women qualify for careers in management. The focus of Chapter 4 is on the obstacles to women's career development in the workplace. It discusses how and why men's and women's career paths differ and assesses possible strategies to tackle the obstacles to women's advancement. Chapter 5 reviews various national policies, programmes and initiatives to promote women in management. The final chapter deals with international action, in particular by the ILO, to promote equal employment opportunities.

Clearly, responsibility for equal opportunity cannot rest in the hands of isolated organizations or enterprises. Governments, employers' organizations, trade unions, civil society organizations and international organizations all need to move in the same direction, actively promoting gender equality in different areas and at different levels.

The ILO gives high priority to promoting gender equality in the world of work. A major concern is to ensure that we have the right labour market statistics, disaggregated by sex, that are needed to track progress and support initiatives worldwide. We also intend to support the process through the more effective use of gender-sensitive indicators, as well as data collection and dissemination on benchmarking and good practices.

Linda Wirth's book is a reflection of our commitment to providing a sound knowledge base on gender equality issues in the world of work. I am certain that everyone interested in and working to promote gender equality will welcome this publication.

Juan Somavia
Director-General
March 2001

---

[1] See ILO: *Breaking through the glass ceiling: Women in management*, report for discussion at the Tripartite Meeting on Breaking through the Glass Ceiling: Women in Management, Geneva, 1997.

CONTENTS

Figures

Tables

ACKNOWLEDGEMENTS

The information on which this book (and the original report) was based comes from a variety of sources. Extensive use was made of publications on women in management in many countries, as well as articles from scholarly journals and from the financial press. ILO publications were frequently consulted. Most of the figures are based on statistics collected by the ILO, UNESCO and other United Nations bodies. In addition, valuable information was supplied by ILO member States, employers' and workers' organizations, research institutions and women's associations, and ILO regional and subregional offices and multi-disciplinary advisory teams. This help is gratefully acknowledged.

I should especially like to thank Jane Zhang, Director of the ILO Bureau for Gender Equality, for her constant support and commitment. I also wish to thank the ILO colleagues who provided valuable assistance in the preparation of the book: Loretta de Luca, formerly of the Salaried Employees and Professional Workers Branch; Ann Herbert of the Conditions of Work Branch; Petra Ulshoefer of the Bureau for Gender Equality; Luesette Howell, formerly of the ILO Bureau of Employers' Activities; Amrita Sietaram of the ILO Bureau for Workers' Activities; Nadejda Veleva, external graphics consultant; and Dorothea Mahnke (an ILO intern who conducted further research on diversity management). Updating and expansion were carried out with the assistance of external consultant Joanna Jackson.

LIST OF ABBREVIATIONS

AFL-CIO	American Federation of Labor and Congress of Industrial Organizations
ASEAN	Association of Southeast Asian Nations
CAHRS	Centre for Advanced Human Resource Studies (United States)
CAPS	Chicago Area Partnerships
CEC	Chinese Employers' Confederation
CEDA	Chinese Enterprise Directors' Association
CEDAW	United Nations Committee on the Elimination of Discrimination against Women
CEO	chief executive officer
CHRC	Canadian Human Rights Commission
ECLAC	United Nations Economic Commission for Latin America and the Caribbean
EU	European Union
EUROSTAT	Statistical Office of the European Commission
EWL	European Women's Lobby
EWMD	European Women's Management Development Network
FAWE	Forum for African Women Educationalists
FTSE	*Financial Times Stock Exchange 100 Companies*
GDI	Gender-related Development Index (United Nations)
GEM	Gender Empowerment Measure (United Nations)
GNP	gross national product
HDI	Human Development Index
HEDCO	Higher Education for Development and Cooperation of Ireland
ICA	International Co-operative Alliance
IPO	initial public offering
IPU	Inter-Parliamentary Union
ISCE-93	International Classification of Status in Employment 1993
ISCED	International Standard Classification of Education
ISCO	International Standard Classification of Occupations
JIWE	Japan Institute of Women's Employment
MBA	master's degree in business administration
MERCOSUR	Mercado Común del Sur (Common Market of the Southern Cone)

NFLS	Nairobi Forward-looking Strategies for the Advancement of Women 1985
NFWBO	National Foundation for Women Business Owners (United States)
NGO	non-governmental organization
OECD	Organisation for Economic Co-operation and Development
SMEs	small and medium-sized enterprises
SNEF	Singapore National Employers' Federation
TQM	total quality management
TUC	Trades Union Congress (United Kingdom)
UIA	Unión Industrial Argentina
UIC-CFDT	Union des Ingènieurs et Cadres – Confédération Française Démocratique du Travail
UNDP	United Nations Development Programme
UNESCO	United Nations Educational, Scientific and Cultural Organization
UNICEF	United Nations Children's Fund
WAM	Women and Mathematics
WEDGE	Women's Entrepreneurship Development and Gender in Enterprise
WIM	Women's Institute of Management (Malaysia)
WIPL	Women in Public Life
WISE	Women into Science and Engineering

GENDER INEQUALITIES IN THE LABOUR MARKET AND IN SOCIETY

1

INTRODUCTION

"Glass ceiling" is a term coined in the 1970s in the United States to describe the invisible artificial barriers, created by attitudinal and organizational prejudices, which block women from senior executive positions. Whether this glass ceiling occurs in the workplace or in politics is essentially a reflection of social and economic gender inequality. With the achievement of educational parity and changes in social attitudes towards men's and women's roles, it had been somehow assumed that women would quickly move up the career ladder. This has proved hard to achieve and no more so than at the top, where the prevalence of male executives tends to perpetuate the glass ceiling and where women often find themselves without the right mix of corporate experience required for senior executive positions.

This chapter reviews some of the gender inequalities that lie behind the phenomenon of the glass ceiling. A major source of discrimination stems from strongly held attitudes towards women's and men's social roles and behaviour. If one compares the effective roles played by women and men rather than looking at women as an isolated group, it becomes apparent that each has different access to resources, work opportunities and status. The consequences of gender inequalities include women being "crowded" into a narrow range of occupations where there is less responsibility and/or lower pay, or having to work part time, where there are fewer opportunities for advancement. While this situation can be explained to some extent by men's and women's perceptions of their respective social roles, these roles have in fact been undergoing substantial changes in recent decades. Labour force participation patterns of men and women, and social attitudes, have been gradually evolving to reflect these.

Since the advent of the women's movement, changes in social acceptance of gender equality have been primarily due to changing perceptions among women and men themselves. The promulgation and enforcement of equal opportunity laws have not only lessened institutional discrimination; they have also had a considerable impact on the awareness of populations. In recent years, women's working lives have become characterized by more continuous labour force participation. Women have entered many of the professions previously reserved for men, and their earnings have become an essential part of household

Table 1.1.   Attitudes of men and women towards working women in the United
States, 1978, 1986 and 1995

Statement	Men/Women	Percentages that strongly agree with statement		
		1978	1986	1995
"In general, women have to be better performers	Women	72	84	77
than men in order to get ahead."	Men	27	31	31
"In general, women are penalized more	Women	38	45[1]	51
for mistakes than men."	Men	17	93[1]	13
"In general, men often exclude women	Women	67	61	65
from informal networks."	Men	59	53	35
"In general, women have an easier time finding	Women	54	81	76
a sponsor or mentor than men do."	Men	37	55	40
"In general, women received their present positions	Women	46[2]	42	25
because they are women."	Men	64[2]	62	39
"In general, women are not serious about	Women	6	18	3
their careers."	Men	17	25	6

[1] 1988 data.
[2] 1972 data.
Source: John P. Fernandez and Julie Davis: *Race, gender and rhetoric: The true state of race and gender relations in corporate America* (New York, McGraw-Hill, 1999), pp. 49 and 61.

income. These changes have led to shifts in societal views about the role of
women in the economy. Table 1.1 illustrates the growth in awareness between
1978 and 1995 of the existence of discrimination against working women in the
United States. A large percentage of those surveyed thought women have to
perform better than men to get ahead. On the other hand, the proportion of those
who believed women received their positions because they were women
decreased from 46 per cent in 1978 to 25 per cent in 1995.

A survey in Japan in the early 1990s showed increasing disagreement by
both men and women with the traditional belief that men should hold jobs and
women should stay at home and do housework.[1] In 1987, 50 per cent of men and
38 per cent of women thought that women should stay at home. By 1990, these
figures were 36 per cent and 24 per cent respectively.

WOMEN'S INCREASING PARTICIPATION IN THE LABOUR FORCE

Labour force feminization continues unabated. Figure 1.1 illustrates the
increases in women's economic activity rates over time from a global perspective
and from the perspective of less-developed and more-developed regions.

At the global level in 1990, 67 per cent of all women aged 20-54 were
economically active. By the year 2010, this figure is expected to reach almost
70 per cent. Regional figures produced by the ILO[2] revealed that in 2000, nearly
58 per cent of women were economically active in Africa, 64 per cent in Asia,
46 per cent in Latin America and the Caribbean, 69 per cent in Europe and 73 per
cent in North America. For the year 2010, these proportions are expected to

Figure 1.1.   Women's economic activity rates for the age group 20-54 in 1950, 1970, 1990 and 2010 (world, more-developed and less-developed regions)

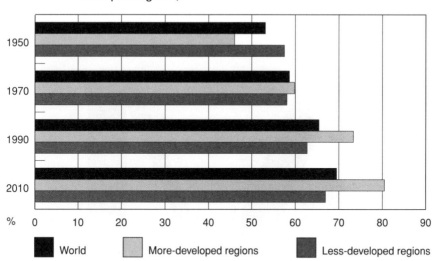

Source: ILO: *Economically Active Population, 1950-2010* (Geneva, 1997), pp. 23, 26 and 29.

remain the same for Asia, and rise by 1 per cent for Africa, Europe and North America, while in Latin America and the Caribbean, women's participation rates will increase by 4 per cent to 50 per cent.

Higher educational levels attained by women coupled with falling fertility rates, particularly in industrialized countries, are contributing to such increases in women's economic activity rates. Another marked trend is that of women spending more of their productive years in the workforce. Periods away from the labour force to give birth and care for children are becoming shorter. In the United States, for example, the proportion of working mothers with children under the age of 3 grew from 34 per cent in 1975 to 57 per cent in 1994,[3] while the percentage of working mothers with children less than a year old was 53.6 in 1998.[4] The labour force patterns of women in many countries are approaching that of men and this can be depicted graphically as an inverted U shape. Figure 1.2 shows how, at the global level, the classic M-shape of women's labour force participation is flattening out and rising. This development is particularly marked in industrialized countries, with the notable exception of Japan, where women have greatly increased their participation but still drop out of the labour force to care for children. In developing countries, the pattern varies from country to country as illustrated in figure 1.3 by the examples of Côte d'Ivoire and India.

Women's share in the labour force is also increasing worldwide, but at a slower pace than their participation rates. By the year 2010, their share will be just over 41 per cent, up from 38 per cent in 1970. In some regions, the increase

Figure 1.2.   M-shape

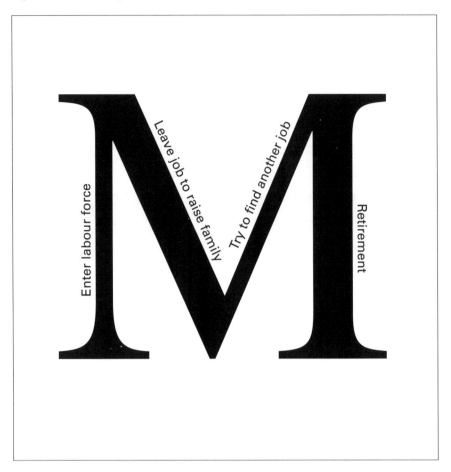

should be more significant (figure 1.4). By the year 2010 in Latin America, women are expected to account for almost 37 per cent of the labour force compared with 24 per cent in 1970. Over the same period, women's share of the job market in North America will grow from 36 per cent to 47 per cent, while in Oceania it is estimated to increase from 33 per cent to almost 45 per cent. In other regions increases should be less striking.[5]

WOMEN'S JOBS IN FLEXIBLE LABOUR MARKETS

Figures 1.3 and 1.4 illustrate the quantitative nature of women's ever-increasing participation in paid employment, but manifest gender inequalities exist in employment status and the quality of jobs held by men and women. Women often have part-time and temporary jobs, while men hold more of the well-paid

Figure 1.3.   Economic activity rates by sex and age group in 1950, 1970, 1990 and 2010 (world and selected countries)

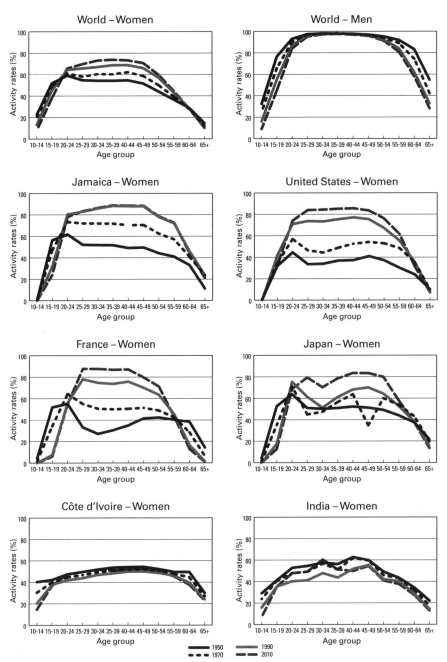

Source: ILO: *Economically Active Population, 1950-2010,* op. cit.

Figure 1.4.   Women's share in the labour force[1] in 1970, 1990, 2000 and 2010 (world and by region)

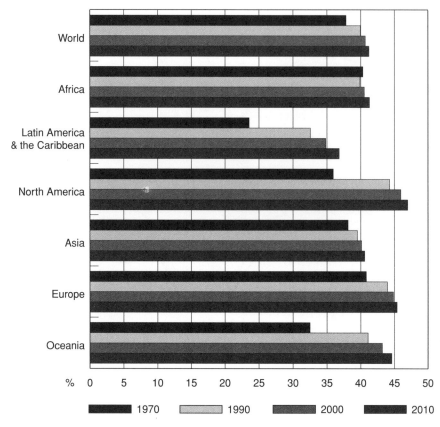

[1] Share as a percentage of economically active population.
Source: ILO: *Economically Active Population, 1950-2010,* op. cit., pp. 1-5.

and secure ones. Women make up the majority of part-time workers (between 60 and 90 per cent), and a large proportion of women who work do so on a part-time basis (figure 1.5). In developing countries, significant proportions of these women work in the informal sector or at home.

Nonetheless, a large proportion of women chooses to or is obliged to work part time because of family responsibilities. Part-time work for women is often triggered by motherhood, while for men it occurs more often in conjunction with labour market entry or exit. For women, the outcome of this labour market segmentation is lower income, limited access to qualified jobs and fewer opportunities for career development. However, the extent of women's part-time work depends not solely on the division of labour in the home but also on the interests and needs of business, and on labour market policies and regulation.[6]

Figure 1.5. Proportion of part-time workers compared with total
employment, 1996-97 (selected countries)

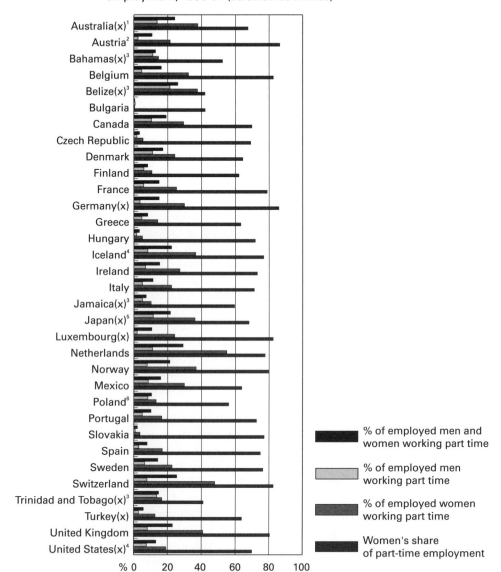

Notes: (x): the data are from 1996.
[1] Refers to actual hours worked. [2] Less than 36 hours. [3] The maximum hours that can be worked to still considered as a part-time worker vary from 32 to 35 hours per week. [4] Wage earners and salaried employees only. [5] Refers to actual hours worked (in ten thousands of persons). Less than 35 hours. [6] Includes those who during the reference period worked 39 hours or less for economic or non-economic reasons.
Source: ILO: *Key Indicators of the Labour Market* (Geneva, 1999), table 5, pp. 139-143.

Involuntary part-time work or time-related underemployment refers to those part-time workers who want and/or seek to work additional hours or who are unable to find full-time employment. This category also includes part- or full-time workers who, during the reference week, work fewer hours than a certain cut-off point, or who work fewer than usual hours for economic reasons. Figure 1.6 shows that women are to a much greater extent likely to find themselves belonging to this category and, accordingly, to the ranks of the underemployed. In general, they account for 50 per cent or more of the category than men do.[7]

Part-time work is not necessarily a secondary form of unemployment as such, but it can be less attractive because of the disadvantages linked to working part time over an extended period. Opportunities for training and promotion are often lost and pension entitlements are lower. Unemployment benefits and sick pay can also be affected.[8]

Differences in unemployment rates for men and women can also be an indicator of gender disparities in the labour market. Unemployment data for men and women point to a mixed pattern depending on the countries involved, and regional differences can be quite pronounced. For the 17 Latin America and Caribbean countries for which data were available for the years 1997-98, unemployment rates for women were higher than for men in 15 of these countries. Moreover, in at least half the countries, the rates for women were two to three times those of men. For 31 European countries, women's unemployment rates were higher than men's in 16 countries during the same period. For the few countries in Africa for which data were available, only Algeria had a lower unemployment rate in 1997 for women (24 per cent) than for men (26.9 per cent). Unemployment rates were considerably higher for women than men in Botswana (1995), Egypt (1995), Mauritius (1995) and Morocco (1996). By contrast, in Asia women had higher unemployment rates than men in only four out of 12 countries for which data were available in the years 1997-98.[9]

Overall, out of a total of 65 countries for which unemployment rates were available in the years 1997-98, some 13 countries had lower unemployment rates for women than men (Australia, Estonia, Hungary, Ireland, Kazakhstan, Lithuania, Poland, Republic of Korea, Russian Federation, Sweden, Turkey, Ukraine and the United Kingdom). In another set of 14 countries, there were only very slight differences between the unemployment rates for men and women during the same period (Azerbaijan, Bulgaria, Canada, Germany, Honduras, Japan, New Zealand, Norway, Philippines, Singapore, Slovenia, Tajikistan, Thailand and the United States).[10]

These data indicate significant gender differences in Africa and Latin America, with women having considerably higher unemployment rates than men. In Asia, unemployment rates tend to be higher for men or similar to those of women in those countries for which data were available (Azerbaijan, Israel, Japan, Kazakhstan, Mongolia, Philippines, Republic of Korea, Singapore, Sri Lanka, Tajikistan and Thailand). In Central and Eastern Europe, many of the countries have similar rates of unemployment for men and women or women

Figure 1.6.   Involuntary part-time work as a percentage of total
employment, 1993-95 or nearest year (selected countries and
areas)

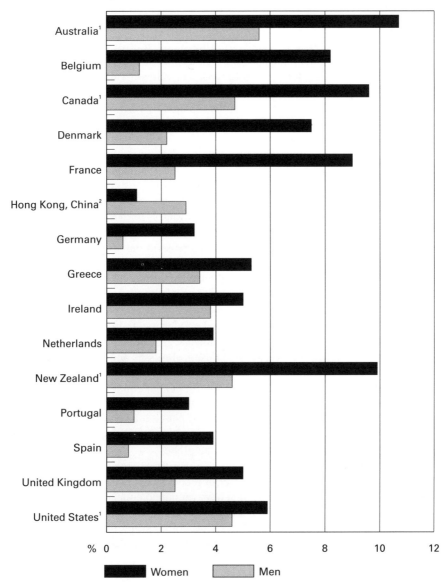

[1] Data are from 1993, and the hours per week are less than 30.   [2] The hours per week are less than 35.
Source: ILO: *Key Indicators of the Labour Market*, op. cit.

have lower rates than men. A notable exception is the Czech Republic, where the unemployment rate of women is 8.2 per cent while that of men is 5 per cent.[11]

MEN'S JOBS, WOMEN'S JOBS: OCCUPATIONAL SEGREGATION

In addition to gender differences in working time patterns, another factor that contributes to gender inequality is that men and women perform different jobs and so-called "women's jobs" are often assigned a lower value in terms of skill requirements and remuneration. Developments in job evaluation methodologies have often demonstrated that many jobs occupied by women in fact require levels of skills, responsibilities, task variation and complexity similar to the higher-paid jobs held by men.

ILO research has found that approximately half of the world's workers are in sex-stereotyped occupations, where one sex predominates to such an extent (representing at least 80 per cent) that these occupations could be considered "male" or "female". The research also noted that there are over seven times as many male-dominated non-agricultural occupations as female-dominated ones.[12] Table 1.2 shows significant changes that have been taking place in a range of job categories in the United States. Overall, an increase in the proportion of women in mainly male-dominated categories has gone hand-in-hand with a decrease in the proportion of women in female-dominated categories. These figures suggest that in the United States at least, there is a slow but steady movement towards a greater occupational diversification for women.

A combination of social attitudes and gender inequality in education and training has largely contributed to occupational segregation, resulting in men and women being streamed into different trades, professions and jobs. This is often referred to as horizontal segregation. Even in Finland, where there is considerable government and social support for gender equality, only 20 per cent of women work in occupations where there is considered to be a balanced male/female employee ratio, i.e. where 40-60 per cent of employees are of the same sex. These jobs represent only 7 per cent of all occupations.[13] The situation is similar in many other countries across the globe.

In the United States, although the percentage of women participating in the labour force has increased dramatically in recent times (from 43.3 per cent in 1970 to 58.7 per cent in 1994), women have remained concentrated in a narrow range of occupations. In 1994, 25 per cent of all employed women were working in administrative support or clerical jobs.[14] A similar situation exists in Canada. Although the proportion of working women increased dramatically in the 1970s and 1980s (from 36 per cent in 1970 to 60 per cent in 1991), they remained concentrated in a narrow range of occupations. In 1984, 33 per cent of all employed women were working in clerical jobs, while only 12 per cent of men worked in any one single major occupational category.[15]

By 1992 in the Republic of Korea, women represented 70 per cent of the workforce in four out of 27 occupational categories: subsistence agriculture and fisheries; life science and health professionals; customer service clerical work;

Table 1.2.   Changes in occupational segregation in the United States, 1974-94

Occupation	Percentage of female employees		Percentage change
	1974	1994	1974-94
Dominated by women			
Cashiers	87.7	79.8	−7.9
Hairdressers	92.4	90.6	−1.8
Librarians	83.7	84.1	−0.4
Registered nurses	98.0	93.8	−4.2
Secretaries	99.2	98.9	−0.3
Social workers	61.3	69.3	8.0
Elementary-school teachers	84.3	85.6	1.3
Therapists	58.3	74.3	16.0
Waiters	91.8	78.6	−13.2
Dominated by men			
Air pilots	1.4	2.6	1.2
Architects	2.8	16.8	14.0
Carpenters	0.7	1	0.3
Computer programmers	22.6	29.3	6.7
Dentists	1.0	13.3	12.3
Engineers	1.3	8.3	7.0
Lawyers	7.0	24.6	17.6
Physicians	9.8	22.3	12.5
Plumbers	0.3	0.7	0.4
Police/detectives	3.1	15.6	12.5
Teachers in third-level institutions	31.3	42.5	11.2

Source: P. Wilson, (ed.): *Salaried and professional women: Relevant statistics* (Washington, DC, AFL-CIO, 1999), p. 9.

agricultural, fisheries and related labour. However, women accounted for less than 5 per cent of workers in five other occupations. These included legislators and senior officials (zero representation), corporate managers (2 per cent female) and physical, mathematical and engineering science professionals (4 per cent female).[16]

Significant changes in women's profiles have, however, taken place during the past 50 years. The reduction of agriculture and growth in manufacturing in the 1950s and 1970s, particularly in industrialized countries, meant that many more women had the opportunity to obtain paid work. During the 1980s and 1990s, those sectors such as the service sector, which had tended to be female dominated, expanded; others, such as heavy industry, which were traditionally male dominated, declined. In Latin America and the Caribbean, for example, women represent between 30 and 40 per cent of the workforce in finance and banking.[17] Over the last decade, women's share of jobs in financing, insurance, real estate and business services has increased in 14 out of the 20 countries for which data were available (figure 1.7).

Not only do men and women have different jobs, but there are also differences in the extent to which they are represented in the hierarchy of

Figure 1.7.   Women's percentage share of jobs in financing, insurance, real estate and business services, 1989-92 and 1996-98 (selected countries and areas)

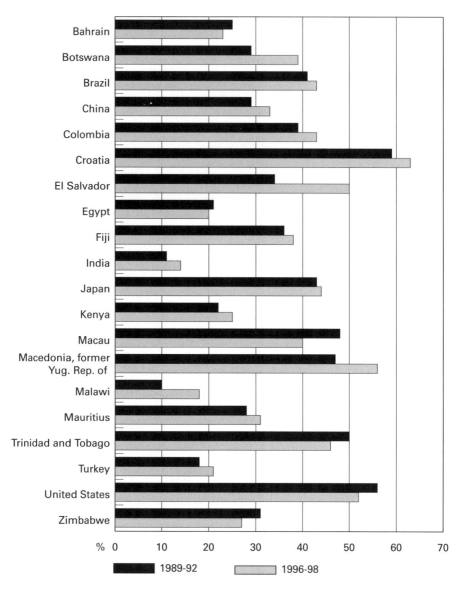

Notes: This corresponds with Major Division 8 of the International Standard Industrial Classification of all Economic Activities (ISIC – Revision 2, 1968). Data are based on: labour force surveys for Brazil, Colombia, Egypt (1995), Japan, Macau, and Trinidad and Tobago; establishment surveys for Botswana, Croatia, El Salvador, Fiji, India, Kenya, Malawi, Mauritius, United States, Zimbabwe and the former Yugoslav Republic of Macedonia; social insurance statistics for Bahrain and Turkey; official estimates for China.

Source: ILO: *Yearbook of Labour Statistics 1999* (Geneva, 1999), table 2B, pp. 105-108.

Table 1.3. Percentage of women employees and women managers in European banks, 1995

	Percentage of women employees	Percentage of women managers				
	Total	Total	Junior management	Middle management	Senior management	Number of banks
Scandinavia	61.5	22.2	38.1	23.8	14.3	7
United Kingdom and Ireland	65.2	24.4	42.8	16.2	6.8	13
Western Europe	45.6	14.0	22.2	11.1	5.0	22
Southern Europe	28.9	7.9	17.5	11.3	5.9	15
Subsidiaries of foreign banks	45.4	20.6	14.7	33.7	11.0	6
Total	46.6	16.1	26.8	16.5	8.4	63

Notes: Scandinavia includes Denmark, Finland and Sweden; Western Europe includes Austria, France, Germany and Benelux countries; Southern Europe includes Greece, Italy, Portugal and Spain; figures for the Republic of Ireland and Northern Ireland are included under the United Kingdom and Ireland; the subsidiaries are of French, German, Dutch and Belgian banks located in Luxembourg, Belgium, Portugal and Greece.

Source: S. Quack and B. Hancké: *Women in decision-making in finance*, Report prepared for the use of the European Commission, Directorate General V, Industrial Relations, Employment and Social Affairs (Wissenschaftszentrum Berlin für Sozialforschung, Berlin, 1997), p. 48.

positions within jobs. Even in occupations dominated by women, men usually occupy the "more-skilled", "responsible" and better-paid positions. For example, in the teaching profession, the majority of teachers are often women but the top administrators are men. Similarly in the health field, doctors and hospital heads are very often men, while most of the nurses and support staff are women. This is commonly referred to as "vertical gender segregation". The movement of women upward through occupational categories to take up more responsible and managerial jobs is hampered by institutional barriers and social attitudes. The "glass ceiling" usually refers to this type of vertical segregation, where recognition of factors such as skill levels, responsibility, pay, status and power is crucial to accessing management positions. Table 1.3 illustrates vertical segregation in banking in Europe. It shows that while there is greater initial female participation in banking jobs in the United Kingdom and Ireland, women appear to have more difficulty in breaking through to higher management. On the other hand, the Scandinavian countries have high initial participation by women and a greater proportion occupying senior management positions. Women are twice as likely to obtain senior management jobs in Scandinavia than in other areas in Europe.

CLOSING THE PAY GAP BETWEEN MEN AND WOMEN

One outcome of occupational segregation is significant pay differences between men and women workers. Although the ILO Equal Remuneration Convention, 1951 (No. 100), has one of the highest rates of ratification of any international

Figure 1.8.   Women's gross hourly wages as a percentage of men's, 1995
(selected European countries)

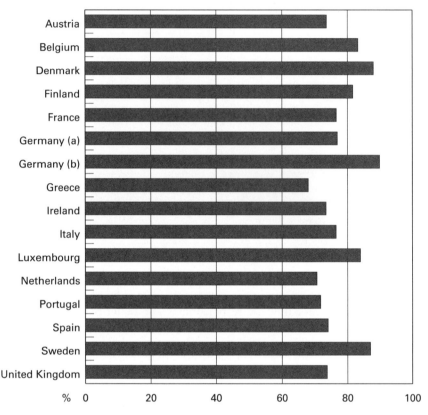

Notes: Data from Austria are from 1996; data from France are from 1994; data from Germany (a) are for old Länder, from Germany (b) from new Länder, including Berlin. For Greece, data apply only to industry.
The data cover all full-time employees in all economic activities except for those working in agriculture, education, health, personal services and administration.
Source: Eurostat: "Statistics in focus: Women's earnings in the EU – 28% less than men's", Population and Social Conditions Press Release No. 6/99 (Luxembourg,1999), p. 3.

labour standard (149 as of 31 December 2000) and the principle of equal remuneration for work of equal value has been incorporated into the labour legislation of many countries, pay differentials continue to be one of the most persistent forms of gender inequality.

The gap is slowly closing but is likely to remain while occupations are still highly segregated by sex. Figure 1.8 reflects the limited progress made up to 1995 in selected countries in Europe. Differences in hours worked by men and women, as well as the inclusion of bonuses and fringe benefits, may also partly explain female/male differentials.

In publishing these figures the Statistical Office of the European Commission (Eurostat) noted that:

> these averages reflect structural differences in the characteristics of working women and men – mostly age, education and occupation. Fewer women than men occupy management positions, which are amongst the best paid jobs. The imbalance in the representation of women or men in certain economic sectors and occupations is one of the determining elements of the gender pay gap.[18]

In the group surveyed, one-third of women working full time were office clerks compared with only 10 per cent of men. Forty-seven per cent of men were manual workers compared with only 18 per cent of women (on average, manual work is better paid than clerical work). Differences in education also affected the figures. Fifty-one per cent of working women had only primary or general secondary-level education compared with 43 per cent of men, while 29 per cent of women had technical secondary education compared with 36 per cent of men.[19] The data also indicated that women's earnings in the 25-29 age group were only 86 per cent of men's. In principle, the women in this group have had equal access to education and work. According to Eurostat:

> ... even for the younger generation there is unequal access to well-paid jobs. Furthermore, when these young women get older, some will make long career breaks and so it is very probable that the pay differences will increase and resemble the ones their mothers are currently experiencing.[20]

ILO data show varying degrees of improvement in women's earnings in countries outside Western Europe. The pay of female employees in Jordan increased significantly as a percentage of men's between 1989 and 1995 (from 81 per cent to 90 per cent). In Ukraine, the proportion jumped from 67 per cent in 1993 to 81 per cent in 1998. Mexico showed an increase from 76 per cent in 1991 to 84 per cent in 1998. Similar, but smaller increases were recorded for Brazil (from 79 per cent in 1989 to 82 per cent in 1997), the Republic of Korea (from 65 per cent to 67 per cent between 1993 and 1998), Japan (from 70 per cent in 1994 to 72 per cent in 1998), Singapore (from 81 per cent in 1989 to 85 per cent in 1997), and Australia (from 90 per cent in 1990 to 93 per cent in 1993).[21]

Some surveys measure pay differences in relation to educational levels of men and women, and often reveal large gaps. In Uruguay, women with a university education earned only 52 per cent of the salary of men with the same educational qualifications. In Argentina, the salaries of women with university degrees were one-third lower in 1993 than those of men with an equivalent education level.[22] In Bolivia, women with a university education in 1990 were receiving 70 per cent of the salary of their male counterparts.[23] A 1997 survey in the United Kingdom found that the starting salaries earned by women graduates were 16 per cent lower than those of their male counterparts and this was in spite of the fact that women appeared to be performing better academically. Of 1,500 graduates surveyed, 64 per cent of the women gained upper-second class or first-class degrees compared with only 55 per cent of men.[24] In the former USSR in 1988, only 7 per cent of women with higher or specialized secondary education occupied managerial posts compared with 48 per cent of men with the same background qualifications.[25] One exception to this trend is Australia, where female graduate starting salaries tend to catch up with those of their male counterparts. They were at their highest level on record in 1998, with female graduates earning 96.8 per cent of the salary of male graduates. Between 1997 and 1998, the median starting salary for female graduates rose by A$1,500 (5.3 per cent) to A$30,000 per annum, while starting salaries for male graduates rose by A$1,000 (3.3 per cent) to A$31,000.[26]

Men and women with higher levels of education earn more than their male and female counterparts with lower educational qualifications. However, the earnings differentials between sexes with the same educational attainment remain substantial. Figure 1.9 illustrates earning gaps between men and women with university education in OECD countries. These figures are similar to those for the overall average pay gap and illustrate that higher education does not systematically reduce gender inequalities in earnings.

In the United States, men with the same education as women earn more; and the higher the level of education involved, the greater the salary gap becomes. In 1993, the median annual income for women with a bachelor's degree was less than that of men with some college education but no degree. Men with a bachelor's degree earned over 27 per cent more than similarly qualified women and men with professional degrees earned almost 38 per cent more than their female counterparts.[27] On the other hand, a British study noted little difference in the hourly pay gap for men and women with university degrees (19 per cent) and those with no qualifications (20 per cent).[28]

Some of these disparities in earnings can be traced to differences in career choices and the amount of time spent by an individual in the labour market, which is often less for women. These differences are also in part due to the fact that women often choose or are steered towards certain types of occupations and even specific types of positions within a given occupation such as management. The extent to which women work part time is also a factor.

RECONCILING WORK AND FAMILY

The gender division of time between work and family is probably the most significant gender issue of all and explains many of the differences between the work patterns and job types of men and women. Time-use studies show that women work longer hours than men in nearly every country. According to a 1995 UNDP report, women perform on average 53 per cent of the total amount of paid and unpaid work in developing countries, and 51 per cent in industrialized countries. In the latter, around two-thirds of women's work is spent on unpaid activities and one-third on paid activities, while the converse is true for men. In developing countries, two-thirds of women's total work burden is also spent on unpaid labour, but less than one-quarter of men's work goes unpaid.[29]

More recent studies for Japan, Australia and Canada confirm these gender differences in time use. In Japan, a 1996 study[30] on the average time use for people over 10 years of age showed that men slept 15 minutes longer than

Figure 1.9.   Mean annual earnings of university-educated women
as a percentage of those of university-educated men in two age
brackets, 1995-96 (selected OECD countries)

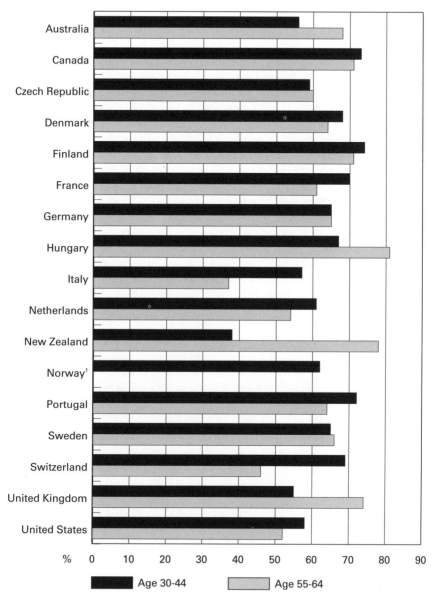

¹ Data not available for age 55-64.
Source: OECD: *Education at a Glance: OECD Indicators 1998* (Paris, 1998), p. 359.

women, but women spent more time on personal care and meals. Paid work and housework showed the biggest differences between men and women. Men worked 2 hours 35 minutes longer than women, but spent only 24 minutes on housework and related activities while women allocated 3 hours 34 minutes to housework per day. Men spent 18 minutes per day more than women on leisure activities. For married couples (aged 15 years and over), the average time spent by men on housework was 28 minutes, while that for married women was 5 hours 9 minutes. For couples with children and parents in the household, the total amount of time women spent on paid and unpaid work was 9 hours 43 minutes compared with the 8 hours spent by their husbands.

In Australia, a 1997 survey[31] found that men and women spent a similar amount of time on necessary activities (sleeping, eating, personal hygiene, and so forth). On average, men spent almost twice as much time as women in paid work or educational/training activities (19 per cent compared with 11 per cent), while women spent nearly twice as much time as men on household work, childcare, shopping, voluntary activities and so forth (21 per cent compared with 12 per cent). These figures show little change since 1992. Men and women continue to spend their day in different ways. On an average day in 1997, men spent 20 per cent of their time on recreation and leisure, 18 per cent on employment-related activities and 7 per cent on domestic activities. Women, on the other hand, spent 18 per cent of their day on recreation and leisure, 13 per cent on domestic work, 9 per cent on employment-related activities and 3 per cent on childcare.

A similar survey conducted in Canada in 1998[32] showed that men and women aged 15 and over both worked a total of paid and unpaid work of 7.8 hours per day averaged over a seven-day week. However, men spent an average of 4.5 hours on paid work and related activities, while the figure for women was 2.8 hours. Men spent 2.7 hours on unpaid work compared with 4.4 hours spent by women. Men and women spent the same amount of time (16.2 hours a day) on personal care and free time.

Although in some countries men are beginning to take a greater share in domestic duties, a study carried out by the Economic Planning Agency in Japan in 1995 (figure 1.10) illustrates the inequality in the hours spent by men and women on housework in five industrialized nations and confirms the wage gap mentioned earlier.

Statistics show that it is easier for men to have both a family and a career. Indeed, many women forgo marriage and children to devote themselves to a career. However, this pattern seems to be more pronounced in industrialized countries than in developing countries. A 1997 survey of managers aged 35 to 54 in the United Kingdom found that 88 per cent of male managers were married compared with 69 per cent of their female colleagues. Twenty-one per cent of women managers had children under 16 years of age, compared with 43 per cent of men.[33] In Germany, a survey of managers found that 43 per cent of the women were unmarried compared with only around 4 per cent of men and 74 per cent of women had no children compared with 57 per cent of men.[34]

Figure 1.10. International comparison of wage differentials and share
of housework by sex (selected OECD countries)

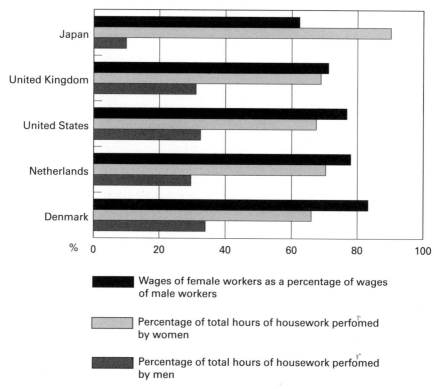

Wages of female workers as a percentage of wages
of male workers

Percentage of total hours of housework perfomed
by women

Percentage of total hours of housework perfomed
by men

Source: Based on Japanese Trade Union Confederation (JTUC-RENGO): *The spring struggle for a better living 1996,*
RENGO White Paper, 1996 (Tokyo), p. 74.

On the other hand, surveys in some developing countries indicate that most
women managers seem to be married with children. For example, a survey of
77 women executives in Colombia found that 23 per cent were single. However,
many of these were under 35 (13 per cent) so they could still possibly marry.
Around 60 per cent of the women surveyed had children.[35] A certain proportion
of women managers reconcile family and a career by delaying having children
until they are well established in their careers and therefore less likely to
encounter major difficulties in re-entering the labour market. They are also more
likely to be in a better financial position to pay for childcare.

> "With a very good education, a dose of intuition and a rigorous organization
> of work, a woman can attain a position of responsibility ... the problem is that
> women are led to believe that they have the right to three things: a career, a
> partner and children. In practice, it is impossible to manage the three things at
> the same time, and the same goes for men."
>
> Source: Interview with a high-level Swiss woman manager, *Journal de Genève,*
> 27 February 1997.

The labour market gender inequalities described in this chapter are part of a broader social and economic context, where cultural and political beliefs and practices perpetuate inequalities of all kinds. Promoting gender equality involves challenging these in order to improve women's access to education and jobs. The next section provides information on efforts by the United Nations to develop indicators for measuring progress in achieving gender equality in society.

GENDER EQUALITY IN SOCIETY: SOCIAL AND ECONOMIC INDICATORS

The 1996 *Human Development Report* of the United Nations Development Programme (UNDP) states that "no society treats its women as well as men".[36] The United Nations has developed a gender-related development index (GDI) to record achievements and monitor progress. It is based on the same set of basic capabilities included in the Human Development Index (HDI) – for example, life expectancy, educational attainment and income – but adjusts the HDI for gender equality. The GDI for 143 countries and HDI for 174 can be seen in Annex I. A positive difference between a country's HDI and GDI rank indicates that it performs relatively better on gender equality than on average achievements alone. Of the 143 countries covered in the 1999 *Human Development Report*, the GDI rank is lower than the HDI rank in 43 countries, indicating the lack of equality in building women's capabilities compared with men's. In 60 of the countries, however, the GDI rank is higher than the HDI rank. As the 1999 report points out, the countries with a higher GDI rank are diverse in terms of economic, cultural and political environment. This suggests that greater gender equality is not dependent upon a certain income level or stage of development and that it can be achieved in varying cultural contexts.[37]

The United Nations has also developed a gender empowerment measure (GEM) which concentrates on participation. It measures gender inequality in key areas of economic and political participation and decision-making; in short, it focuses on women's opportunities. It thus differs from the GDI, which is more an indicator of gender inequality in basic capabilities. Annex I ranks the GEM estimated for 102 countries. The ranking shows that some developing countries outperform much richer industrial nations in terms of gender equality in political, economic and professional activities. For example, countries such as Japan and France come behind Costa Rica, Cuba, the Czech Republic, Ecuador and South Africa.[38]

While the GDI and GEM are useful indicators, there are some drawbacks to comparing these figures. One example of this is that one of the factors on which the indexes are based is the real gross national product (GNP) per capita and the data used for this come from the latest year available. The date of the latest data available can vary considerably from country to country.

The UNDP *Human Development Report 1999* also discusses the aspects of care and labour in gender discrimination. It notes that life expectancy rates are positively affected by care in different forms, such as social support and social relationships. For example, unmarried adults have higher mortality rates than married ones and, according to the United Nations Children's Fund (UNICEF), children in a caring environment fare better in terms of health than those who lack this attention.[39] It is not only the weak and sick that need care to prosper; even the healthiest of adults need a certain amount of care. A deficit in care services not only destroys human development, but it also undermines economic growth.[40] That these factors are overlooked has considerable implications for gender equality, as women still carry the main responsibility for care. Gender discrimination is perpetuated through the lack of value placed on women's caring role in society.[41] Moreover, the ongoing changes in markets, in part due to globalization, tend to be based on a short-term perspective on investments. As managers, women are affected by the common assumption that in the event of building families they will bear the main burden of responsibility arising out of this. Thus, there is not the same degree of investment in women. They are less likely to receive the same encouragement or career advice through mentoring as men. Often they are not placed in visible lower-management positions or given important projects; the latter are normally given to men who are assumed to remain as dedicated and as available even when they start a family.

CONCLUSION

Labour market inequalities between men and women explain many of the difficulties women face in pushing against the glass ceiling. Wage disparities arising out of occupational segregation, which in turn are linked to the disproportionate gender division between paid employment and unpaid care work, perpetuate the image of women as "secondary" workers. Gradual movements towards diversification in occupations for women and the closing of the wage gap have been noted. However, to quicken the pace on the road to gender equality, diversification in occupations for men will be required. In addition, there will have to be a greater sharing of family responsibilities between women and men. To support such developments, the world community will need to find a greater balance between achieving economic and social objectives so that men and women everywhere can enjoy "human development" on an equal footing.

Notes

[1] Japan Institute of Labour: *White Paper on Labour 1991: Present state and problems of females and young workers – Outline of the analysis* (Tokyo, 1992), p. 34.

[2] ILO: *Economically Active Population 1950-2010*, Vols. II-V (Geneva, 4th edn., 1998; on diskette).

[3] P. Wilson (ed.): *Salaried and professional women: Relevant statistics* (Washington, DC, AFL-CIO, 1999), p. 9.

[4] US Department of Labor: "Employment of mothers with infants". http://stats.bls.gov/opub/ted/1999/Jun/wk2/art02.htm.

[5] ILO: *Economically active population* 1950-2010, op. cit.

[6] ILO: *Gender! Partnership of equals* (Geneva, 2000), p. 50.

[7] ILO: *Key Indicators of the Labour Market 1999* (Geneva, 1999). This publication seeks to provide constituents with information on economic activities, such as the size and composition of the labour force and hours of work. There is also a focus on specific groups of workers such as women and youth.

[8] ILO: *Gender!*, op. cit., p. 50.

[9] ILO: *Yearbook of Labour Statistics 1999* (Geneva, 1999), table 3A, pp. 451-470.

[10] loc. cit.

[11] loc. cit.

[12] R. Anker: *Gender and jobs: Sex segregation of occupations in the world* (Geneva, ILO, 1998), p. 207.

[13] E. Hänninen-Salmelin and T. Petäjäniemi: "Women managers, the challenge to management? The case of Finland", in N. J. Adler and D. N. Izraeli (eds.): *Competitive frontiers: Women managers in a global economy* (Cambridge, Mass., Basil Blackwell, 1994), p. 177.

[14] Wilson, op. cit., p. 6.

[15] C. Andrew et al.: "Women in management: The Canadian experience", in Adler and Izraeli, op. cit., p. 377.

[16] M. Roh, Korean Women's Development Institute: Statement to the 41st Session of the United Nations Commission on the Status of Women, Panel on Women and the Economy, New York, Mar. 1997, p. 3.

[17] Inter-American Development Bank: *Women in the Americas: Bridging the gender gap* (Washington, DC, 1995), p. 65.

[18] Eurostat: "Average EU woman earns a quarter less than a man", Press Release No. 48/99 (Luxembourg, June 1999), p. 1. See http://europa.eu.int/ comm/eurostat.

[19] ibid., p. 2.

[20] loc. sit.

[21] ILO: *Yearbook of Labour Statistics 1999*, op. cit., table 5A, pp. 823-893.

[22] Consejo Nacional de la Mujer: *Resúmen ejecutivo, síntesis y actualización del informe nacional sobre la situación de la mujer en la última década en la República Argentina* (Buenos Aires, 1995).

[23] M. O. Aliaga de Torres (Confederación de Empresarios Privados de Bolivia): *La participación de la mujer en el campo empresarial*, Paper prepared for the Seminario Regional para las Organizaciones de Empleadores en América Latina, Cartagena, 21-24 Sep. 1992, p. 7.

[24] Survey by Barclays Bank reported in *Financial Times*, 29-30 Mar. 1997.

[25] A. Posadskaya and N. Zakharova: *To be a manager: Changes for women in the USSR*, Discussion Paper No. 65, Training Policies Branch (ILO, Geneva, 1990), p. 4.

[26] Office for the Status of Women: "Facts about women". http://osw.dpmc.gov.au/content/resources/women_aus.html.

[27] American Federation of Labor and Congress of Industrial Organizations (AFL-CIO): *Current statistics on white-collar employees* (Washington, DC, 1995), p. 27.

[28] I. Bruegel: "Globalization, feminization and pay inequalities in London and the UK", in J. Gregory et al.: *Women, work and inequality: The challenge of equal pay in a deregulated labour market* (New York, St. Martin's Press, 1999), p. 78.

[29] "Women's invisible contribution to the global economy estimated at eleven trillion dollars says UN report. Women's work goes unpaid, unrecognised and undervalued", Press Release on UNDP: *Human Development Report 1995*. http://www.undp.org/hdr/1995/hdr95en2.htm.

[30] H. Mikami: *Time use survey in Japan* (Tokyo, Statistics Bureau and Statistics Center Management and Coordination Agency, 1999).

[31] Australian Bureau of Labour Statistics: *How Australians use their time, 1997* (Canberra, 1998).

[32] Statistics Canada: *Overview of the time use of Canadians in 1998*, General Social Survey, Catalogue No. 12F0080XIE (Ottawa, 1999).

[33] K. Charlesworth: *A question of balance? A survey of managers' changing professional and personal roles* (London, Institute of Management, 1997), p. 7.

[34] Survey by the *Union de Leitenden Angestellten* (Managerial Union of Employees in Germany), 1997.

[35] R. B. González: *Participación de la mujer ejecutiva en Colombia*, Working paper commissioned by the ILO (Bogotá, ILO, 1996), p. 5.

[36] United Nations Development Programme (UNDP): *Human Development Report 1999* (New York and Oxford, Oxford University Press, 1999), p. 11.

[37] ibid., p. 132.

[38] ibid., pp. 132-133.

[39] ibid., p. 77.

[40] ibid., p. 79.

[41] ibid., p. 80.

WOMEN IN PROFESSIONAL AND MANAGERIAL JOBS

2

INTRODUCTION

Over the last few decades, women have attained educational levels comparable to those of men in many countries and have been increasingly hired in jobs previously reserved for men. They have responded to expanding opportunities and invested themselves particularly in business, administration and finance. Women today represent over 40 per cent of the global workforce and have been gradually moving up the hierarchical ladder of organizations. Yet typically, their share of management positions does not exceed 20 per cent, and the more senior the position involved, the more glaring is the gender gap. National surveys reveal that in the largest and most powerful companies worldwide, women's share in top positions is limited to a mere 2 to 3 per cent.

The term "glass ceiling" illustrates well the point that when there is no objective reason for women not rising to the very top as men do, there exists inherent discrimination in the structures and processes of both organizations and society in general. Qualified and competent women look up through the glass ceiling and can see what they are capable of achieving, but invisible barriers prevent them from breaking through. The glass ceiling may exist at different levels depending on the extent to which women progress in organizational structures, and this is commonly represented by a pyramidal shape as in figure 2.1. In some countries or companies, the glass ceiling may be closer to the corporate head, while in others it may be at junior management level or even lower still.

The nature of women's career paths is a major factor blocking women from top positions. At junior management levels, women are usually placed in functions which are regarded as "non-strategic", for example human resources and administration, rather than in line and management jobs that lead to the top. Often, this is compounded by women being cut off from both the formal and informal networks that are necessary for advancement within organizations. For women with family responsibilities, upward movement may be further hampered as they struggle to satisfy the needs of both career and family.

In the last two decades, improvements in the educational qualifications of women and the fact that many women have increasingly been delaying marriage and childbearing have created a pool of women worldwide both qualified and

Figure 2.1.   The glass ceiling in the organizational pyramid

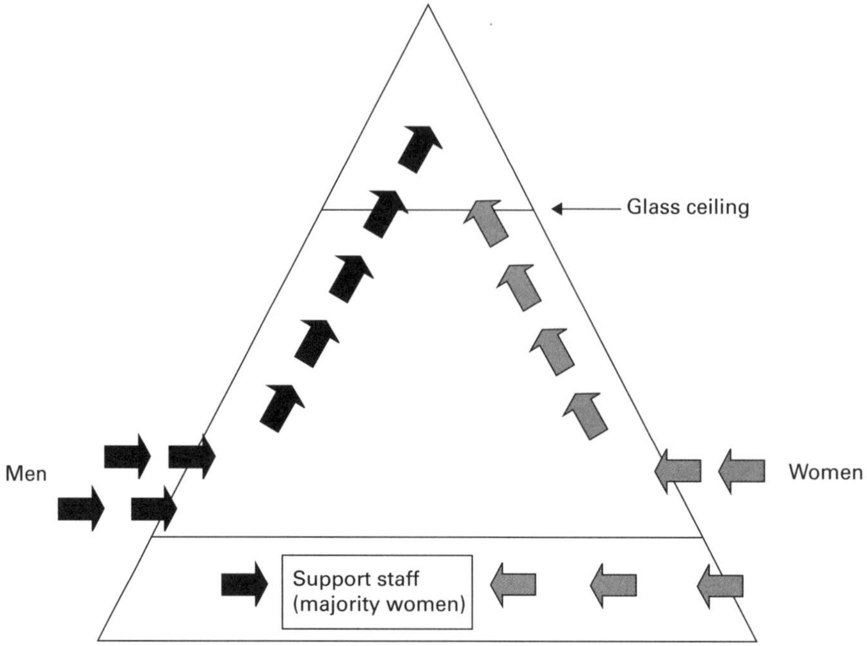

Source: ILO: *Economically Active Population, 1950-2010* (Geneva, 1997), pp. 23, 26 and 29.

ready for professional and managerial jobs. At the same time, growth in the public sector and the services sector and the introduction of equality laws and policies in many countries have provided opportunities for qualified women to occupy lower- and middle-level management posts. These changes have paved the way for their taking up and aspiring to more senior management positions. While employment in the public sector has recently declined in many countries, this to some extent has been offset by growth in the services sector.

Women's interest in professional and managerial work and the predicted shortages of highly qualified managers have not, however, resulted in women obtaining senior executive positions in significant numbers. The glass ceiling continues to limit women's access to senior management and to management positions in those sectors and areas which involve more responsibilities and higher pay.

This chapter presents statistical data on the situation of women in professional and managerial positions. It examines the position of women managers in the private and public sectors, especially at senior levels, and looks at women's impact on politics. Trends relating to women operating their own businesses are also identified. Differences between the salaries of male and female managers are noted, as are the obstacles experienced by women in trying to break through the glass ceiling.

STATISTICAL ISSUES INVOLVED IN CLASSIFYING PROFESSIONAL AND MANAGERIAL EMPLOYEES

Until recently, much of women's work has been undervalued or unrecognized. While more systematic efforts are being made by the United Nations system and governments to value and account for women's work in national statistics, research on women in management is a relatively new field and comparisons over time and across countries are limited. National studies on the issue usually cite general statistics on the percentage of women holding management positions in private companies or the public sector. Some surveys provide data for women at different management levels. In general, however, cross-country comparisons are difficult to make, as studies are often restricted in focus (for example on large corporations or the public sector) and coverage (excluding, for instance, small- and medium-sized enterprises – SMEs).

The situation is further complicated by the range of definitions employed and the non-availability of statistics for different countries over time. National classifications of occupations vary considerably, and the definition of "manager" in some countries can broadly cover all types of managers in the public and private sectors. In others, classifications are more detailed and categorize managers by area (for example, finance managers, production managers and sales managers) or by type of organization (large, medium, small and so forth). The term "manager" may also include administrative staff that are just below junior-level managers. In France, the term *cadre* is broad and covers managers and professional staff:

> a *cadre* is not necessarily a hierarchical supervisor responsible for the work of subordinates. ... The term refers more to a level of organizational status than to a job category with specific task responsibilities. It applies to an employee with a university degree representing four or five years of study (the equivalent of a master's degree) or to an employee who has climbed the ladder and acquired a *cadre* position through her or his work and continuing educational experience.[1]

In Canada, supervisors in clerical, sales, services and production sectors are included in the definition of "manager". In the United States, certain management-related occupations are included in the occupational group of administrative and managerial workers. For example, administrators in education (55 per cent of whom are women) in the United States are included in this group, whereas in other countries, they may be included in the professional and technical category.[2]

ILO data collected on the basis of the International Standard Classification of Occupations (ISCO) constitute the most complete set of data available for making broad international comparisons. Until 1988, ISCO-68 was the system used. This was then updated by the adoption of ISCO-88 by the 14th International Conference of Labour Statisticians in 1987.[3] In this system, managers are no longer included in the same category as administrative workers, although they are still broadly classified in a category entitled "legislators, senior officials and managers" (Major Group 1). Professionals too are no longer grouped with technical and related workers and are classified in a single category

(Major Group 2). An increasing number of countries are now providing data under the 1988 classification system, making comparisons over time possible for a larger number of countries. Data collected under either ISCO-68 or ISCO-88 do not, however, enable international comparisons to be made of women's and men's positions at different levels and types of management. In particular, they do not permit an analysis of women's position in private-sector management. Such data can only be found in studies based on national classifications of occupations and in specific surveys or in other research targeting particular sectors or companies.

The ILO has also developed the SEGREGAT database, which provides data on employment by sex and detailed occupational groups for 40 countries for the years in and around 1970, 1980 and 1990.[4] These countries provided data to the ILO based on their own occupational classifications which, in many cases, were revised over time. While it is difficult to compare such data across countries, some of the national classifications do provide more detailed data by sex for different levels of management and for managers in various sectors.

In this chapter, the figures and tables based on ILO data represent statistics provided to the ILO by the largest possible number of countries in the most recent year or years available. In some cases, data are grouped for one- to three-year time periods in order to include a greater spread of countries across all regions. In most cases, it was difficult to include countries from the African region owing to the lack of available data. In other cases, it was not possible to include certain countries as they are still providing statistics to the ILO under the ISCO-68 classification. Moreover, data were not always broken down by sex for some countries. Other factors which restricted the selection of more countries included switches in the last few years from ISCO-68 to ISCO-88, and changes in data series and methodologies over time. In short, the main criteria for the selection of countries were the availability and comparability of data.

WOMEN IN PROFESSIONAL JOBS

Women working in the financial and professional services are found in a wide variety of occupations: as administrators and managers, as scientists, engineers, architects, lawyers, accountants, economists, statisticians and information technology specialists. Together with their male counterparts, they are well qualified, possess a high degree of technological know-how and often occupy positions of authority. Financial and professional employees play an essential role in business, the economy and society. Yet, as salaried employees they share many of the concerns of other workers with regard to job security, the effects of new technology, work organization and working time. These so-called "knowledge workers" often do not have the benefit of collective organization through trade unions to defend their interests in the new environments created by constantly changing modern economies driven by information technology (IT). Achieving equal opportunities between men and women is just as much of a challenge for financial and professional employees as it is for workers in other sectors. An ILO compendium of principles and good practices for the conditions of work and employment of professional workers[5] declares that women and men should have the right on equal terms to receive education and training for jobs demanding high qualifications, and that they both should enjoy equality of opportunity and treatment for career advancement.

Progress in gender equality in the labour market is best reflected in women's entry into professional positions. Between 1997-98 in the 23 countries for which data were available, women occupied close to half or more of professional jobs in many instances (figure 2.2). This represents a distinct movement towards overall parity for professional jobs, although it is clear that there are considerable variations from one profession to another.[6] Within the professional category, women are concentrated in certain occupations for which pay rates are often lower. As was pointed out in ILO research:

> in the United States in 1991 almost one-half of women in the professional and technical category worked in only two occupations: nurses and teachers (15.9 per cent and 32.5 per cent of all women professional and technical workers respectively). In Japan, 46.6 per cent of women professional and technical workers were in these same two occupations in 1990 (25.3 per cent as nurses and 21.3 per cent as teachers). In both India and Hong Kong, China, over 80 per cent of women professional and technical workers are either nurses or teachers.[7]

From the data in figure 2.2, it appears that with few exceptions there has been little change over the last five years or so. This is to be expected for those countries close to parity, but for others such as Austria, Denmark, Germany, the Netherlands, Singapore, Spain and the United Kingdom, only limited progression in women's entry to professional jobs is evident from the data. This is somewhat surprising for countries such as Germany, Spain and Singapore, where there has been a significant increase in the number of professional jobs: Germany, by 28 per cent; Singapore, by 77 per cent; Spain, by 31 per cent. The growth in the number of professional jobs does not appear to have opened up more opportunities for women in these countries, suggesting that the implementation of gender equality policies has not kept pace with economic expansion.[8]

WOMEN IN MANAGERIAL JOBS: THE FIGURES

Legislative, senior official and managerial jobs represent only a relatively small proportion of the total workforce. Figure 2.3 indicates a range of 2 to 16 per cent for such jobs in the 29 countries for which data were available in 1998. In certain countries such as Canada, Estonia, Lithuania, the Netherlands, New Zealand, Singapore and the United Kingdom, management as an occupational category has grown significantly since the 1970s. The developing tertiary sector and growth in the state sector mostly account for this trend. The expansion in these sectors has often given more opportunities to women and, while they remain under-represented, their increase in this occupational category has exceeded increases in the labour force as a whole. This partly explains their high share of management positions in these countries.

Figure 2.2.   Women's percentage share of professional work,[1]
1993-95 and 1997-98 (selected countries)

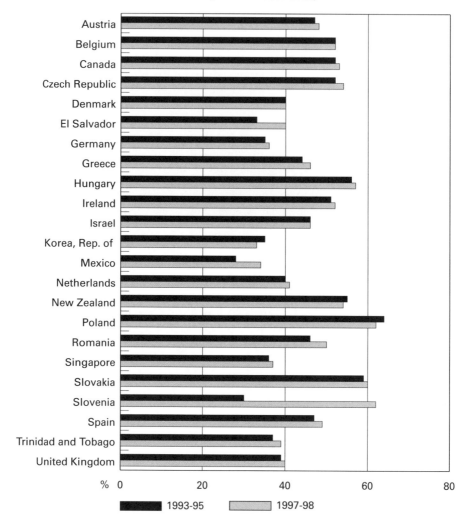

Notes: 1993-98: Canada, Germany, Mexico, New Zealand, Trinidad and Tobago, Singapore, Slovenia, United Kingdom; 1993-97: Czech Republic, Greece, Ireland, Republic of Korea; 1994-98: Denmark, Romania, Slovakia, Spain; 1995-98: Austria, Hungary, Netherlands, Israel, Poland; 1995-97: Belgium, El Salvador.

[1] International Standard Classification of Occupations (ISCO-88), Major Group 2: Includes physical, mathematical and engineering science professionals, physicists, chemists, mathematicians, statisticians, computing professionals, architects, engineers, life science and health professionals, nurses, teachers at all levels, business professionals, legal professionals, social science and related professionals, writers and creative or performing artists and religious professionals.

Source: ILO: *Yearbook of Labour Statistics 1999* (Geneva, 1999), table 2C, pp.187-240.

Figure 2.3. Percentage of people employed in legislative, senior official and managerial positions,[1] 1998 (selected countries)

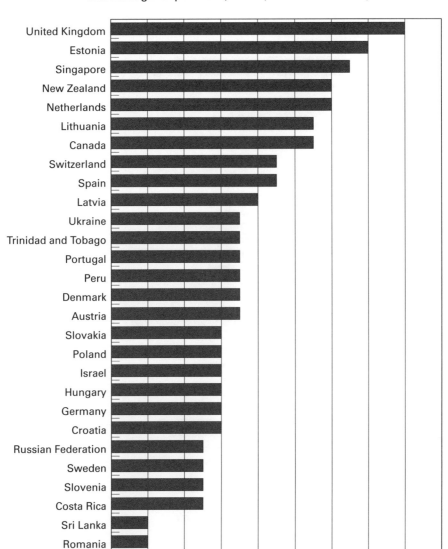

Note: Figures are for individuals aged 15 and over except for Sri Lanka (10+); Costa Rica (12+); Lithuania and Peru, urban areas (14+); Spain, Sweden and the United Kingdom (16+).

[1] ISCO-88, Major Group 1: Includes legislators, senior government officials, traditional chiefs and heads of villages, senior officials of special interest organizations, corporate managers, directors and chief executives, production and operations department managers, other department managers and general managers.

Source: ILO: *Yearbook of Labour Statistics 1999*, op. cit., table 2c, pp. 187-240.

Figure 2.4. Women's percentage share of legislators, senior officials and managers[1] and their share of total employment, 1998-99 (selected countries)

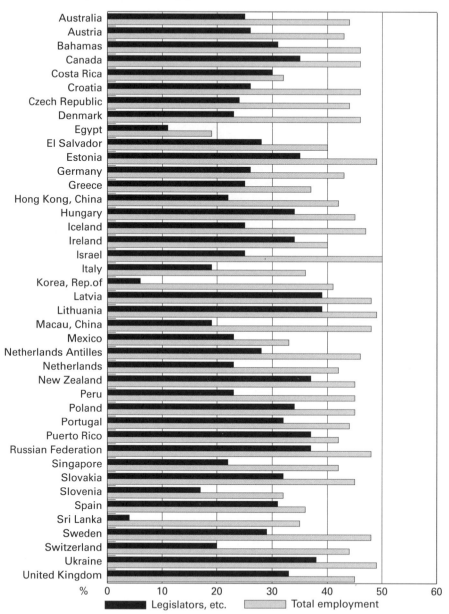

Note: See figure 2.3.
[1] See note 1 to figure 2.3.
Source: ILO: *Yearbook of Labour Statistics 2000*, table 2c, pp. 187-240.

Despite the statistical limitations mentioned earlier in this chapter, ILO data clearly show a pattern of women holding a smaller proportion of management positions compared with men in most countries. Figure 2.4 shows that in nearly half the 41 countries for which statistics were available, women typically held between 20 and 30 per cent of legislative, senior official and managerial positions. In 16 of the 41 countries women held between 31 and 39 per cent of such jobs. Statistics based on the earlier ISCO-68 classification system of administrative and managerial jobs show greater variation, ranging from under 10 per cent to over 40 per cent (figure 2.5). These figures often contrast sharply with the high and increasing levels of labour force participation by women worldwide, as also shown in figure 2.5.

It is notable that countries in Central and Eastern Europe, along with those such as Canada and New Zealand, rate the highest in terms of women's share of the labour market and also in terms of the number of legislative, senior official and managerial positions held by women. However, the proportion of managerial jobs held by women still lags behind their share of overall employment (figure 2.4). Policies to support working mothers meant that women have traditionally held a high proportion of professional and managerial jobs in the countries of Central and Eastern Europe. The data in figures 2.2 and 2.4 reflect their continued presence in these jobs. The progression of the women's movement over the past decades in a number of industrialized countries such as Australia, Canada, New Zealand, the United Kingdom and the United States has also accelerated women's entry into a wider range of professions and managerial jobs in these countries.

In another set of countries in which women held over 40 per cent of total employment, their share of legislative, senior official and managerial jobs was less than 30 per cent. In Denmark and Israel for example, women proportionally held half as many such jobs compared with their share of the total labour market. In these countries, rising participation rates of women have not always resulted in women gaining access to the better-paid and more qualified jobs.

While women's share of overall employment is lower in a number of developing countries, there appears to be less discrepancy in their access to professional and managerial jobs than in some industrialized countries such as Austria, Germany and Switzerland. Even the Scandinavian countries, which are well known for high levels of women's participation in political decision-making and for their generous family support systems, have a low ranking due to the low participation of women in private-sector management jobs and the high degree of occupational segregation, just as elsewhere in the world. Such figures reflect the persistent inequities in the quality and nature of women's jobs compared with men's jobs in the labour market.

It is notable that the proportion of women in management positions appears to be more significant in some developing countries (Colombia, Costa Rica, the Philippines and Venezuela) than in certain industrialized countries. In Mexico, a 1997 government report estimated that the participation of women in executive management positions (presidents, director-generals and general managers) of

Figure 2.5.   Women's percentage share of administrative and managerial
               positions,[1] and their share in total employment, 1997-98
               (selected countries)

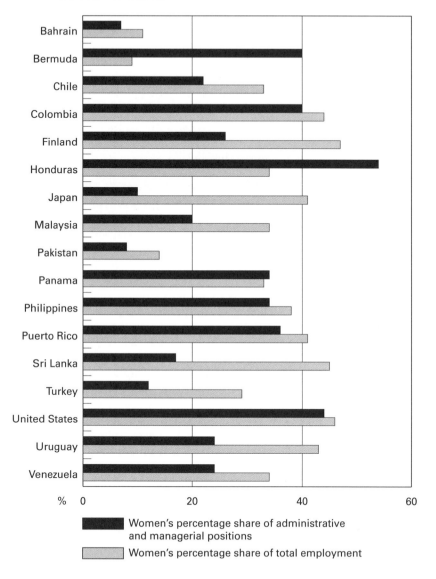

Notes: (1) All countries: Employed people aged 15 years and over except for Honduras and Sri Lanka (10+), Colombia and Turkey (12+), and Puerto Rico and the United States (16+).   (2) Data based on establishment surveys in Bermuda and Sri Lanka, excluding the northern and eastern provinces of the latter.   (3) Data based on social insurance statistics in the private sector in Bahrain.
[1] ISCO-68, Major Group 2: Including legislative officials, government administrators and managers. Data based on labour force surveys.
Source: ILO: *Yearbook of Labour Statistics 1999*, op. cit., table 2C, pp.187-240.

public or private institutions or companies was 12.1 per cent. At the next level down in the private sector (directors, managers and administrators), the participation of women was estimated at 19.8 per cent.[9] Even though general labour force participation rates of women are lower in these countries, many working women seem to be well educated and prepared for professional occupations, and their skills are in demand. In addition, managerial women in developing countries have better access to childcare and household assistance due to extended family systems and the availability of inexpensive domestic help.

Surveys of businesses often report lower figures for women's share of management positions at around 10 per cent or less. A 1992 survey in Germany of 343 companies employing a total of roughly 1.5 million workers found that 7 per cent of their technical and managerial staff were women. Figures by sector in this survey showed that women had a higher share of managerial positions in the services sector (15 per cent) than in other sectors (5 per cent).[10] According to a 1995 survey of over 300 companies in the United Kingdom,[11] just over 10 per cent of managerial jobs were held by women, while an ILO study on women managers in the Russian Federation found 6 per cent of women as heads of national organizations.[12] A 1999 survey of 1,738 major companies in Argentina found that, out of a total of 12,598 executives, 1,222 or 9.7 per cent were women.[13]

In Switzerland, national statistics from 1996 reveal that women held 10 per cent of management positions in sectors representing 80 per cent of professional workers. In the same year, a smaller survey of 97 Swiss companies found that almost 9 per cent of management jobs were held by women, but that over a quarter of the companies had no women managers.[14] In 1998, the Swiss statistical office reported that 12.3 per cent of women employees held managerial positions compared with 24.5 per cent of men.[15]

Other surveys have found somewhat higher proportions. A recent survey of 553 companies in Colombia found that 23.7 per cent of director positions were held by women.[16] One in Brazil covering over 1 million establishments found that women had increased their share of management positions from 12 per cent in 1985 to 17 per cent in 1988.[17] In Uruguay, the figure for women managers reported in 1994 was 20 per cent.[18]

UNEVEN AND SLOW PROGRESS FOR WOMEN IN MANAGEMENT

Even though the figures just presented do not match women's overall share of the labour force, it has to be recognized that women worldwide are gradually increasing their share of managerial work. However, the pace of change is slow and progress has generally been uneven, as is illustrated in figure 2.6.

Over the last five years or so, there have been increases in the share of managerial positions held by women in 13 out of the 24 countries for which data were available. The percentage rise has mostly been only between 1 and 3 per cent, but in a few countries, it has been more significant: in El Salvador, this has been from 26 to 35 per cent; in Ireland, from 19 to 27 per cent; in New Zealand,

Figure 2.6.   Women's percentage share of legislators, senior officials and
managers,[1] 1993-95 and 1997-98 (selected countries)

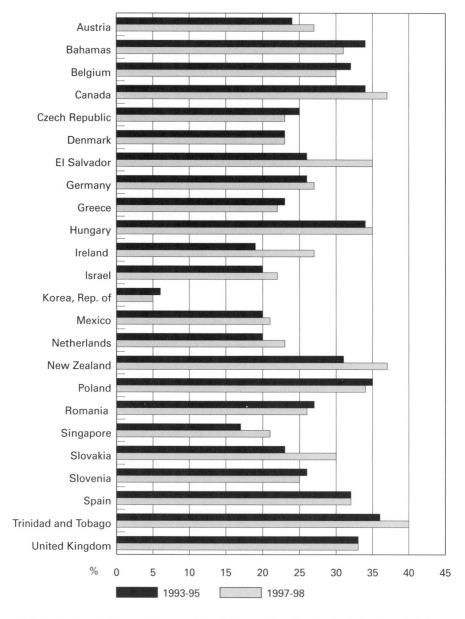

Notes: 1993-98: Canada, Germany, Mexico, New Zealand, Singapore, Slovenia, Trinidad and Tobago, United Kingdom; 1993-97: Bahamas, Czech Republic, Greece, Ireland, Republic of Korea; 1994-98: Denmark, Romania, Slovakia, Spain; 1995-98: Austria, Hungary, Netherlands, Israel, Poland; 1995-97: Belgium and El Salvador.

[1] See note 1 to figure 2.3.

Source: ILO: *Yearbook of Labour Statistics 1999*, op. cit., table 2c, pp. 187-240.

from 31 to 37 per cent; in Slovakia, from 23 to 30 per cent. It is notable that in some countries, such as Denmark, Spain and the United Kingdom, there has been no change, while in others there has even been a decline (Belgium, Czech Republic, Greece, Republic of Korea, Poland, Romania and Slovenia). The evident lack of significant progress in women obtaining managerial positions reflects the complexity of issues to be addressed in order to overcome labour market discrimination and dismantle the glass ceiling. Social and cultural attitudes, coupled with dramatic economic changes that exist in transition countries or which emerged during the financial crisis that affected Asia, explain to some extent the problems women may face in competing for managerial positions.

ILO data compiled on the basis of national classifications of occupation (not internationally comparable) show that, in Canada, the proportion of women managers rose from 13 per cent in 1970 to 25 per cent in 1980 and 40 per cent in 1990. In Mexico, women accounted for 16 per cent of public-sector officials and private-sector managers in 1980 and 19 per cent by 1990. In Hungary, they increased their share as managers in business from 16 per cent in 1980 to 25 per cent in 1990. Other countries, however, registered a much slower rate of change. For example, the proportion of women managers and entrepreneurs in Germany increased only from 16 to 17 per cent between 1976 and 1989.[19]

National surveys confirm these trends. A 1995 White Paper on working women published by the Prime Minister's Office in Japan reported that women's share in professional and technological occupations grew from almost 31 per cent in 1950 to 42 per cent in 1990; in managerial jobs it jumped from just over 1 per cent to 9 per cent during the same period.[20] In Thailand, 19 per cent of managers were women in 1990 compared with 8 per cent in 1974.[21] In Singapore, the proportion increased from 22 per cent in 1992 to 27 per cent in 1996,[22] while in Colombia, it reached 37 per cent in 1996, up from 27 per cent in 1990 and 14 per cent in 1980.[23] In 1998, women in Australia comprised 27.3 per cent of managers compared with 17.2 in 1990.[24] In the United States, women constituted just 4.4 per cent of managers in 1900. This slowly increased to 16 per cent by 1970, at which stage the trend accelerated so that by 1992, the figure had reached 41.5 per cent.[25]

Even though the proportion of women in management has doubled or even tripled in certain countries, it remains generally low. In 1970, women formed 3 per cent of managers and officials in Tunisia and this increased to 9 per cent by 1989.[26] The proportion of administrative and managerial positions in Pakistan held by women more than doubled from 4 per cent to 9 per cent between 1989 and 1997. In Niger, the percentage rose from 3 per cent in 1986 to 8 per cent in 1991. For women in Bahrain, the share increased from 4 per cent to 7 per cent between 1989 and 1997.[27] In some countries, there has been little or no change in women's share of management. In Japan, there was a 2 per cent increase between 1989 and 1998 (from 8 per cent to 10 per cent) and in Bangladesh, women's share of administrative and managerial jobs remained static at 5 per cent between 1989 and 1996.[28]

In some countries, twofold or threefold increases in the number of administrative and managerial jobs does seem to have given women more opportunities. The number of these kinds of jobs doubled in Turkey between 1989 and 1998, and women's share increased from 6 per cent to 12 per cent during the same period. During the same period in Malaysia, a threefold increase in such jobs was accompanied by a near doubling of the share for women (from 11 per cent to 20 per cent).[29]

WOMEN AT THE TOP

Few women gain access to the highest positions as executive heads of organizations and, despite some improvements, many would claim that the pace of change is still far too slow given the large number of qualified women in the labour market today. Where figures are available, they show women holding from 1 per cent to 5 per cent of top executive positions. In the United States, where women are as equally qualified as men and constitute around 46 per cent of the workforce, they were shown by a 1996 survey (*Fortune 500*) to hold only 2.4 per cent of executive positions and form a mere 1.9 per cent of top earners among the largest companies. By 1999, these figures had improved, with 5.1 per cent of executive management positions being held by women while only 3.3 per cent of the highest-paid officers and directors were women.[30] In contrast, a survey in Australia revealed no change over recent years in the 1.3 per cent figure of executive directors who were women.[31]

While it must be acknowledged that time is still needed for women at junior and middle management levels (those in the "pipeline", so to speak) to move into executive positions, the fact remains that women are not moving quickly enough nor in sufficient numbers into line or strategic positions. Yet this factor is crucial for enlarging the pool of women aspiring to senior positions and for building a critical mass of senior women for networking and providing role models for those down the line. Speeding up women's movement towards the top requires that recruitment and promotion methods be objective and fair. Above all, there has to be awareness and commitment from directors of companies as to the benefits for their organizations from promoting women to high-level managerial positions.

Statistics on women in the most senior positions vary considerably depending on whether surveys target only the largest organizations or include all kinds of organizations. Comparison of "jobs at the top" across countries is clouded by the use of such terms as "senior management", or "top-level management", which can include managers just below the highest executive positions. Similarly, the scope of the term "director" is broad and can vary according to the context and level of directorship.

Women seem to experience the most difficulty in obtaining executive jobs in large corporations, even though they often have greater opportunities at junior and middle management levels in these same corporations. This is clearly illustrated by the case of Japan where women directors of companies in general (including SMEs) increased from 9 per cent in 1970 to 13 per cent in 1990. Despite this, there was hardly a crack in the glass ceiling of Japanese corporate structures as women's share of management of corporations only increased from a minimal 1 per cent to 2 per cent in the same period.[32] Similarly, a survey submitted to the Swedish Government in 1998 showed that 99.6 per cent of managing directors of companies registered on the Swedish stock exchange were men.[33]

Data on the largest corporations in the United States provide strong evidence that women still experience great difficulty in obtaining positions at the very top in those firms. In 1999, almost 12 per cent of corporate officers of *Fortune 500* companies were women, up from 10 per cent in 1996. However, women held little more than 5 per cent of the highest-ranking corporate positions such as chairperson, vice-chairperson, chief executive officer (CEO), president and so forth.[34] One reason contributing to this is that few senior women are in the so-called "line" positions that involve profit-and-loss or revenue-generating responsibilities, and which are critical for advancement to the highest levels. In 1999, men still held 93.8 per cent of line jobs in the United States.[35] Similarly, in Canada men held 93.6 per cent of line jobs in 1999.[36] One positive trend in the United States is the declining proportion of companies that have no women or only one woman corporate officer. The percentage of companies with no women in such positions declined from 23 per cent to 21 per cent between 1995 and 1999, and those with only one dropped from 33 per cent to 23 per cent in the same period. Moreover, the proportion of companies with more than one female corporate officer increased from 44 per cent to 56 per cent during this period.[37] In Canada, however, 43.6 per cent of companies had no female corporate officers and only 26.6 had multiple female officers in corporate positions by 1999.[38]

> "I am now working for companies and charging an extremely good daily rate. I think they see me as an ally in this situation and yet the same men that hire me and pay me well won't promote women from within their own organizations. What is going on here, I ask myself? They seem to truly value my skills as long as I am not a part of their own organization. I'm non-threatening."
>
> Source: M. E. Reeves: *Suppressed, forced out and fired: How successful women lose their jobs* (London, Quorum, 2000).

In Brazil, a 1991 survey of major corporations found that women comprised only around 3 per cent of top executives: 3.5 per cent in the 300 largest national private groups, 0.9 per cent in the 40 largest state-owned groups, and 0.5 per cent in the 40 largest foreign-owned companies (see figure 2.7). Figures were similar for women as directors, managers and department heads in the highest salary brackets of Brazilian companies. In 1989, they represented 6 per cent of managers overall: 4 per cent of the directors in finance, real estate and insurance companies; 3 per cent of production, research and development managers; 6 per cent of financial, commercial and publicity managers.[39]

Figure 2.7.   Women's percentage share of senior executive positions in major
corporations, Brazil, 1990

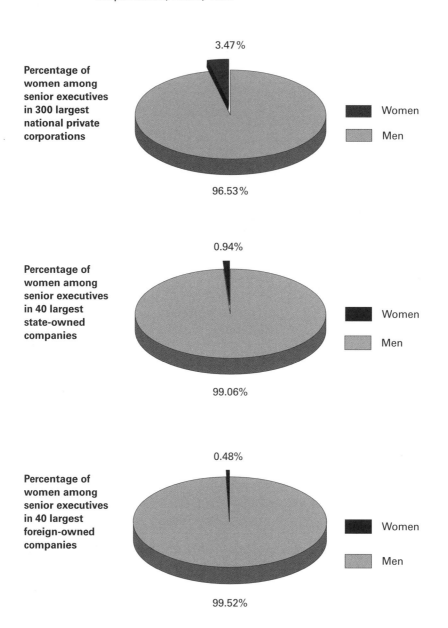

Source: S. de Avelar: *Women in economic decision-making in Brazil: A glass ceiling report* (New York, 1994).

In the United Kingdom, the total number of managers and administrators was 4,306,000 in 1999. Of these, women constituted almost 33 per cent.[40] But there was still a glass ceiling apparent at the highest levels. A 1998 survey of over 584 different companies in the United Kingdom found that 3.6 per cent of directors were women: of these, 10.7 per cent were function heads and 16.2 per cent were department heads. By 1999, the percentage of women directors had increased to 4.5 per cent.[41] Another survey indicated that among *FTSE 100 (Financial Times Stock Exchange 100)* companies, women accounted for only 4 per cent of directors and held under 2 per cent of executive directorships.[42] In 1995, the proportion of women as senior executives and board directors in the 70,000 largest German companies was between 1 per cent and 3 per cent, while their share of senior and middle management was 6 per cent and 12 per cent respectively. In associations, administrative bodies and organizations, they held 9 per cent of senior managerial positions.[43]

A recent French government report cited a 1997 study[44] of the 5,000 leading enterprises in France, which found that women comprised 1,680 of the 26,700 managers (6.3 per cent). The same study showed that women represented 2 per cent of the chief executive officers of these companies, 4.7 per cent of executive managers and 7.6 per cent of managers overall.

The situation is more encouraging in certain countries. A study in Jamaica found an eleven-to-one ratio of women to men at boardroom level,[45] while in Chile, women held 8 per cent of director and high-level executive positions in 1996.[46] A survey of private-sector boards in Australia reported an increase in the number of women on these boards from 7.6 per cent in 1998 to 8.3 per cent in 1999. This compares with a figure of 4 per cent in 1996.[47] Surveys focusing on senior management (not just the very top jobs) report higher proportions of women holding management positions. In the Netherlands, women increased their participation in senior management from 10 per cent in 1979 to 18 per cent in 1990[48] and in Canada, women's presence in senior management across all sectors was 15.9 per cent in 1998 compared with an availability rate of 20.8 per cent for qualified women.[49]

In Finland, female managers most often work below board level as personnel, marketing or financial managers and women's share in these positions reached 11 per cent in 1994.[50] In Australia, women on average increased their share of senior management jobs from 8 per cent in 1994 to 11 per cent in 1996. They fared best in industries employing large numbers of women, such as health and community services and the hotel and catering industry.[51] In Argentina, women occupied close to 7 per cent of senior management jobs according to a 1995 survey.[52]

WOMEN MANAGERS IN THE FINANCIAL, BUSINESS AND BANKING SECTORS

In the area of finance, women have certainly increased their share of management positions, although at a varying pace. ILO data show that, in the United States, women increased their share in financial management from 19 per cent in 1970 to 45 per cent in 1991, a proportion similar to that of managers in general. National statistics in the United States show that, by 1995, women comprised just over 50 per cent of all financial managers.[53]

According to ILO data, the proportion of women working in middle management in the financial services of large organizations in France increased from 15 per cent in 1982 to 26 per cent in 1990, a greater increase than that achieved by women in management overall. In the United Kingdom, the share of women among financial managers rose from 11 per cent to 17 per cent during the 1980s. In Hungary, the proportion of women among chief accountants and economic managers was already as high as 64 per cent in 1980, but increased further to 75 per cent in 1990.[54]

Some national studies reflect similar trends. In Colombia, while there were more women managers in industry (25 per cent) than in any other sector in 1996, their share had hardly changed since 1990. However, the proportion of women among managers in the financial sector rose from 20 per cent in 1990 to 24 per cent in 1996.[55] Interestingly, in Colombia's finance sector, women represented 13 per cent of the executive directors in Medellin and 8 per cent in Bogotá. When it came to the industrial sector, they represented 8 per cent of the executive directors in Medellin and 1 per cent in Bogotá.[56] In Brazil, women's share of director-level positions in financial, real estate and insurance companies was 8 per cent in 1988, but was 15 per cent in financial, commercial and publicity management for the same year.[57] In Germany, women represented 9 per cent of senior and middle management in the service sector in 1995. In financial institutions, however, their share of this management level was only 4 per cent.[58]

Women have made significant inroads at senior levels in finance and banking in Australia and Canada. In Australia, their proportion of senior management was just under 9 per cent in 1996, while in the business services sector they represented almost 25 per cent of managers and just over 14 per cent of senior management.[59] In Canadian banking, women's representation in middle management was almost 56 per cent in 1996 and over 15 per cent at the most senior levels — a fivefold increase since 1987.[60] In Malaysia, women almost doubled their representation as financial brokers between 1983 and 1994 (from 19.3 per cent to 34.6 per cent).[61]

Table 2.1 illustrates women's progress in a survey of European banks at all levels of management except at the most senior level, where the percentage of women on the board of directors actually decreased slightly between 1990 and 1995. Considering how few women existed at the lower levels in 1990, it is possible that there were not enough female candidates to maintain or increase the participation of women over the following five years. There was also a

Table 2.1.   Proportion of women in executive positions in European banks, 1990 and 1995

	Women as percentage of managers		Percentage of banks without women at this level		No. of banks
	1990	1995	1990	1995	1990-95
Board of directors	5.0	4.9	51.5	51.1	47
Executive committee	0.9	3.4	91.5	78.7	47
Directors/divisional heads	1.6	4.9	65.8	52.6	38
Directors/departmental heads	10.4	13.5	31.3	25.0	32

Source: S. Quack and B. Hancké: *Women in decision-making in finance*, Report prepared for the use of the European Commission, Directorate General V, Industrial Relations, Employment and Social Affairs (Berlin, Wissenschaftszentrum Berlin für Sozialforschung, 1997), p. 48.

Table 2.2.   Share of women at decision-making level in EU ministries of finance, 1994-95[1]

Position	Percentage of women holding this position
Ministries of finance	5.9
State secretaries	8
Heads of departments	6.5
Heads of treasury	0

[1] Data for Austria and Denmark are from 1996.
Source: Based on Quack and Hancké, op. cit., p. 6.

marked drop in the proportion of banks without women managers at all levels except at board of director level.

Finance ministries, central banks and banking supervisory agencies are among the most important political institutions with regard to the coordination and regulation of the financial system. These institutions not only determine the access of companies and individuals to credit, but also influence overall economic development, monetary stability and employment growth. Female representation at this level can therefore be seen as crucial to democracy and key to the development of gender equality in the labour market and society as a whole. The very specific educational background required in these institutions (in some cases it is necessary to have attended certain well-reputed educational institutions)[62] can be an obstacle to women's participation in these areas. Table 2.2 presents data from the European Union which illustrate how women are largely excluded from this area of decision-making. It should be noted that these figures are only indicative as many differences exist in the organization of Finance Ministries in EU member States.

The two major stock exchanges in Europe, based in London and Paris, show increasing female participation in financial decision-making. The London Stock Exchange is not only the largest in Europe, but also one of the three largest in the world. In comparison to the rest of the financial sector, women play a relatively significant role in decision-making at this stock exchange. One-third (five) of the board is female, as is half (two) of the executive directors. These figures may in part be due to early efforts in the area of positive action in British banks and the London subsidiaries of banks from the United States.[63]

The Paris Bourse is the second largest stock exchange in Europe and its importance is increasing both nationally and internationally. The institution appears to be an almost exclusively male arena, with only one woman out of 17 members of the board and no women among the six executive directors. This may partly reflect a "pipeline" problem, as it was not until 1973 that women gained access to the prestigious French universities known as the *Grandes Ecoles*. Just as is often the case with Oxford and Cambridge in the United Kingdom, it is only through the *Grandes Ecoles* in France that a career in finance at this level becomes possible. The first women who graduated from these institutions are now progressing to the lowest decision-making levels of the Bourse: 15 out of 41 of these directors are women. It may therefore be only a matter of time before female representation improves at higher levels.[64]

WOMEN MANAGERS IN THE PUBLIC SERVICE

The public service sometimes offers women greater opportunities for access to senior managerial positions than other sectors. Women have been a little more successful in the civil service than in the private sector in the United Kingdom, occupying 9 per cent of the top three levels and almost 8 per cent of chief executive jobs in local government.[65] In Canada, the share of women executives in the public service increased from 24.9 per cent in 1997 to 26.9 in 1998. However, they were still considered to be under-represented when compared with their presence in the major feeder groups, such as scientific and professional employees, where their representation is 33.1 per cent.[66] In the Turkish public service, women formed 32 per cent of division chiefs (middle management positions) in 1996. At higher levels, women held 12 per cent of general directorships and just over 2 per cent of under-secretary positions.[67] In Australia, 30.9 per cent of government board positions were held by women in 1998.[68]

In developing countries, women likewise have greater chances of obtaining management positions in the public service. In the Philippines, women increased their share of government executive positions from 15 per cent in 1990 to 29 per cent in 1994.[69] By 1985 in Thailand, 46 per cent of civil servants were women and 30 per cent of these women were classified as senior officials. Women occupied 26 per cent of administrative and management positions and 6 per cent of the executive positions in the civil service.[70] In Chile, women occupied 12 per cent of senior positions in 13 ministries in 1995. At lower levels of management, their share was 24 per cent. The share of senior executive jobs was, however, only 2.5 per cent.[71] In Bulgaria, 30 per cent of junior-level executive posts were held by women and 13 per cent of senior state officials were women.[72]

In other areas of public service, women can be well represented. According to an Azerbaijan report to CEDAW, one-third of all the employees of the State

Figure 2.8.   Percentage of women managers in the United Kingdom
by function group, 1998

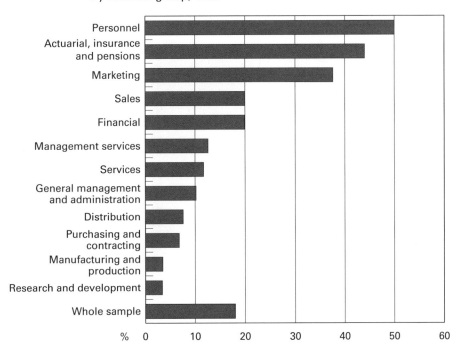

Source: Institute of Management/Remuneration Economics: *National Management Survey*, June 1998 (a survey
of 25,952 firms).

and economic machinery of the country were women in 1994.[73] In a similar
report from Mexico, statistics show that 20 per cent of supreme court judges,
12 per cent of circuit court judges and 23 per cent of district magistrates were
women.[74] In Bulgaria in the early 1990s, women constituted almost 50 per cent
of the country's public prosecutors.[75]

"GLASS WALLS"

In what is a mirror of occupational segregation patterns, women managers tend
to be concentrated in certain sectors. Most women managers in the United
Kingdom are to be found in retail distribution, followed in descending order by
the hotel and catering sectors, banking and finance, medicine and health
services, and then the food, drink and tobacco industries. But women are
increasingly entering management in non-traditional sectors such as manufacturing, insurance and banking.[76] In terms of functions, a 1998 survey
(figure 2.8) in the United Kingdom found that women constituted 50 per cent of
all personnel managers, 44 per cent of actuarial, insurance and pensions
managers and 37.6 per cent of marketing managers. At the other end of the scale,

Table 2.3.   Percentage of men in male-dominated managerial and professional occupations, various years (selected countries and territories)

Country/territory	Year	Architects, engineers and related technicians	Legislative officials and govt. administrators	Managers
OECD				
Australia	1990	94.1	83.3	93.9
Canada	1990	89.6	64.8(x)	59.5
Finland	1990	85	58.3(x)[1]	75.3(x)
France	1990	87.2	n.a.	85.8
Germany (Federal Rep. of)	1989	95.3	78.9(x)	78.4(x)
Italy	1981	95.4	87.6[1]	65.2(x)[2]
Netherlands	1990	95.4	n.a.	86.6
New Zealand	1986	91.7	84.7	82.4
Norway	1990	87.8	54.2(x)	82.83
Spain	1990	92.9	86.2	91.0
Switzerland	1980	98.5	94.0	94.2
United States	1991	88.1	54.5(x)	53.9(x)
North Africa and Middle East				
Bahrain	1981	96.1	93.0	95.1[3]
Egypt	1986	94.4	88.5	88.6
Iran, Islamic Rep. of	1986	95.8	87.5	100
Jordan	1979	98.8	95.6	95.53
Kuwait	1985	97.9	95.9	96.3
Tunisia	1989	86.8	89.8	90.9
Asia				
China	1982	82.3	n.a.	89.7
Fiji	1991	95.1	68.1(x)	77.1(x)
Hong Kong, China	1986	96.3	92.3	90.6
India	1981	98.4	98.2	97.6
Japan	1990	97.6	98.3	90.8
Korea, Rep. of	1983	98.3	n.a.	n.a.
Malaysia	1980	92.2	80.3	93.2

Notes: n.a. indicates that no comparable occupation was available for comparison.   (x) Indicates an occupation which is not male-dominated, i.e. where less than 80 per cent of the workers are male.   [1] Government administrators only.   [2] Includes managers and directors in public/private companies, in addition to administrative employees with managerial functions.   [3] Includes working proprietors.

Source: R. Anker: *Gender and jobs: Sex segregation of occupations in the world* (Geneva, ILO, 1998), pp. 258-61.

they constituted only 3.4 per cent of research and development managers and 3.5 per cent of manufacturing and production managers. At director level, 18 per cent of personnel directors and 13 per cent of marketing directors were women. However, despite the size of the sample of this survey, no female directors were identified in areas such as marketing and production, purchasing and contracting, or insurance and pensions.[77]

Women executives, administrators and managers in the United States are more likely than men to be employed in the service, insurance, real estate, public administration and finance sectors. In 1995, 42 per cent of women administrative and managerial workers were employed in the service sector compared with 30 per cent of men.[78] Women managers were less likely to be employed in manufacturing, professional services and other services. Similarly, in Brazil, women managers were more concentrated in the public utilities and in financial and commercial management than in manufacturing or research and production.[79] In Argentina, a 1999 survey revealed that 35 per cent of women executives were concentrated in commercial management, followed by 16 per cent as personnel managers and 14 per cent as managers in accounting and financial control.[80]

According to ILO research, legislative officials, government administrators and managers are occupational groups that have become less male dominated over the last two decades. They went from being male dominated in 75 out of 83 country examples to 63 out of the 83.[81] Table 2.3 illustrates the extent of male domination in managerial and certain professional occupations, using data from national occupational classifications.

In those large organizations where women have managed to reach high-level managerial positions, they are often restricted to areas less central or strategic to the organization, such as human resources and administration. The increase in women's share of personnel and labour relations managerial positions in the United States over a 20-year period was higher than in other areas of management (from 21 per cent in 1970 to 58 per cent in 1991). Similarly, data for France show higher overall increases for women in personnel management than in other areas, with the percentage of women personnel managers in large companies increasing from 25 per cent in 1982 to 38 per cent in 1990. In Finland, the proportion of female personnel managers increased dramatically from 17 per cent in 1971 to 70 per cent in 1990.[82]

It is still extremely difficult for women to move laterally into strategic areas such as product development or finance and then upwards through the central pathways to key executive positions in the pyramidal structure that is characteristic of large organizations. Sometimes these barriers are called "glass walls" and the concept is illustrated by figure 2.9.

WOMEN IN POLITICS

When it comes to political representation, women also experience a glass ceiling effect although in some cases, such as in the Scandinavian countries, they have managed to climb higher than in the corporate world of the private sector. In 1999, for example, Finland elected its first woman President. The world average for women representatives in national parliaments stood at 13 per cent in 1999, with 13.4 per cent of these in the single or lower house and 10.9 per cent in the upper house or senate.[83] The first woman to hold the highest office within the world organization of parliaments was elected as President of the Inter-Parliamentary Union (IPU) Council in 1999.[84] In 1999, there were five women commissioners in the European Commission, bringing the female participation

Figure 2.9.　The glass ceiling and glass walls in the organizational pyramid

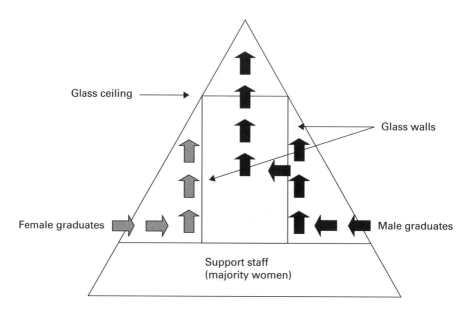

Source: ILO: *Economically Active Population, 1950-2010* (Geneva, 1997), pp. 23, 26 and 29.

to 25 per cent. One of these five women is in charge of budgetary issues, a particularly male-dominated sector as previously mentioned.[85]

In political life, women also tend to be concentrated in certain areas. Figure 2.10 and table 2.4 show how women are remarkably absent from holding higher responsibilities in the fields of finance and foreign affairs, and in security and defence. Women have found it easier to penetrate social, family, health and labour affairs, areas more closely related to women's perceived social roles and therefore usually considered more suited to women. A good example is to be found in the Government of Bulgaria in 1994: there were no women ministers, but four women vice-ministers headed the Ministry of Labour and Social Affairs, the Ministry of Health, the Ministry of Culture and the Ministry of Education and Science.[86]

Figure 2.11 indicates the "glass-ceiling effect" with regard to women in government both at ministerial and sub-ministerial level in all regions. In quite a number of countries, less than 10 per cent of ministers were women, with some having no women ministers at all. In a few countries, over 20 per cent of ministers were women. In 1998, Sweden achieved gender parity at the ministerial level with half of its 22 ministers being women. The data in figure 2.11 provide a varied picture of women in government, from which it is difficult to draw conclusions. While total female representation may be fairly high in a country, it may be concentrated almost entirely at ministerial level. In other

Figure 2.10. Indicative survey of posts of presidents of parliamentary committees held by women, world overview (based on information for 97 countries, in percentages)

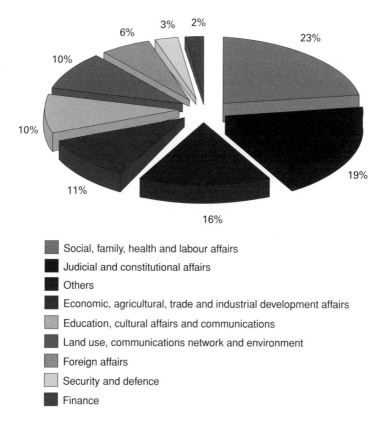

☐ Social, family, health and labour affairs

■ Judicial and constitutional affairs

■ Others

■ Economic, agricultural, trade and industrial development affairs

☐ Education, cultural affairs and communications

■ Land use, communications network and environment

☐ Foreign affairs

☐ Security and defence

■ Finance

Source: Inter-Parliamentary Union (IPU): *Men and women in politics: Democracy still in the making – a world comparative study* (Geneva, 1997), p. 107.

instances, representation at ministerial level is stronger than at the sub-ministerial level. Moreover, countries range from having low representation at both levels to having strong representation at both levels. It should be noted, though, that there is not necessarily a correlation between the wealth of a country and the level of representation of women in government.

EARNINGS GAPS BETWEEN FEMALE AND MALE MANAGERS

The male/female differences in management noted above also contribute to earnings differentials. Furthermore, although rates of pay may be similar, actual earnings can vary because of the different salary packages offered to managers, which provide various fringe benefits and access to certain schemes for boosting

49

Table 2.4.   Women in committees of the European Parliament: Parliamentary term
              1999-2004

Committee	Chairwoman	No. of members	No. of women	Percentage of women
Women's Rights and Equal Opportunities	Yes	38	34	89.5
Environment, Public Health and Consumer Policy	Yes	59	32	54.2
Culture, Youth, Education, Media and Sport	No	35	15	42.9
Employment and Social Affairs	No	54	21	38.9
Petitions	No	30	9	30.0
Industry, External Trade, Research and Energy	No	60	18	30.0
Legal Affairs and the Internal Market	Yes	35	10	28.6
Citizens' Freedoms and Rights, Justice and Home Affairs	No	43	12	27.9
Economic and Monetary Affairs	Yes	45	12	26.7
Development and Cooperation	No	35	9	25.7
Fisheries	No	20	5	25.0
Budgets	No	45	11	24.4
Budgetary Control	No	21	5	23.8
Agriculture and Rural Development	No	38	9	23.7
Constitutional Affairs	No	30	7	23.3
Regional Policy, Transport and Tourism	No	59	11	18.6
Foreign Affairs, Human Rights, Common Security and Defence Policy	No	65	11	16.9
Total	4	712	231	32.4

Source: European Commission: *Women in decision-making*, data from the European Database, updated 15 Sep. 1999.

bonuses. Earnings gaps may also reflect differences in seniority and the concentration of women in low-paid managerial sub-groups.

In the United Kingdom in 1996, women professionals were the least disadvantaged group of women workers, with weekly earnings approaching 83 per cent of those of men. Women managers, however, earned only 71 per cent of male managers' weekly salaries, which was even lower than the figure of 74 per cent for all occupations.[87] According to a 1998 survey of 25,952 people employed by 584 organizations, these differences had continued to persist. However, female managers' pay rose more quickly – a 7.7 per cent increase compared with 6.8 per cent for men. The average female manager was 37 and reportedly earned £31,622 annually, whereas the average male manager was

Figure 2.11. Percentage of government positions occupied by women, 1996
(selected countries by region)

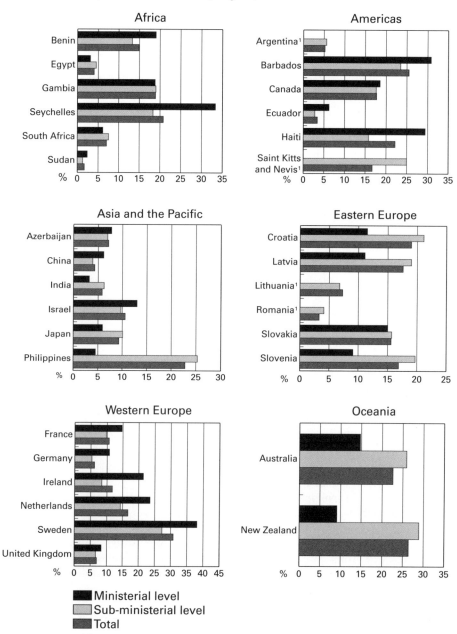

Ministerial level
Sub-ministerial level
Total

[1] No ministerial posts were occupied by women.

Source: United Nations: Data compiled by the Division for the Advancement of Women of the United States Secretariat, based on information from the Worldwide Government Directory (Bethesda, Maryland, Jan. 1996).

43 and earned £37,235. However, the situation was less positive at boardroom level with female directors receiving pay increases of 7.4 per cent compared with male directors who received increases of 10.3 per cent. The average female director was 41 years old and earned £66,711 annually, while her male counterpart was 48 years old and earned £94,742 (42 per cent more).[88]

In Finland, female managers were paid 35 per cent less on average than men,[89] and a large-scale survey in Brazil also found considerable pay differences between the sexes, with women managers sometimes earning only half the salary of their male counterparts.[90] In New Zealand, only 28 per cent of all women legislators, administrators and managers received over $NZ40,000 in 1996 compared with 58 per cent of all men occupying the same positions.[91] In 1995, women's salaries in Uruguay were 57 per cent of men's in the banking and finance sector. In managerial positions, the female/male ratio in earnings was even lower, with women earning only 47 per cent of men's salaries.[92] In Australia, the weekly income of women managers and administrators was a high 88 per cent of their male counterparts in 1998.[93]

Median weekly earnings of women managers in the United States are rising compared with their male counterparts, but still remain lower. In 1999, their pay was 84 per cent of men's, up from 68 per cent in 1995.[94] There are, however, variations depending on the type of activity or sector. Data analysed in 1997 by the National Committee on Pay Equity in the United States found that male managers in the medical and health sector received US$854 per week compared with the US$632 received by female managers – a weekly difference of US$222. Similarly, in the education and related fields sector, where women likewise formed more than 50 per cent of all employees, male administrators earned US$950 per week while female managers earned US$662 – a US$288 difference. The gender gap was even greater for marketing, advertising and public relations managers, with male managers earning US$1,059 a week compared with the US$736 earned by female managers – a US$323 difference.[95] Interestingly, a 1998 survey found that 2.7 per cent (double the 1995 figure) of women were among the five most highly paid officers at *Fortune 500* companies.[96]

The pay gap at managerial level also varies by country. According to the Korean Women's Development Institute, the average monthly wage of women workers in 1995 was 58 per cent that of men's. However, differentials varied considerably according to occupations. The figure for legislators, senior officials and managers was 83 per cent, followed by 72 per cent for professional occupations. A 1988 study found that 62 per cent of the female/male wage differential in the Republic of Korea was due to gender-based discrimination.[97]

OBSTACLES TO BREAKING THROUGH THE GLASS CEILING

Table 2.5 gives an overview of the obstacles experienced by personnel managers and other managers surveyed in European banks. A significant proportion of the respondents considered family obligations and the pre-

Table 2.5.   Obstacles to the recruitment and promotion of women to junior, middle and senior management positions in Europe: Viewpoints of personnel managers and female bank managers (in percentages)

Answers of personnel (male and female) managers in banks			Statement	Answers of female bank managers		
Junior management	Middle management	Senior management		Junior management	Middle management	Senior management
43.4	**20.7**	**17.2**	**No, there are no barriers**[1]	**11.4**	**2.0**	**1.4**
56.6	**79.3**	**82.8**	**Yes, there are barriers**[1]	**88.6**	**98.0**	**98.6**
			Personal barriers:[2]			
30.0	17.4	16.7	Not the right education	34.7	21.9	21.9
33.3	21.7	8.3	Lack of further training	29.8	25.3	11.0
6.7	17.4	31.3	Lack of experience	36.3	38.4	29.5
73.3	63.0	45.8	Family obligations	61.3	58.2	44.5
			Structural barriers:[2]			
10.0	4.3	6.3	Gender bias in promotion	4.0	6.8	17.8
10.0	21.7	16.7	Career starts in specialized management tracks	5.6	8.9	11.0
13.3	15.2	25.0	Informal promotion without advertising	17.7	25.3	30.1
			Cultural barriers in organizations:[2]			
10.0	10.9	10.4	Prejudices of personnel managers	19.4	24.0	21.2
3.3	17.4	18.8	Insufficient personal contacts	15.3	28.8	39.7
56.7	58.7	68.8	Male values dominate corporate culture	38.7	56.2	77.4
			Basis of calculations:			
53	58	58	Total respondents (N)	140	149	148
30	46	48	Respondents who listed at least one barrier (N)	124	146	146
74	114	119	No. of answers	326	429	444
2.5	2.5	2.5	Average no. of answers/ respondents	2.6	2.9	3.0

Notes: The figures in **bold** refer to over 355 of respondents who replied positively to the statement.   [1] Calculated on the basis of all respondents. Percentages add up to 100 per cent.   [2] Calculated on the basis of respondents who listed at least one barrier. Since multiple answers could be given, percentages do not add up to 100 per cent.

Source: Quack and Hancké, op. cit, p. 51.

dominance of "male values" in corporate culture to be the main obstacles to career advancement for women. The nature of the obstacles blocking women's progress to higher management varies, however, from those encountered at lower levels. Higher-ranking female bank managers seem to experience discrimination to a greater extent, both in terms of structural and cultural barriers, where insufficient personal contacts and dominance of "male values" adversely affect their advancement.[98]

The difficulties women face in reaching the top are also reflected in the higher levels of education and effort often demanded of them. A survey of businesses in Jamaica found that women had more years of schooling before joining the labour force than had men. They also advanced faster than men in middle-level management. Though a relatively high proportion of them (10 per cent) reached senior management positions, it took them significantly longer to do so than men.[99]

The hurdles facing women aspiring to management jobs can be so formidable that they sometimes abandon efforts to make it to the top of large firms. They often take their energy and know-how to smaller and more flexible companies or set up their own businesses. By 1996 in Sweden, approximately 20 per cent of start-up companies were being run by women and by 1999 in the United States, 38 per cent of all firms were run by women.[100] In Australia, women make up 35 per cent of the country's 1.3 million small business operators, and the growth rate of female small business operators from 1995 to 1997 was three times that for men.[101]

A recent survey in Ireland by a large multinational computer company showed that women clearly felt that the glass ceiling was still intact. As a consequence, many women have been starting their own companies, with between 35 and 40 per cent of all new businesses being owned by women. According to the survey, 64 per cent of Irish women in business earn half or more of the family income and 24 per cent are sole providers for their families.[102] Figure 2.12 shows increases over the last decade in the percentage of women employers in 18 countries for which data were available. In countries such as Australia, Canada, Finland, Thailand and the United States, over 30 per cent of all businesses are now owned or operated by women.

There is also a trend towards a growth in women-owned businesses in Africa, Asia and South America. In Western Asia, for example, the number of self-employed women rose from 22 per cent in 1970 to 30 per cent in 1990. The figures for Latin America over the same period are very similar (from 22 per cent to 34 per cent), while those for North Africa are lower (from 8 per cent to 21 per cent).[103] According to the National Foundation for Women Business Owners (NFWBO), firms owned by women around the world can account for between one-quarter and one-third of businesses in the formal sector and probably have an even stronger presence in the informal sector.[104] In Brazil, for example, it is thought that women run over 30 per cent of small and micro-businesses.[105] A United Nations study covering the Latin American region notes that micro-businesses and self-employment are a major source of employment and income for women and that between 30 per cent to 60 per cent of all micro-businesses in the region are operated by women.[106]

The fragility of women's advancement to management positions, however, is reflected in the fact that gains can be somewhat dampened by economic recession and restructuring, or by reductions in societal supports for women. For example, the recent bursting of the "economic bubble" in Japan resulted in companies hiring far more men than women. A survey of companies revealed that the proportion hiring male-only graduates increased from 50 per cent in 1992 to 62 per cent in 1996, while at the same time companies hiring both men

Figure 2.12. Percentage of women employers,[1] 1989-91 and 1997-98
(selected countries)

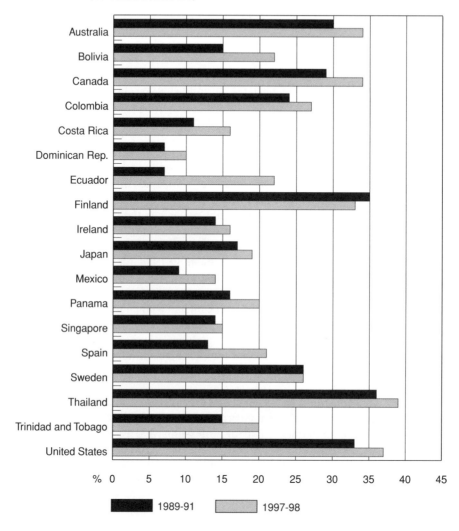

Note: Based on labour force sample surveys for all countries except for the Dominican Republic, where it is based on official estimates.

[1] International Classification of Status in Employment 1993 (ISCE-93), Group 2 (Employers). Canada and the United States includes Group 3 (own-account workers). The ILO defines *self-employment jobs* as those jobs where the remuneration is directly dependent on the profits from the goods and services produced. The incumbents make the operational decisions affecting the organization or delegate such decisions while retaining responsibility for the welfare of the organization. *Employers* are defined as those workers who, working on their own account or with one or more partners, hold the type of job defined as a "self-employment job" and, in this capacity, on a continuous basis have engaged one or more people to work for them in their business as employees. *Own-account workers* are those workers who, working on their own account or with one or more partners, hold the type of job defined as a "self-employment job" and have not engaged any employees on a continuous basis.

Source: ILO: *Yearbook of Labour Statistics 1999*, op. cit., table 2D, pp. 241-264.

and women graduates fell from 45 per cent to 37 per cent.[107] In addition, policies such as affirmative or positive action[108] are being strongly challenged through the courts in Europe and the United States.

Despite indications that women's labour is increasingly in demand, only a relatively small number of companies are investing in women's career development. Such companies believe that promoting women produces more talent and therefore more long-term profitability. As competent and qualified women become harder to attract and retain, companies promoting women today expect to gain advantages over the longer term. Moreover, making women visible at the top can provide a competitive edge in selling services and products to the growing number of women customers.

Indications that more such developments can be expected are to be found in a study from the United States, which examined the positive performance impact of women's presence on the boards of companies making initial public offerings (IPOs).[109] The study notes that when such companies go public, the initial stock price is based on factors not related to their current financial performance. Instead, one of the criteria used to determine the initial value is the composition of the senior management team, and its gender balance in particular is becoming an increasingly significant element. In 1988, there were no women on the boards of 134 companies going public. In 1993, 27 per cent of 535 IPO companies surveyed had women in their senior management teams. Of companies that went public in 1996, 41 per cent had women on their boards. The study found that, "having women on the top management team results in higher earnings and greater shareholder wealth", and that it is the mix of women and men on the board that results in higher long-term performance. The study also points to the trend for women to leave large corporations for smaller entrepreneurial firms.

A principal constraint on the level and type of labour market participation of women is the responsibility they carry for raising children and performing household tasks. An important feature of professional and especially managerial work is the extended working hours that seem to be required to gain recognition and eventual promotion. It can be practically impossible to reconcile the long hours often required of management staff with the amount of time needed to care for a home and children, not to mention care of the elderly. Yet, the availability of part-time managerial work is rare. In this context, time is very much a gender issue. Women who desire both a family and a career often juggle heavy responsibilities in both domains. Those who opt for part-time work early in their careers may find their advancement hampered, even after a return to full-time employment, since their male counterparts will have invested heavily in career building during the same period.

CONCLUSION

While women have captured an ever-increasing share of the labour market, improvements in the quality of women's jobs have not kept pace. This is reflected in the smaller representation of women in management positions, particularly in the private sector, and their virtual absence from the most senior jobs. Wage differences in male and female managerial jobs stem from the reality that even when women hold management jobs, they are often in less strategic lower-paying areas of a company's operations. They are also linked to the fact that women managers tend to be younger on average, as most senior jobs tend to be dominated by older men. Despite the persistent inequalities at managerial level, the continuous entry of women into higher-level jobs has been noted in this chapter, although they remain under-represented in senior management. With few exceptions, the main challenge appears to be the sheer slowness in the progress of women into senior leadership positions in organizations, which suggests that discrimination is greatest where the most power is exercised. However, the growth in entrepreneurship and increasing numbers of women running their own businesses, both large and small, heralds a different future for societies. The economic power gained by women will play a key role in the struggle to sweep aside gender inequalities in all walks of life.

Notes

[1] E. Serdjénian: "Women managers in France", in N. J. Adler and D. N. Izraeli (eds.): *Competitive frontiers: Women managers in a global economy* (Cambridge, Mass., Basil Blackwell, 1994), p. 193.

[2] In this book, the terms "junior", "middle", "senior" and "executive" are used for convenience when referring to the various levels of management.

[3] Resolution III concerning the revision of the International Standard Classification of Occupations; published as ILO: *ISCO-88: International Standard Classification of Occupations* (Geneva, 1990).

[4] For the ILO publication based on these data, see R. Anker: *Gender and jobs: Sex segregation of occupations in the world* (Geneva, ILO, 1998).

[5] See ILO: *Conditions of work and employment of professional workers: Compendium of principles and good practices* (Geneva, 1990).

[6] The coverage in Chapter 3 of the educational choices made by students explains the concentration of men and women in certain professions and jobs.

[7] Anker, op. cit., p. 164.

[8] ILO: *Yearbook of Labour Statistics 1999* (Geneva, 1999), pp. 213, 220 and 222.

[9] United Nations Committee on the Elimination of Discrimination against Women (CEDAW): *Third and fourth periodic reports of the States parties: Mexico* (May 1997), para. 148.

[10] *Gleichbehandlung von Männern und Frauen im Arbeitsleben: Umfrage der Bundesvereinigung der Deutschen Arbeitgeberverbände*, Survey conducted by the Confederation of German Employers' Associations, 1992.

[11] Institute of Management/Remuneration Economics: *National management salary survey*, cited in the Trades Union Congress (TUC): *Professional and managerial staffs: Trends and prospects*, Report prepared by the Labour Research Department for the Professional and Managerial Staffs Symposium, Feb. 1997, p. 13.

[12] A. Posadskaya and N. Zakharova: *To be a manager: Changes for women in the USSR*, Discussion Paper No. 65, Training Policies Branch (Geneva, ILO, 1990), p. 4.

[13] N. Muscatelli: "Las mujeres sólo ocupan el 10% de los cargos directivos", in *El Clarín* (Buenos Aires), 15 Aug. 1999, p. 26.

[14] Office fédéral de la statistique: *Vers l'égalité? La situation des femmes et des hommes en Suisse*, Deuxième Rapport Statistique. http:www.statistik.admin.ch/stat_ch/ber03/sake/ftfr03.htm.

[15] loc. cit.

[16] S. Ramirez: "En las altas esferas", in *Fempress*, No. 206, Dec. 1998, p. 6.

[17] S. de Avelar: *Women in economic decision-making in Brazil: A glass ceiling report*, Working paper prepared for an Expert Group Meeting on Women and Economic Decision-Making organized by the United Nations Division for the Advancement of Women, New York, Nov. 1994.

[18] S. Ferreira and R. Corbo: *Situación actual del empleo de las mujeres en el Uruguay* (Montevideo, Ministry of Labour and Social Security, National Employment Office,1996).

[19] ILO: SEGREGAT database.

[20] *Japan Labor Bulletin* (Tokyo, Japan Institute of Labour), 1996, Vol. 35, No. 5, p. 1.

[21] S. Siengthai: *Women and economic decision-making in international financial institutions and transnational corporations in Thailand*, Paper prepared for the Expert Group Meeting on Women and Economic Decision-Making in International Financial Institutions and Transnational Corporations, United Nations Division for the Advancement of Women, Boston, Mass., 11-15 Nov. 1996.

[22] Information provided to the ILO by the Singapore National Employers' Federation (SNEF), Mar. 1997.

[23] R. B. González: *Participación de la mujer ejecutiva en Colombia*, Working paper commissioned by the ILO (Bogotá, ILO, 1996), p. 1.

[24] Affirmative Action Agency: *Annual Report 1997-98* (Sydney, 1999).

[25] E. A. Fagenson and J. J. Jackson: "The status of women managers in the United States", in Adler and Izraeli, op. cit., table 23.1, p. 389.

[26] ILO: SEGREGAT database.

[27] ILO: *Yearbook of Labour Statistics 1999*, op. cit., table 2C, pp. 197-240.

[28] ibid.

[29] ibid.

[30] Catalyst: "Catalyst census posts solid gains in percentage of women corporate officers in America's largest 500 corporations: Women continue to lag far behind men in line officer positions". http://www.catalystwomen.org/press/release111199.html.

[31] Commonwealth Office for the Status of Women: "Australian Women". http://osw.dpmc. gov.au/content/resources/publications.html.

[32] ILO: SEGREGAT database.

[33] U. Koch: "Equality issue lands on the manager's desk", in *Nordic Labour Journal*, Vol. 2, 1998, p. 10.

[34] Catalyst: "Catalyst census posts solid gains ...", op. cit.

[35] idem: "1999 Catalyst census of women corporate officers and top earners". http:// www.catalystwomen.org/press/factscote99.html.

[36] idem: "Catalyst census finds few women corporate officers". http://www.catalystwomen. org/press/release020800.html.

[37] idem: "1999 Catalyst census of women corporate officers ...", op. cit.

[38] idem: "Catalyst census finds few women corporate officers ...", op. cit.

[39] de Avelar, op. cit.

[40] United Kingdom Central Statistical Office: *Labour Force Survey: Quarterly Bulletin* (London, Feb. 1999).

[41] Institute of Management/Remuneration Economics: *National management survey*, cited in TUC, op. cit., p. 13.

[42] Labour Research: "Women knock on the boardroom door", cited in TUC, op. cit., p. 13.

[43] Verlag Hoppenstedt GmbH: Various press releases (Darmstadt, Dec. 1995).

[44] J. Laufer and A. Fouquet: *Effet de plafonnement des carrières de femmes cadres et accès des femmes à la décision dans la sphère économique* (Groupe HEC, Centre d'études de l'emploi, Service des droits des femmes, 1997), cited in "Femmes dans les lieux de décision", Avis du Conseil économique et social sur le rapport présenté par Mme Michèle Cotta au nom de la section du travail, Mandature 1999-2004, Séance des 19 et 20 décembre 2000, in *Journal Officiel de la République française*, Année 2000, No. 18, Dec. 2000, p. II-89.

[45] Survey conducted by the Jamaica Employers' Federation, cited in C. Thomas: *Report to the OAS on the Caribbean subregion*, Oct. 1996.

[46] L. Pardo: "La mujer en las decisiones económicas", in M. E. Valenzuela (ed.): *Igualdad de oportunidades para la mujer en el trabajo* (Santiago, Servicio Nacional de la Mujer, 1996), p. 179.

[47] Commonwealth Office for the Status of Women (OSW), Background and Statistics Section of the OSW website: *Australian women* (Canberra, 2000). http://osw.dpmc.gov.au/content/resources/women_aus.html.

[48] ILO: SEGREGAT database.

[49] See Canadian Human Rights Commission (CHRC): "Employment equity: Assessment of progress for designated groups", in *Annual Report 1999* (Ottawa, 2000).

[50] Ministry of Social Affairs and Health, Finland: *Equal rights, equal responsibilities, equal opportunities* (Helsinki, 1994), p. 7.

[51] Affirmative Action Agency: *Annual Report 1995-96* (Sydney, 1996).

[52] Muscatelli, op. cit.

[53] US Department of Labor, Bureau of Labor Statistics: *Employment and Earnings*, Jan. 1996.

[54] ILO: SEGREGAT database.

[55] González, op. cit., p. 4.

[56] Ramirez, op. cit., p. 6.

[57] de Avelar, op. cit.

[58] Verlag Hoppenstedt GmbH, op. cit.

[59] Affirmative Action Agency, op. cit., p. 23.

[60] CHRC: *Annual Report 1996* (Ottawa, 1996).

[61] S. L. Mei Ling: *Strategies to reach the top for women in management: Perspectives from ASEAN*, Working Paper No. 114, Salaried Employees and Professional Workers Branch (Geneva, ILO, 1997), table 8, p. 18.

[62] S. Quack and B. Hancké: *Women in decision-making in finance*, Report prepared for the use of the European Commission, Directorate General V, Industrial Relations, Employment and Social Affairs (Berlin, Wissenschaftszentrum Berlin für Sozialforschung, 1997), p. 30.

[63] ibid., p. 29.

[64] ibid., p. 30.

[65] Institute of Management/Remuneration Economics: *National management survey*, cited in TUC: *Professional and managerial staffs*, op. cit., p. 14.

[66] See CHRC: "Employment equity…", op. cit.

[67] CEDAW: *Second and third periodic reports of States parties: Turkey*, CEDAW/C/TUR/2-3 (Sep. 1996), p. 66.

[68] Commonwealth Office of the Status of Women: "Facts about women". http://osw.dpmc.gov.au/content/resources/facts.html.

[69] CEDAW: *Fourth periodic report of the States parties: The Philippines*, CEDAW/C/PHI/4 (July 1996), p. 47.

[70] S. Siengthai and O. Leelakulthanit: "Women in management in Thailand", in Adler and Izraeli, op. cit., p. 165.

[71] Universidad de Chile: *Las mujeres en la toma de decisiones económicas* (Santiago, 1995).

[72] CEDAW: *Second and third periodic reports of the States parties: Bulgaria* (Nov. 1994), p. 19.

[73] idem: *Report by Azerbaijan to initial report* (Sep. 1996), para. 99.

[74] idem: *Third and fourth periodic reports of the States parties: Mexico* (May 1997), para. 141.

[75] idem: *Second and third periodic reports of the States parties: Bulgaria* (Nov. 1994), para. 72d.

[76] V. Hammond and V. Holton: "The scenario for women managers in Britain in the 1990s", in Adler and Izraeli, op. cit., p. 227.

[77] Institute of Management: "Small business pay gap widens", press release relating to Institute of Management/Remuneration Economics: *National management salary survey*, June 1998. http://www.inst-mgt.org.uk/institute/press/smallbu.html.

[78] US Department of Labor, Women's Bureau: "Facts on working women". http:// gatekeeper. dol.gov/dol/wb/public/wb_pubs/wmgt.htm.

[79] de Avelar, op. cit.

[80] Muscatelli, op. cit.

[81] Anker, op. cit., pp. 390-91.

[82] ILO: SEGREGAT database.

[83] Inter-Parliamentary Union (IPU): *Women in national parliaments*, (Geneva, Nov. 1999).

[84] idem: "First woman president of IPU council", Press Release No. 8, Berlin, 16 Oct. 1999.

[85] European Women's Lobby (EWL): "News-update", No. 7, Jul./Aug. 1999. See also European Commission: "Women in decision-making", data from the European Database, updated 15 Sep. 1999.

[86] CEDAW: *Second and third periodic reports of the States parties: Bulgaria* (Nov. 1994), para. 69.

[87] Reported in TUC, op. cit., p. 14.

[88] Institute of Management: "Small business pay gap widens", op. cit.

[89] Ministry of Social Affairs and Health, Finland, op. cit., p. 7.

[90] de Avelar, op. cit.

[91] Statistics New Zealand figures based on 1996 census of population and dwellings (Auckland, 2000).

[92] Ferreira and Corbo, op. cit.

[93] Australian Bureau of Statistics: "ABS survey finds more males in high paid jobs", press release, Canberra, 25 Mar. 1999. http://www.abs.gov.au/ausstats/abs@.nsf/Lookup/NT00002E6A.

[94] US Department of Labor, Women's Bureau Publications: "Median annual earnings for year-round full-time workers by sex in current and real dollars 1951-98". http://www.dol.gov/ dol/wb/public/wb_pubs/achart.htm.

[95] AFL-CIO: "The pay gap by occupation". http://www.aflcio.org/women/a_z.htm.

[96] Catalyst: "1999 Catalyst census of women corporate officers...", op. cit.

[97] M. Roh, Korean Women's Development Institute: Statement to the 41st Session of the United Nations Commission on the Status of Women, Panel on Women and the Economy, New York, Mar. 1997, pp. 2-3.

[98] Quack and Hancké, op. cit., pp. 49ff.

[99] I. Gershenberg: "Gender, training, and the creation of a managerial elite: Multinationals and other firms in Jamaica", in *Journal of Developing Areas* (Macomb), 1994, Vol. 28, No. 3, p. 321.

[100] C. Brush: "Women's entrepreneurship", in ILO Enterprise Forum: *A new spirit of organization: Articles and cases* (Geneva, ILO, 1999), p. 142.

[101] Commonwealth Office of the Status of Women: "Facts about women 2000". http:// osw.dpmc.gov.au/content/resources/facts.html.

[102] IBM: *The Celtic tigress grows and proposes an agenda for change* (Dublin, May 1998).

[103] Brush, op. cit., p. 142.

[104] National Foundation for Women Business Owners (NFWBO): "Characteristics of women entrepreneurs worldwide are revealed", *Research summary* (Washington, DC, 5 Mar. 1999).

[105] de Avelar, op. cit.

[106] United Nations Economic Commission for Latin America and the Caribbean (ECLAC), Women and Development Unit: *The challenge of gender equity and human rights on the threshold of the twenty-first century* (Santiago, May 2000), p. 27.

[107] S. Imada: "Female labor force after the enforcement of the equal employment opportunity law", in *Japan Labor Bulletin* (Tokyo), 1996, Vol. 36, No. 8.

[108] "Affirmative action" and "positive action" are used interchangeably in this book. The first term tends to be used in the United States, South Africa and Australia, whereas the second is more commonly used in Europe.

[109] See T. M Welbourne: *Wall Street likes its women: An examination of women in the top management teams of initial public offerings*, Working Paper 99-07, Centre for Advanced Human Resource Studies (CAHRS). http://www.ilr.cornell.edu/depts/cahrs/PDFs/WorkingPapers/WP99-07.pdf., p. 3.

IMPROVING WOMEN'S QUALIFICATIONS AND OPPORTUNITIES: A KEY ELEMENT IN BREAKING THROUGH THE GLASS CEILING

3

INTRODUCTION

Just how well prepared are women for management jobs? Undoubtedly women's education, training and life experience are increasingly equipping them with the necessary qualifications and skills to aspire to and be selected for top positions. Despite persistent differences in educational levels, the gender gap is closing in many areas. Overall enrolment figures worldwide show that the number of women reaching higher levels of education is approaching or even exceeding that of men, and this should theoretically allow women more access to management jobs in years to come.

The pursuit of universal education over the last decades has contributed to the rising educational levels of women worldwide. At the same time, increases in women's labour force participation have led to a higher value being placed on women's contribution to family income. Together with changing social attitudes, this has created a more enabling family and social environment for young women to achieve better education. Furthermore, the expansion of the service sector and of service jobs, in which there has traditionally been a high concentration of women, has opened new horizons, motivating women to seek qualifications for the kind of jobs to which they have easier access. Job growth, generated by new information technologies such as the Internet, is creating new opportunities and women are increasingly taking advantage of such developments to create and run businesses.

It has to be recognized, however, that significant gender differences continue to exist in the nature and quality of education and training. These can represent real obstacles for many women, both at the recruitment stage and later in their careers. Improving the quality of women's education largely depends on support from the family and community in encouraging young women and providing them with the same educational and training opportunities as young men. Indeed, young women have increasingly been encouraged to undertake further education to increase their chances of finding employment later, though the focus of this education tends to be at lower educational levels. In contrast, young men are often prompted to take on higher-level studies of longer duration. This situation is gradually changing in many countries, but the problem of gender choice remains: young women still tend to select particular fields of study and young men others. Thus, many women can end up lacking the right educational profile to enable them to enter and advance in certain professional and managerial careers.

This chapter examines these educational trends, and highlights the ongoing improvements in the academic achievement levels of young women, which reach or even surpass those of young men in certain areas. A slow but steady shift towards young women entering more scientific and technological subject areas is also notable. These changes are already affecting the type of professions women are opting for and will influence the gender composition of professional and managerial occupations in the future.

THE IMPROVED EDUCATIONAL ACHIEVEMENTS OF YOUNG WOMEN

Progress in the levels and educational qualifications achieved by young women clearly demonstrate their intellectual capacity to perform as well as young men. The main differences between the groups lie in the choices of subject areas they make as they progress to higher levels of education. Standardized assessment tests in the United Kingdom show that girls are outperforming boys academically at ages 7 and 14 in English, home economics, French, and craft design and technology, while in maths and science there is little difference between the two groups. In school examinations taken at ages 15-16, young women have consistently outperformed young men, while at advanced-level examinations (ages 17-18), they have at least matched them and since 1980 have frequently done better. In particular, young women have been achieving slightly higher-level passes in physics, chemistry and technology – although fewer young women take these subjects than young men do.[1] While all students are required to take English and at least one science subject, gender choices are already apparent at upper-secondary school level. In Scotland, for example, twice as many female students as male students achieved a grade A to C pass at the higher level in biology in 1995, while the reverse was true for physics.[2]

European Union (EU) data even show trends for more female students than male students overall to graduate from upper-secondary education in 8 out of 14 countries for which data were available (see figure 3.1). However, female students obtained more general upper-secondary school-leaving certificates while male students obtained more vocational ones (see figures 3.2 and 3.3).

In the United Kingdom, the myth that boys catch up with girls in education at higher levels (GCSE and A-level studies) has not been borne out by the facts. It was shown that females had built up an increasing lead over their male counterparts, "in all subject areas except science and maths where they are even in results".[3] In the United Republic of Tanzania in the early 1990s, male students were performing better than their female peers in secondary school examinations. At university level, however, the drop-out rate in maths and science between 1982 and 1992 was lower for young women than for young men, and their performance levels were higher.[4]

Figure 3.1. Overall number of female graduates per 100 male graduates
at upper-secondary level in selected EU Member States, 1995-96

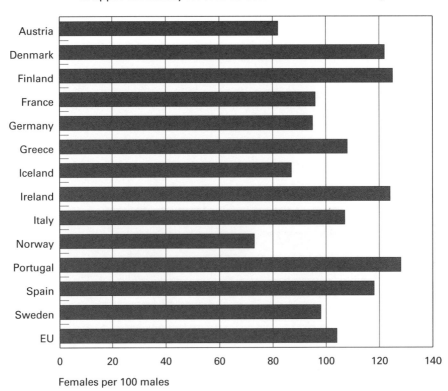

Females per 100 males

Notes: The data for Ireland do not include students completing secretarial and commercial courses in independent private schools, graduates of publicly aided agricultural colleges and graduates of catering and apprenticeship programmes. For Sweden, adult and special adult education is excluded.

Source: European Commission: *Education across the European Union: Statistics and indicators 1998,* Eurostat, Theme 3 (Brussels, 1998).

Mexico shows higher figures for female attendance at intermediate and higher intermediate levels of education. Between the early 1980s and the early 1990s, the number of females per 100 males increased from 89 to 94. However, this may in part be due to an increased drop-out rate amongst males rather than improved female participation.[5] The figures for Bulgaria are also encouraging. In 1997 young women totalled 50.4 per cent of secondary school students and as much as 74.1 per cent of students at higher-grade institutes (at the non-academic level).[6] Of the 30,500 students in technical secondary education in Azerbaijan in 1996, a full 61 per cent were female.[7]

At higher levels of education, women worldwide are catching up with men in terms of numbers, as can be seen in figure 3.4. By 1999 in the United States, women represented 44 per cent of the Yale Medical School entry-level class and were earning more bachelors' and masters' degrees than men.[8] In many

Figure 3.2.   Female graduates per 100 male graduates at upper-secondary
level in selected EU Member States (general education), 1995-96

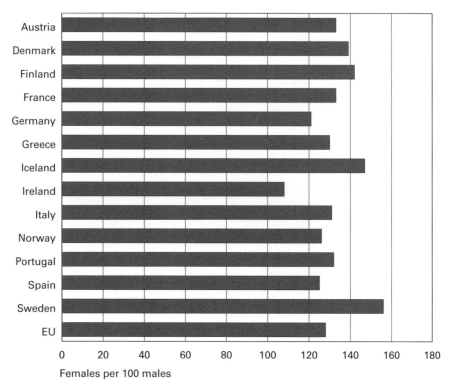

Females per 100 males

Notes: See figure 3.1.
Source: European Commission: *Education across the European Union...*, op cit.

European countries, the percentage of young women with a university education
is also increasing more rapidly than the percentage of similarly qualified men.
In a number of these countries, the share of young women with university
degrees is actually higher than that of young men.

Table 3.1 shows that developed countries have the best percentage (52.7 per
cent) of female enrolments at the third level in 1996, while the least developed
countries have the lowest percentage at 26.7 per cent. Developing countries are
rapidly catching up with the developed countries and show, with an increase of
4.9 per cent, the most significant improvement in participation for female
enrolments at the third level.

In Japan, women's enrolment in four-year colleges and universities has been
gradually increasing since 1975 when it stood at 21.6 per cent of the total. Ten
years later this had only increased to 23.9 per cent but since the enactment of a
1985 law on equal employment opportunity which encouraged women to invest
more in their education, the figure jumped to 27.9 by 1990.[9] In Uruguay, more

Figure 3.3. Female graduates per 100 male graduates at upper-secondary level in selected EU Member States (vocational education), 1995-96

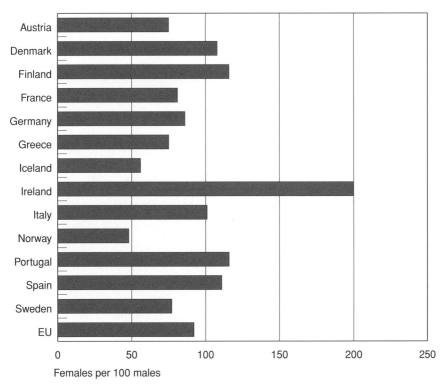

Females per 100 males

Notes: See figure 3.1.
Source: European Commission: *Education across the European Union...*, op. cit.

women than men had achieved higher levels of education in 1994, with their share reaching 56.9 per cent.[10] In Mexico, 82 per cent of all students who enrolled in higher education in 1994-95 were women.[11] By 1996, Bulgaria had more women than men (54.3 per cent) enrolled in universities and other educational institutes providing academic degrees.[12]

The share of university degrees awarded to women is also rising. In the United States, women are being awarded more degrees than in previous years (see figure 3.5). The US Department of Education reports that since 1982, the number of bachelors' degrees awarded to women has exceeded those awarded to men. Since 1986, the number of masters' degrees awarded to women began to exceed those obtained by men and it is expected that by the year 2000, the total number of doctoral degrees awarded to women and men will be equal.[13] As part of this increase, there has been a rise in degrees awarded to women in such areas as business and medicine (figure 3.6).

Figure 3.4. Women's percentage share of enrolments at third-level institutions, 1985 and 1996 (worldwide and by region)

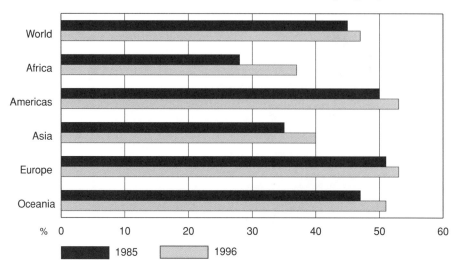

Notes: Data cover ISCED levels 5, 6 and 7 provided at universities, teacher training colleges and higher professional schools.

Source: UNESCO: *Statistical Yearbook 1998* (Paris, 1998), pp. 2-14.

Table 3.1. Women's percentage share of enrolment at third-level institutions,[1] 1985 and 1996 (least-developed, developing and developed countries)

Type of country	1985	1996
Least developed countries	26.1	26.7
Developing countries	36.0	40.9
Developed countries	50.4	52.7

[1] ISCED levels 5, 6 and 7 provided by universities, teacher training colleges and higher professional schools.

Source: UNESCO: *Statistical Yearbook 1998* (Paris, 1998), sec. 2:14-2:15.

This trend also appears in other countries. In 1990, Australian women obtained 34.5 per cent of doctoral degrees compared with 13.7 per cent in 1977, and their share of masters' degrees doubled in the same period (from 19 per cent in 1977 to 41 per cent in 1990). In Poland, women were awarded 11 per cent of all doctoral degrees in 1955 but 29 per cent in 1991.[14] Since 1986, there have been twice the number of female graduates as male graduates at Al Ain University in the United Arab Emirates.[15]

Despite growing gender equality in the number of enrolments undertaken and degrees awarded, women are still concentrated in the lower levels of tertiary education (colleges, institutes and so forth) and often for courses of shorter duration. Young men, on the other hand, attend university-type institutions, and for longer periods. One common fear of women is that an investment in

Figure 3.5.   Percentage of degrees obtained by women at institutions of higher education by type of degree, 1990 and 1996 (United States)

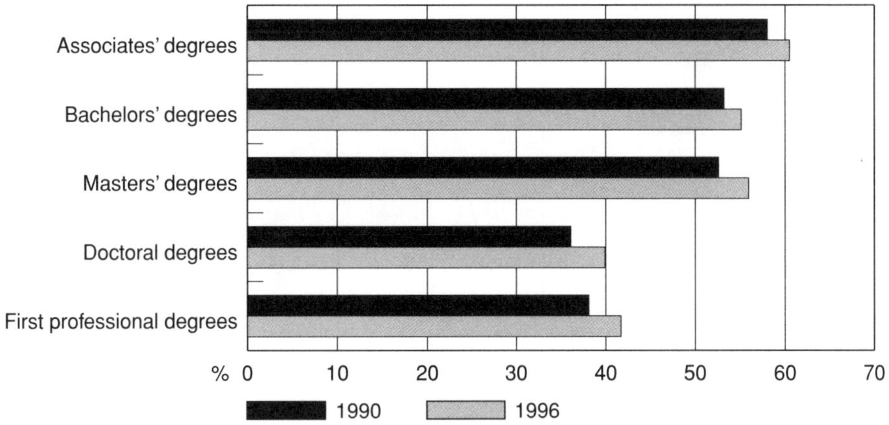

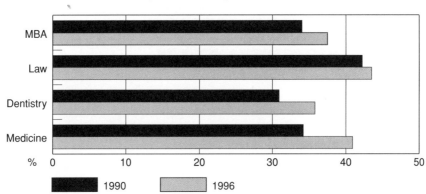

Source: D. Furchtgott-Roth and C. Stolba: *Women's figures: An illustrated guide to the economic progress of women in America* (Washington, DC, AEI Press, 1999), pp. 85-87.

Figure 3.6.   Percentage of degrees awarded to women by subject area, 1990 and 1996 (United States)

Source: Furchtgott-Roth and Stolba, op. cit., pp. 87-99.

education will not result in the career opportunities they expect. For example, a recent Swedish survey found that only 5 per cent of female economists were reaching senior positions compared with 24 per cent of male economists. Of those with classics degrees, 13 per cent of men reach senior positions compared with only 3 per cent of women.[16] Figure 3.7 shows that, in general, there are fewer female science graduates than male science graduates, but this gap is less pronounced in lower-level non-university institutions. In Japan, there are nearly twice as many women science graduates of such institutions as men, while in the

Figure 3.7.   Number of science graduates per 100,000 individuals in the labour force, men and women aged 25-34, 1995 (OECD countries)

A. Non-university tertiary education

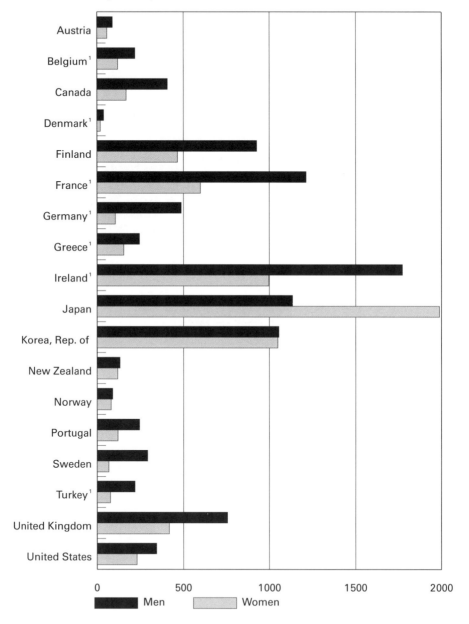

Figure 3.7. (cont.)

B. University-level education

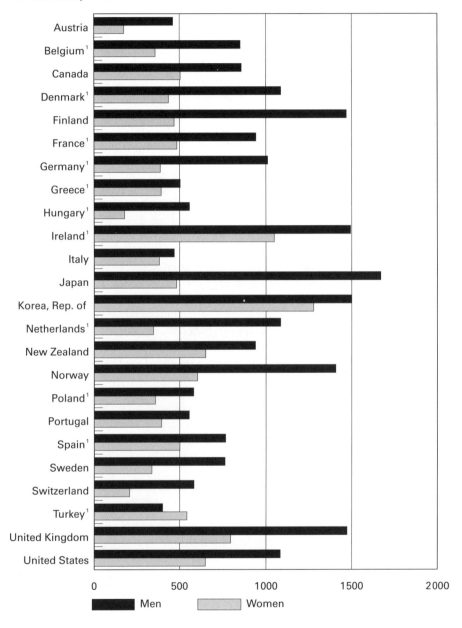

¹ 1993 data.

Source: OECD: *Education at a Glance: OECD Indicators 1996* (Paris, 1996).

case of university-level science graduates, men are almost four times as numerous as women.

NEW GENDER CHOICES IN CAREERS

Gender choice of study areas contributes to differential outcomes in the professional profiles of men and women. Even if the quality of education is high across all the disciplines, the fact that men and women graduate in different areas already sets the stage for dividing occupations into typically "male" or "female" jobs.

Gender choice is generally more pronounced in higher education and in university studies. In the OECD countries, young men tend to favour maths, computer science, engineering and architecture, and young women generally account for 30 per cent or less of those with qualifications within these categories. Exceptions to this trend include Italy and Portugal, where women obtain around 50 per cent of the qualifications awarded in maths and computer science. On the other hand, young women dominate medicine in many countries, being awarded up to 80 per cent of all such degrees. Women continue to be in the majority graduating in the humanities, usually taking 60 per cent to 70 per cent of these degrees. In many countries, natural science, law and business qualifications seem to be relatively evenly divided between women and men. Figures 3.8 and 3.9 illustrate these trends in OECD countries.

An ILO study found a 12 per cent female participation rate in technical programmes (science and technology, engineering, agriculture, environmental studies and technical teacher training) among 20 polytechnic institutions across a group of African countries (Botswana, Gambia, Ghana, Kenya, Malawi, Nigeria, Uganda, the United Republic of Tanzania and Zambia).[17]

Studies suggest that such gender choices are based on sex-role socialization by families and societies.[18] Employers are also influenced by views that tend to classify jobs as being more "suitable" for women or men. Such differential treatment in the labour market is readily perceived by young people, who adapt their choice of profession and the subjects they study accordingly. In this way occupational segregation is perpetuated.

> "As a student in the Electronics and Telecommunications Department of the Technical College I was very scared because I had an opinion that men were extra intelligent especially in the more difficult lessons in engineering. Fortunately there was another female student in electrical engineering who in high school had been in co-education. She encouraged me by saying that I should not be scared of boys, that their reasoning and learning capability was just the same as girls. I took her words and continued with my studies and did very well in my three years. There were times where I ranked first in overall performance."
>
> A telecommunications engineer in Africa.
>
> Source: ILO: *Women in technical trades*, op. cit., p. 20.

Gender choices are, however, gradually changing and women are increasingly enrolling in so-called technical areas. For example, Japanese

Figure 3.8.   Percentage of university-level qualifications in different subject
               categories by sex, 1996 (OECD countries)

A. Natural sciences

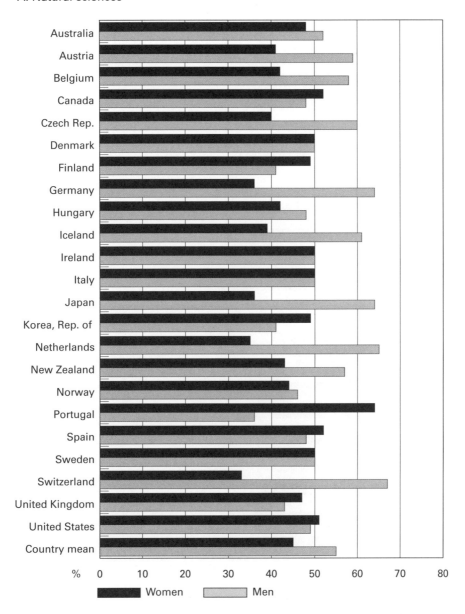

Figure 3.8. (cont.)

B. Maths and computer science

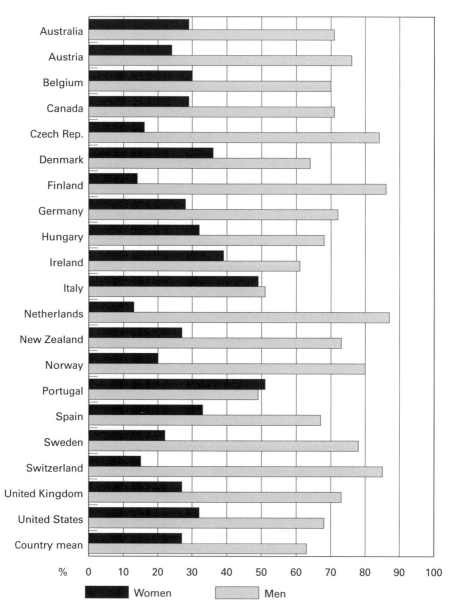

Figure 3.8. (cont.)

C. Medicine

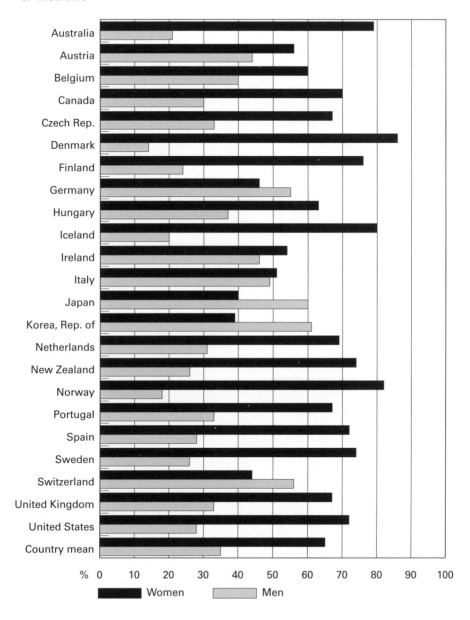

Figure 3.8. (cont.)

D. Engineering and architecture

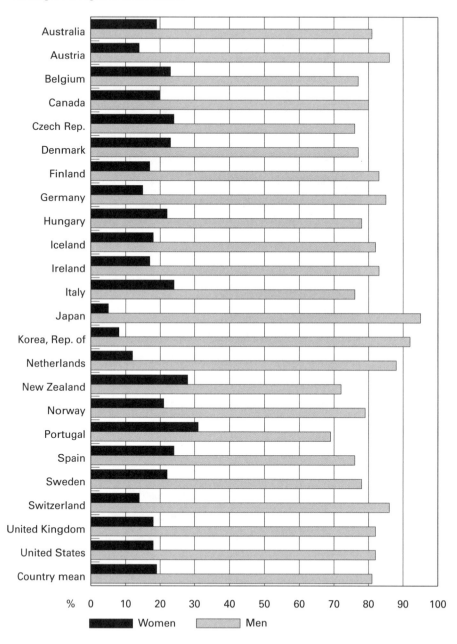

Figure 3.8. (cont.)

E. Business and law

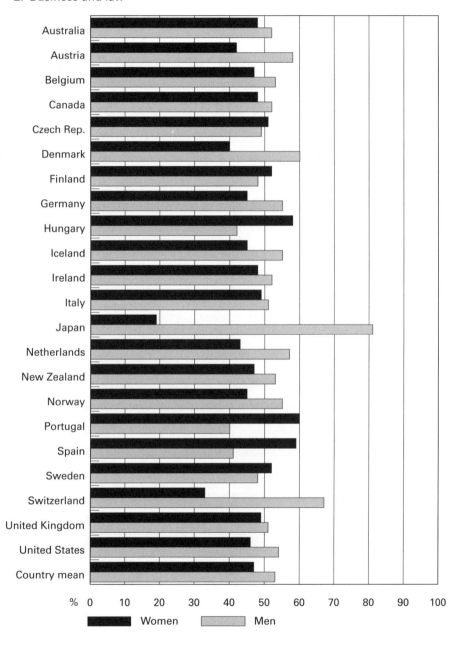

Figure 3.8. (cont.)

F. Humanities and general

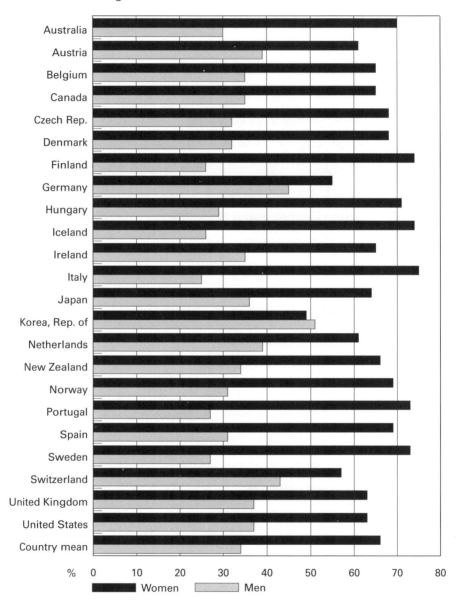

Notes: For Iceland (maths and computer science), data are not applicable because the category does not exist. For Japan (maths and computer science, and medicine) and the Republic of Korea (maths and computer science, and business and law), data are included in another category.

Source: OECD: *Education at a Glance: OECD Indicators 1997* (Paris, 1997), pp. 340-431.

Figure 3.9.   Percentage of non-university qualifications in different subject categories by sex, 1996 (OECD countries)

A. Natural sciences

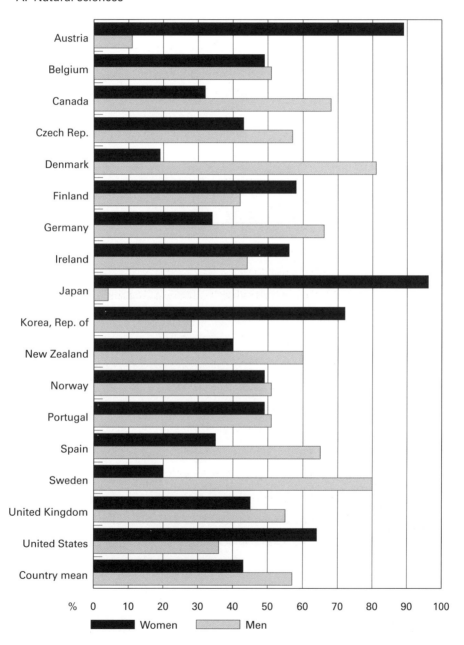

Figure 3.9. (cont.)

B. Maths and computer science

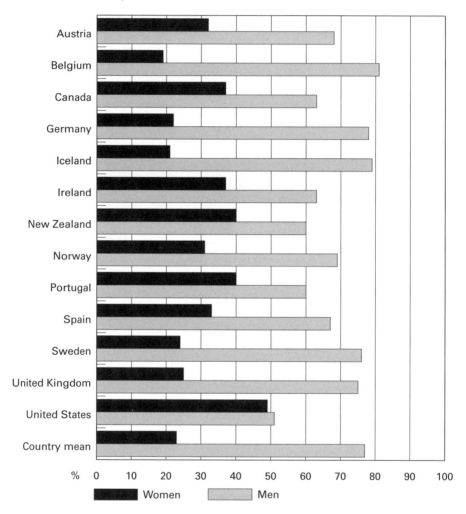

Figure 3.9. (cont.)

C. Medicine

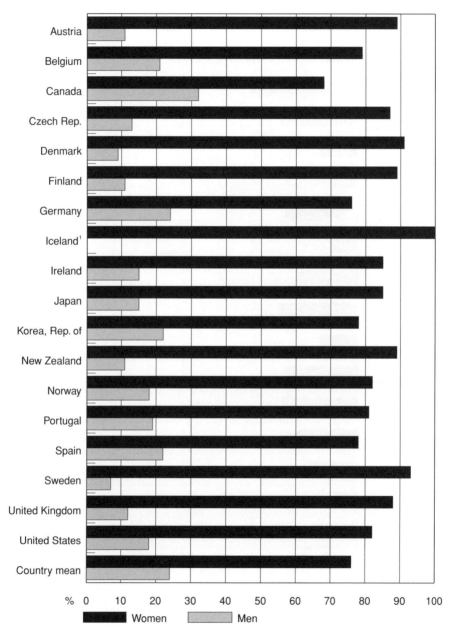

¹ Zero value for men.

Figure 3.9. (cont.)

D. Engineering and architecture

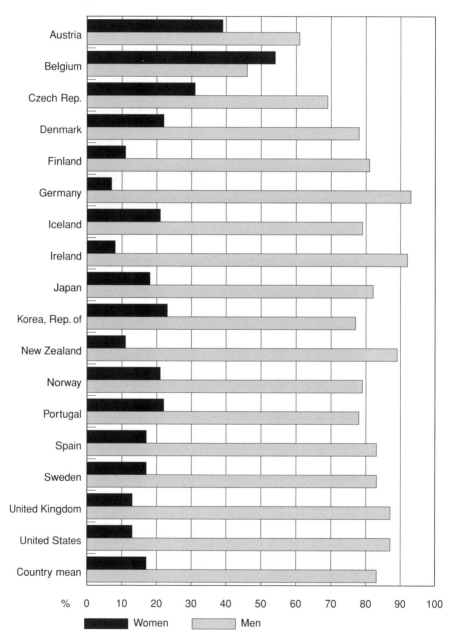

Figure 3.9. (cont.)

E. Business and law

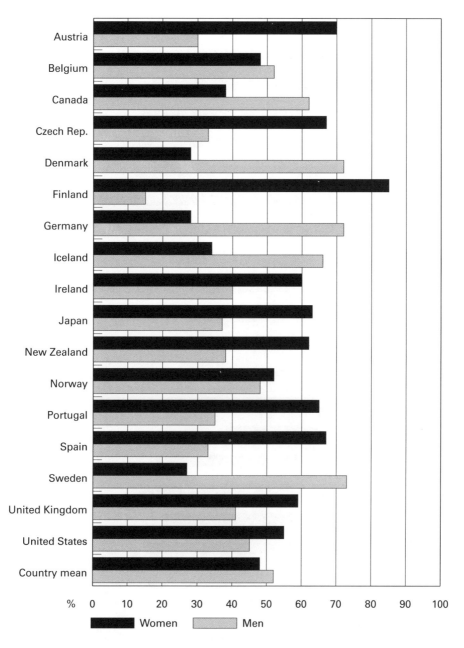

Figure 3.9. (cont.)

F. Humanities and general

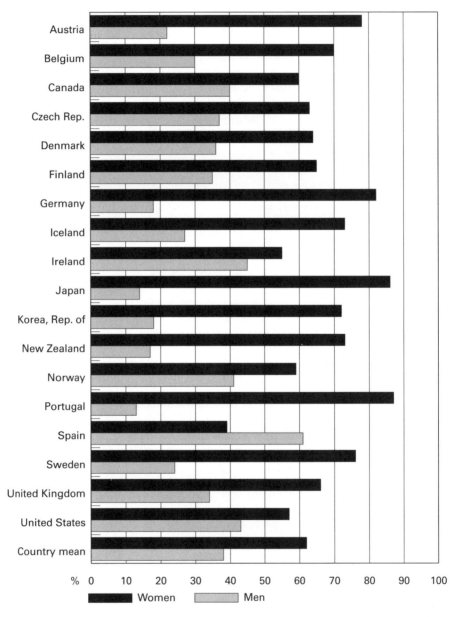

Notes: For maths and computer science, data for Czech Republic are not applicable because the category does not exist; for Denmark, because the magnitude is negligible; and for Japan, because the data are included in another category.

Source: OECD: *Education at a Glance: OECD Indicators 1997* (Paris, 1997) pp. 340-431.

women are preparing themselves more for career jobs in business, with an increasing proportion of women majoring in the social sciences, science, maths and engineering.[19]

In France, while the overall share of women's enrolments in university studies rose from 49 per cent in 1974 to 55 per cent in 1985, their representation in economics jumped from 33 per cent to 49 per cent in the same period. Similarly, the proportion of women in Turkish universities almost doubled from 19 per cent to 37 per cent between 1968 and 1990. The increase in their proportion in specific disciplines was even more significant: engineering (from 7 per cent to 22 per cent); maths and natural sciences (from 22 per cent to 46 per cent); agriculture and forestry (from 10 per cent to 33 per cent).[20]

A Bulgarian survey from 1991 showed that women constituted 28.6 per cent of all technical scientists, 5.26 per cent of those with doctoral degrees and 30.4 per cent of professors within the field. Of medical scientists, women formed 48.2 per cent of the total. Within this field, 7.26 per cent of women held doctorates and 36 per cent were professors.[21]

It is clear that in many countries, study and occupational choices are gradually broadening for women. There seems, however, to be little indication of a parallel evolution for men. Though they have always had a wider choice, few are moving into subject areas traditionally regarded as "female". Moreover, women are only beginning to move into non-traditional areas and gender bias remains strong in engineering and technology at higher education levels. The proportion of women enrolled in engineering in third-level education has traditionally been extremely low. Over the last 10 to 15 years there has been some progress, although women's share remains minimal in most countries (figure 3.10). Out of the 19 selected countries for which UNESCO data were available, most had a very low (10 per cent or less) or low (30 per cent or less) percentage of women among engineering students in 1990. By the mid- to late 1990s, even though their share had doubled in some countries, the overall percentages remained modest: in the Islamic Republic of Iran it increased from 4 per cent to 11.7 per cent and in Uganda from 5.7 per cent to 8.8 per cent. In a few countries, increases brought women's share to relatively higher levels. In Tunisia, for instance, it rose from 12.2 per cent in 1990-91 to 25.6 per cent in 1995-97. It should also be noted that even in 1990-91, several countries stood out for the high proportion of women enrolled in engineering courses. These included Albania (29.8 per cent), Cuba (30.8 per cent) and Nicaragua (27.3 per cent).

Maths is another area where women are making inroads. Figure 3.11 gives an idea of the extent to which women are specializing at the highest levels in maths and computer science. Data for which UNESCO statistics were available for the years 1996-97 indicate that women obtained 30 per cent or more of primary degrees in maths in these countries (figure 3.11). In several countries (including Estonia, the former Yugoslav Republic of Macedonia, Mongolia, Romania, Saudi Arabia and Slovenia), women were awarded 50 per cent or more of such degrees. But a number of Eastern European countries actually show

Figure 3.10. Percentage of women engineering students attending third-level institutions, 1990-91 and 1995-97 or nearest years (selected countries)

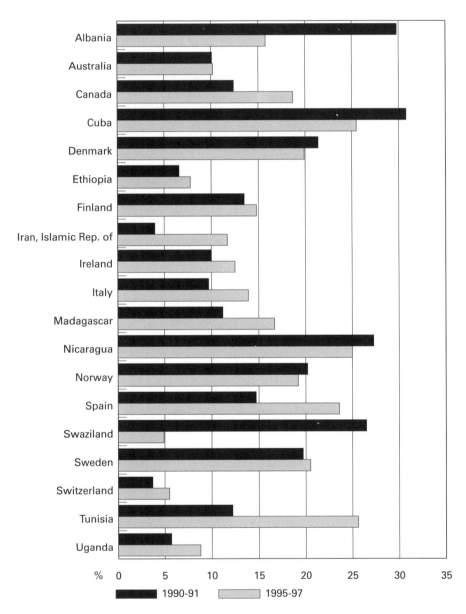

Notes: Revised version of ISCED, adopted by the General Conference of UNESCO at its 29th Session, Nov. 1997.
For Australia, Canada, Denmark, Finland, Ireland, Italy, Norway, Sweden and Switzerland, 1995-97: change in data coverage in total. For the Islamic Republic of Iran, 1995-97: private universities not included.
Source: UNESCO: *Statistical Yearbook 1998* (Paris, 1998), sec. 3, pp. 262-341.

Figure 3.11. Percentage of primary degrees (ISCED 6) in maths and computer
science awarded to women, 1996-97 or nearest years
(selected countries and territories)

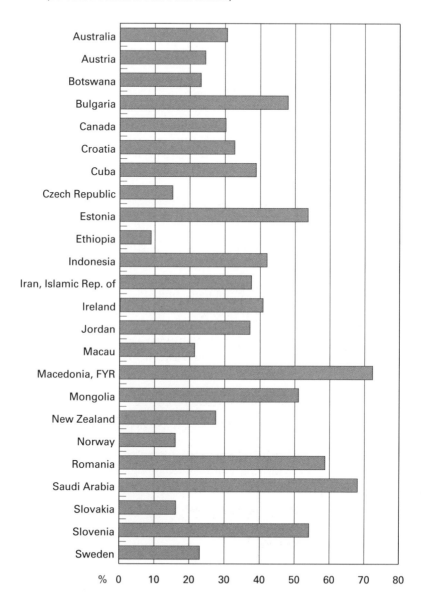

Source: UNESCO: *Statistical Yearbook 1998* (Paris, 1998), sec. 3, pp. 345-389.

decreases in the number of women graduating in maths and computer science since 1994-95. The proportion of women obtaining primary degrees in Estonia decreased from 66 per cent of the total to 53.7 per cent. The decrease over the same period in the Czech Republic was from 24 per cent to 15 per cent, and in Bulgaria from 51 per cent to 47.9 per cent. Figure 3.12 indicates that a significant number of women are also gaining postgraduate degrees in maths and computer science.

Individual country studies reflect similar patterns with regard to gender choice and subject areas. In the United Kingdom, the percentage of female undergraduates enrolled in engineering and technology increased from 3 per cent in 1972 to 14 per cent in 1992; for business and administration studies, the percentage increased from 35 per cent to 42 per cent in the same period. In 1992, the proportion of female doctoral candidates in engineering and technology was 14 per cent, and in maths 16 per cent. In contrast, women's share in education was 49 per cent and 52 per cent in medicine-related studies.[22]

A strong movement of women into the areas of commerce and business administration is also notable in quite a few countries (figure 3.13). In most of the 22 countries for which sex-disaggregated enrolment statistics were available, women's share of higher-level business administration enrolments was already high or relatively high in 1990, but in most of them it increased further over the following years. In a few countries there were significant increases. Swaziland had the most marked increase, jumping from 45.7 per cent to 64.5 per cent in 1995. It was followed by the Islamic Republic of Iran (from 20.9 per cent to 27.5 per cent) and Australia (from 40.7 per cent to 49.8 per cent). Similarly, earlier UNESCO data showed increases of 16 per cent between 1990 and 1994 in Italy and an increase of 18 per cent between 1990 and 1996 in the Republic of Korea.[23]

STRATEGIES TO WIDEN THE EDUCATIONAL CHOICES OF GIRLS AND WOMEN

Efforts to encourage and facilitate young women's entry into non-traditional subject areas at all levels have concentrated on four main areas:

- Elimination of sex-role stereotyping in educational curricula.
- Awareness-raising on educational choices.
- Promotion of gender equality in the teaching profession.
- On-the-job training.

Each of these is now discussed in turn.

Eliminating sex-role stereotyping in educational curricula

No matter the subject, educational materials have often presented images of traditional social, domestic and occupational roles for both men and women. From an early age, children thus develop notions of male and female roles which are anachronistic. While social roles constantly evolve as societies change,

Figure 3.12. Percentage of postgraduate degrees (ISCED 7) in maths and computer science awarded to women, 1996-97 (selected countries)

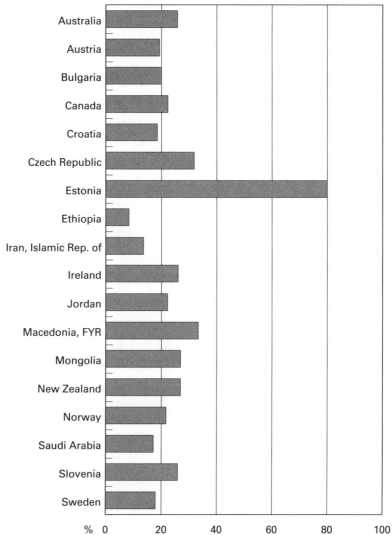

Source: UNESCO: *Statistical Yearbook 1998* (Paris, 1998), sec. 3, pp. 345-389.

school texts do not always reflect the latest developments. A child's mother nowadays may be working as a bank manager or a laboratory technician, but school textbooks still often portray women only in traditional occupations such as nurses and secretaries. In implementing equality policies and laws, a number of countries have undertaken to review and systematically reduce sex stereotyping at all levels in the curricula of educational institutions.

Figure 3.13. Percentage of female business and administration students in third-level education (ISCED 7), 1990-91 and 1995-97 or nearest year (selected countries)

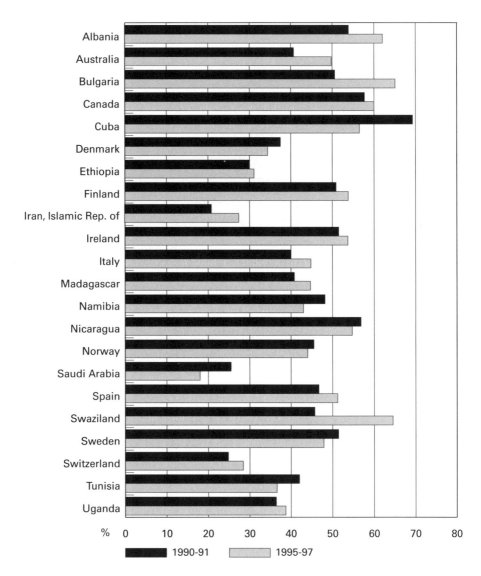

Notes: For Australia, Canada, Denmark, Ireland, Italy, Norway, Spain, Sweden and Switzerland, 1995-97: change in data coverage in total. For the Islamic Republic of Iran, 1995-97: private universities not included.

Source: UNESCO: *Statistical Yearbook 1998* (Paris, 1998), sec. 3, pp. 345-389.

In Slovenia, there has been a notable move away from depicting men's and women's careers in stereotypical ways in school textbooks. Typical male and female domestic roles, such as the man reading the newspaper while the woman cooks, are no longer portrayed in school textbooks. Even though most textbooks and exercise books still use the first person masculine singular or plural in a generic sense, attempts have been made to use both the masculine and feminine form of address, and the issue of language is still under discussion.[24] An initiative has also been undertaken in Azerbaijan to revise the content of textbooks to remove stereotypical images of women.[25]

In Argentina, a national programme to promote equality of opportunity for women and men in education was launched during the 1990s. The central aim of the programme is to integrate into the education system a focus and values that promote gender equality while highlighting women's historical contribution in all fields of public life. The main actions to be undertaken include the following:

- Modifying curricula to ensure that women's participation in all areas of society is properly reflected.
- Promoting more equality, reciprocity and mutual respect between the sexes.
- Sensitizing teaching staff in order to promote non-discriminatory attitudes and practices in teaching and vocational guidance.
- Promoting women's participation in scientific and technological areas and training them to take up positions of responsibility.
- Stimulating research on the socio-educational status of women and vocational guidance in order to diversify educational and employment options of both sexes.[26]

In Costa Rica, a 1990 law prohibits the use of educational content, pedagogical methodologies or instruments that assign men and women social roles contrary to the social equality and complementarity of the sexes, or which depict women as subordinates. Furthermore, it requires the State to promote the concepts of shared responsibility with regard to family rights and obligations, and also with regard to national solidarity. These values must be incorporated in all educational materials and programmes and reflected in teaching methods.[27] In a similar vein to Costa Rica, Mexico reported to the United Nations in 1997 that the Ministry of Public Education was drawing up a plan for the revision of the content of teaching materials and teaching methods in order to eliminate sex-stereotyped images of women and men.[28]

In an another effort to counter stereotyping, the Department of Education and Training in the province of Manitoba in Canada regularly screens all textbooks and support materials from kindergarten to senior secondary levels. This is done through material selection procedures based on a specific methodology. Non-sexist language is one of the many criteria used.[29]

"We have in mind a technology film about ... developing a gas fire or something like that rather than developing a testing technique for an off-shore structure. The evidence is that things which are more closely related to human benefit seem to be more motivating for the girls in science and technology, so we bear this in mind."

Manager, British Gas, United Kingdom.

Source: S. McRae et al.: *Women into engineering and science: Employer's policies and practices* (London, Policy Studies Institute, 1991), p. 19.

The way post-secondary educational courses are advertised also has a role to play, particularly in how they may appeal or not appeal to young women. Studies conducted by management schools in the United Kingdom indicate that their courses are usually promoted as being a worthwhile investment for future promotion and higher salaries (money and status). When the Manchester Management School marketed its master's degree in business administration (MBA) courses as oriented towards developing "people skills" in addition to catering for the perceived "harder" subjects (accounting or statistics), the number of women students increased sharply. The proportion of women students enrolled in its part-time MBA course doubled from 26 per cent to 52 per cent between 1993 and 1996.[30]

Awareness-raising on educational choices

As much occupational segregation is perpetuated by gender choices made at school, efforts to overcome it often focus on encouraging young women to take an interest in non-traditional subject areas. A range of actors is crucial to achieving this. First and foremost, parents, family and friends play major roles in pointing children in certain directions. Second, the local community, teachers and the media can also significantly influence the views not only of children, but also of the family. Third, business and industry can play an important part in terms of their approach to recruitment and training, and also through their input into educational institutions and the local community. Finally, government initiatives can influence all these partners through awareness-raising programmes and by providing incentives to employers.

In 1996, Opportunity 2000, a group of British companies promoting equal employment opportunities, brought employers and educators together to examine how more young women could be persuaded to take up science, engineering and technology careers. Two key objectives were identified. First, stereotypes about the capabilities of young women and men needed to be challenged at school – particularly at primary level – and employers, teachers and parents had a role to play in this regard. Second, the image of engineering and science careers, rooted as these have been in the Industrial Revolution of the eighteenth and nineteenth centuries, had to be changed. Recommendations on how to achieve these objectives included the following:

- an employers-schools partnership in developing science and careers education in curricula;
- mentoring girls and providing them with more role models;
- improving teachers' knowledge of the world of science, engineering and technology;

- raising the priority given to vocational guidance; and
- improving the quality of practical work experience where it forms part of the curricula.[31]

In the United Kingdom, various government campaigns and initiatives were launched in the early 1980s to boost the numbers of young women selecting science and engineering careers by encouraging them to reflect on their choice of subjects for advanced study and future careers.[32] These included the "Women into Science and Engineering" (WISE) campaign, the "Engineering Award" scheme, "Opening Windows" and "Insight". These efforts were apparently fruitful, as there was a 59 per cent increase in the number of young women taking up advanced-level maths between 1978 and 1985. Furthermore, according to a survey by the Engineering Council, the proportion of women entering science and engineering degree courses increased from 8 per cent to 10 per cent between 1982-83 and 1985-86. The Engineering Council estimates that by 2010, there will be at least 17,000 female chartered and technical engineers compared with the 2,700 noted in 1985.

In 1991, Industry Canada produced a motivational and instructional video, called *Rap-O-Matics: Catch the beat of science and maths*, for students aged 11 to 15. The purpose of the video was to encourage young people, particularly girls, to keep up their maths and science courses throughout high school. As a further measure, the Canadian Committee on Women in Engineering was created with government support in 1990 to examine the situation of women in engineering. In 1992, it published a report, *More than just numbers*, with recommendations ranging from changing the attitudes of educators, employers and the engineering profession to addressing gender equality issues through training programmes. The implementation of these recommendations by both the public and private sectors is being monitored by Industry Canada. In 1994, the Manitoba Department of Education and Training distributed a directory of innovative programmes and resources (*Expanding choices*) to all school divisions with the aim of improving the interest of girls in maths and science. A video, *Raising young voices*, was produced in British Columbia and distributed in 1995 together with discussion guides that examine the impact of gender socialization on the self-image and aspirations of young women.[33]

In the Republic of Korea, encouraging schools to educate young women in industrial design and computer skills is one of the measures envisaged in a five-year plan adopted by the National Assembly to implement the Women's Development Act. The Korean Women's Development Institute reports that funding will also be provided for science and engineering courses to be extended to women's universities.

In Ghana, the education service organizes "gender sensitization" training for teachers and one-day science workshops for girls in primary and secondary schools. It also organizes annual two-week science, technology and maths workshops for girls. These "science clinics", as they have been dubbed, aim to expose girls to science issues and to provide them with hands-on experience. The programme includes such things as field trips, encouraging students to work on their own projects, offering guidance and counselling on science and maths careers, and providing access to women professionals working in scientific fields. Girls also travel from neighbouring countries to attend the science clinics.[34] Since the programmes began, there has been a 20 per cent increase in the number of girls pursuing science and maths at secondary level and many girls attending the clinics have been opting for careers in pure and applied sciences, particularly engineering.[35]

Employers and special interest organizations have also been joining forces in various countries to raise awareness. In the mid-1990s, a project in the United States targeted 200 classroom teachers and administrators in grades 6-12 in maths, science and computer science, using a "train-the-trainer" model. The project was funded by the National Science Foundation, with assistance from a number of large corporations. It is estimated to have reached 77,000 girls and the initiative has produced several interesting results. In one after-school computer laboratory, the ratio of boys to girls increased from 25:2 to 1:1; in another school, the percentage of girls enrolling for physics classes increased from 46 per cent to 62 per cent, while the percentage enrolling in an introductory calculus class rose from 45 per cent to 71 per cent; in yet another school, girls signed up for physics classes for the first time in 12 years.[36]

Voluntary associations have also been very active in this sphere. In the United States, "Women and Mathematics" (WAM), an advisory and mentoring programme run by the Mathematical Associations of America, aims to motivate and inspire young women to work towards careers in maths, science and technology. In 12 states, women who use maths in their jobs volunteer to mentor students and/or talk with teachers, counsellors, parents and students about maths and the need for a strong mathematical background in many traditional and emerging careers.

The Danish equal status council has tried to broaden the debate on gender equality in education by, among other things, starting a discussion on the situation of boys in schools. It has also emphasized the importance of changing attitudes towards both sexes and of treating them equally. One of the council's projects focused on making equality a priority theme in all subjects and age groups, including at the pre-school stage. This was a departure from earlier initiatives to attract girls to certain subjects. In higher education, the creation of courses combining technical and scientific or commercial subjects with those from the humanities, such as languages, has attracted a large number of female students.[37]

An Australian report to UNESCO identified, "the need for a paradigm shift away from asking what is wrong with girls and women to questioning what it is about the environment of science, engineering and technology that does not attract and retain the interest of girls and women".[38] It has been argued that women are less attracted to technical subjects and applied sciences as they are seen to be more objective and instrumental, and therefore less people oriented.[39]

Promoting gender equality in the teaching profession

The promotion of gender equality in the education system at all levels is potentially a powerful strategy for influencing the gender choice of subjects and careers by girls and young women. Greater awareness and equality in the appointment and promotion of teaching staff at primary, secondary and higher education levels will no doubt foster an "enabling environment" where both girls and boys can develop to the full their individual potential and interests without undue pressure to conform to gender stereotypes. Moreover, when more women are appointed to higher positions and within non-traditional areas, they will provide important role models for future generations of young people.

Yet women in the teaching profession face similar obstacles to those in other sectors in terms of academic preparation, training, recruitment and promotion. In many countries, there is obviously a glass ceiling working against women employed in higher education. Table 3.2 shows that even though the representation of women amongst university students is high worldwide, their proportion among university staff is much lower.

Analysis of teaching staff within universities usually shows women to be at the bottom of the pyramid, disproportionately occupying the more junior and less secure and untenured teaching positions. Despite steady improvements, by 1995 in the chemistry departments of those colleges in the United States that granted bachelor of science degrees, women held only 10 per cent of full professorships, 25 per cent of associate professorships and 37 per cent of assistant professorships. For universities granting PhDs, the corresponding figures were only 5, 15 and 23 per cent respectively.[40]

The need to ensure women's input into educational policy decisions and their implementation is another important argument for increasing women's presence among higher-level teaching staff of educational institutions. There has indeed been a gradual increase of female staff in higher education in many countries. In China, for example, the percentage of women faculty members at regular institutions rose from 11 per cent in 1950 to almost 30 per cent in 1991.[41] Yet here too, obstacles preventing women from reaching senior positions remain. While the pool of women with doctoral degrees in the United States increased from 16 per cent in 1972 to about 36 per cent in 1990, there was a smaller increase in women hired by universities and colleges – a 6.5 percentage point change overall between 1972 and 1989-90.[42]

Affirmative action measures have been advocated for improving the situation of women in teaching, particularly at university level. An increasing number of educational institutions are adopting programmes in this respect. These include the following measures:

- the inclusion of women on selection committees;
- the preferential appointment of women with equal qualifications to university-level teaching positions until a 50 per cent quota is reached;
- the granting of in-house promotions so that women can have a greater chance of professorships;

Table 3.2.   Women as a percentage of total staff and student bodies in third-level institutions, 1995-97 or nearest year (selected countries by region)

Region/country	Percentage female teaching staff	Percentage female students
Africa		
Algeria	24	44
Botswana	28	47
Eritrea	25	13
Guinea	4	9
Madagascar	29	46
Malawi	30	25
Swaziland	32	45
Americas		
Brazil[1]	38	52.9[2]
Cuba	45	60
Guyana	29	56
Nicaragua	36	53
Asia		
Cambodia	17	16
Iran, Islamic Rep. of	27	37
Korea, Rep. of	22	32
Lao People's Dem. Rep.	34	33
Mongolia	29	61
Philippines	57	57
Singapore	25	46
Sri Lanka	33	44
Arab States		
Jordan	13	42
Kuwait	16	66
Lebanon	33	49
Qatar	33	73
Saudi Arabia	29	47
Western Europe		
Germany[4]	24	42[3]
Switzerland[4]	13	41
Central and Eastern Europe		
Albania	39	60
Bulgaria	42	53
Estonia	39	56
Lithuania	42	54
Moldova, Rep. of	35	50
Romania[5]	37	49

[1] Data from 1994. [2] Figures exclude ISCED level 7 for female students but not for total. [3] Does not include students at ISCED level 7 for which registration is not required. [4] Figures from 1993-94 as others were unavailable. [5] Figures from 1996-97 as others were unavailable.

Source: UNESCO: *Statistical Yearbook 1998*, op. cit., pp. 229-260.

- the creation of funded chairs for women;
- the allocation of half of all grants for doctoral degrees to women;
- the monitoring of the entry and exit of women academics;
- the setting up by universities of childcare centres nearby; and
- the setting up of compulsory reporting systems to governments.

These measures play an important role because the actual recruitment and selection procedures for university appointments have been criticized as not being sufficiently strict, objective and fair.

"The selection and promotion procedures of most Australian universities are sufficiently under-regulated to permit considerable latitude. With few requirements to justify their decisions, most committees continue to appoint or promote people like themselves – usually men."

Felicity Allen, Senior lecturer in Applied Psychology, Monash University, Australia, quoted in Lie et al., op. cit., p. 22.

In Norway, various initiatives were launched in the 1980s to strengthen women's presence among higher education staff. The official government policy on gender equality includes as a primary goal an increase in the number of women in research and senior positions in the universities. The rationale behind this is that women are an important resource and can offer new perspectives to the scientific community. In 1986, the Government set aside funds for the appointment of qualified women to full professorship positions in universities. In 1981, the Research Council of Norway instituted a quota system to increase the number of women scholarship holders pursuing doctoral degrees. Quotas are also used to women's advantage where they are under-represented (40 per cent or less) in a discipline or within specific staff categories within each discipline. However, they are used only where candidates have approximately the same qualifications. Progress is noticeable in different areas. For example, at the University of Oslo, where the teaching hierarchy used to be completely dominated by men, women's representation on faculty councils increased from 25 per cent in 1980 to 33 per cent in 1993. By 1993, 18 per cent of department heads were women, as were two deans and two associate deans. In the Academic Collegium, which has the final voice in policy decisions, female representation increased in the same period from 38 per cent to 44 per cent.[43]

The Commonwealth Secretariat has identified several strategies for improving the position of women in higher education. These include the review of appointment and promotion procedures, the provision of legislative and infrastructure support, special programmes for women to handle different jobs and move into non-traditional areas, and institutional and government support. The Secretariat advocates broad measures to assist women in coping with their multiple roles and to help them become more competitive. In addition, it is trying to facilitate change in the administrative and management structures of universities. In order to build a network of core trainers who could develop readily available and user-friendly training materials, the Secretariat commissioned six training modules. These were evaluated and revised in 1995 and 1996 at two pan-Commonwealth workshops that were attended by senior women managers and trainers. The modules address the following areas: management development for women; women's studies as a catalyst for the advancement of women; managing personal and professional roles; women and research; women in leadership positions; and women and university governance.[44]

On-the-job training

Vocational training systems and on-the-job training may actually reinforce occupational segregation based on gender. Countries such as Austria, Germany, Norway, Sweden and Switzerland are well regarded for their vocational training programmes. However, an ILO report notes that the gap between male and female graduation rates is particularly high.[45] In Norway, a major reform of the vocational training system is under way in order to extend it to both female- and male-dominated job areas. Employer-funded training is an area not usually directly covered by equality of opportunity policies, except for the public sector. However, women's access to such training is critical for their own advancement and for organizations to maximize women's contribution. The fact that many women work part time is also a factor preventing their access to on-the-job training. For women moving up the ladder in managerial jobs, access to formal management training programmes offered by employers is critical, as are more informal processes such as gaining experience in a range of tasks and being included in networks, both within and outside the organization. For women entrepreneurs, networking with others is an important source of learning on how to manage a business. An increasing number of programmes directly assist women entrepreneurs, especially in developing countries, to gain access to management training, marketing techniques and identification of credit options.

CONCLUSION

Equal access for young women and men to education, vocational training and on-the-job training is an essential prerequisite for women to obtain more highly skilled and better-paying jobs. Until a sufficient number of women have the qualifications and skills required for moving into "men's" jobs, they cannot constitute the critical mass in organizations needed to ensure that all women, not just the exceptional few, have the chance to advance. Yet gender-based study choices made by students, their families and employers will continue to be the norm unless special measures are taken to encourage different choices. Young women need to be encouraged to take up studies in non-traditional subjects and in areas of future job growth. Young men also need to be increasingly prepared for understanding changing gender roles and the implications for their own professional, social and family lives. This requires a multifaceted, well-integrated approach that involves education curricula, teacher training, vocational training advisory services, the media, and the setting of targets and legal obligations for employers. Once in a job, women should have equal access to continuous technical and professional upgrading so that they can compete for higher-level jobs later on.

Notes

[1] United Kingdom, Department of Education and Employment: *Third Report of the United Kingdom of Great Britain and Northern Ireland*, United Nations Convention on the Elimination of Discrimination Against Women, July 1995, pp. 50-51.

[2] See Equal Opportunities Commission: *Some facts about women 1999: Great Britain (Manchester)*.

[3] S. Vinnicombe and N. L. Colwill: *The essence of women in management* (London, Prentice Hall, 1995), p. 6.

[4] V. G. Masanja: *Girls, mathematics and science: Problems and strategies to overcome them*, Paper presented to the Seminar on Girls' Education in Anglophone Africa, Nairobi, 16-20 May 1994, organized by the Forum for African Women Educationalists (FAWE) and Higher Education for Development and Cooperation of Ireland (HEDCO).

[5] CEDAW: *Second and third periodic reports of the States parties: Mexico* (May 1997), para 194.

[6] idem: *Second and third periodic reports of the States parties: Bulgaria* (Nov. 1994), para 78.

[7] idem: *Second and third periodic reports of the States parties: Azerbaijan* (May 1997), para 45.

[8] D. Furchtgott-Roth and C. Stolba: *Women's figures: An illustrated guide to the economic progress of women in America* (Washington, DC, AEI Press, 1999), p. 22.

[9] L. N. Edwards: "The status of women in Japan: Has the equal opportunities law made a difference?", in *Journal of Asian Economics*, Vol. 5, No. 2, 1994, p. 222.

[10] S. Ferreira and R. Corbo: *Situación actual del empleo de las mujeres en el Uruguay* (Montevideo, Ministry of Labour and Social Security, National Employment Office, 1996).

[11] CEDAW: *Second and third periodic reports of the States parties: Mexico* (May 1997), para. 195.

[12] idem: *Second and third periodic reports of the States parties: Bulgaria* (Nov. 1994), para. 78.

[13] E. A. Fagenson and J. J. Jackson: "The status of women managers in the United States", in N. J. Adler and D. N. Izraeli: *Competitive frontiers: Women managers in the global economy* (Cambridge, Mass., Basil Blackwell, 1994), pp. 390-391.

[14] S. S. Lie et al.: *World Yearbook of Education 1994: The gender gap in higher education* (London and Philadelphia, Kogan Page, 1994), pp. 15 and 145.

[15] Vinnicombe and Colwill, op. cit., pp. 125-126.

[16] U. Koch: "Equality issue lands on the manager's desk", in *Nordic Labour Journal*, Vol. 2, 1998, pp. 9-10.

[17] ILO: *Women in technical trades* (Geneva, 1990), p. 20.

[18] See M. E. Corcoran and P. Courant: "Sex-role socialization and occupational segregation: An exploratory investigation", in *Journal of Post Keynesian Economics*, 1987, Vol. 10, No. 3.

[19] Edwards, op. cit., p. 224.

[20] Lie et al., op. cit., p. 163.

[21] CEDAW: *Second and third periodic reports of the States parties: Bulgaria* (Nov. 1994), para. 81.

[22] Lie et al., op. cit., p. 175.

[23] UNESCO: *Statistical Yearbook 1996* (Paris, 1996).

[24] CEDAW: *Consideration of reports submitted by States parties under Article 18 of the Convention: Slovenia* (Sep. 1995), p. 25.

[25] CEDAW: *Second and third periodic reports of States parties: Azerbaijan* (May, 1997), para. 103.

[26] D. Bertino et al.: *Reorientación profesional para la mujer*, Working paper for the Interdepartmental Project "La Igualdad de las Mujeres en Materia de Empleo" (Geneva, ILO, 1994), pp. 17-18.

[27] ibid., p. 104.

[28] CEDAW: *Second and third periodic reports of the States parties: Mexico* (May 1997), paras. 80-81.

[29] The methodology referred to is the three-stage Canadian Exchange of Instructional Materials Analysis model, referred to in CEDAW: *Consideration of reports submitted by States parties under Article 18 of the Convention: Canada* (Oct. 1996), p. 112.

[30] *Financial Times*, 1 July 1996.

[31] Opportunity 2000: "How employers can attract girls into science education". http://www.Int.ac.uk/orgs/opp2000/chap3.htm.

[32] See McRae et al., op. cit.

[33] CEDAW: *Consideration of reports ... Canada*, op. cit., pp. 111 and 137.

[34] Forum for African Women Educationalists (FAWE): *Newsletter* (Nairobi), May 1995, Vol. 3, No. 3, p. 24.

[35] A. Odaga and W. Heneveld: *Girls and schools in sub-Saharan Africa: From analysis to action*, World Bank Technical Paper No. 298, African Technical Department Series (Washington, DC, World Bank, 1995), p. 7.

[36] UNESCO: *World Education Report 1995* (Paris, 1995), p. 75.

[37] CEDAW: *Third periodic reports of the States parties: Denmark* (May 1993), pp. 15-16.

[38] UNESCO: *World Science Report* (Paris, 1996), p. 316.

[39] E. M. Byrne: *Investing in women: Technical and scientific training for economic development*, Training Discussion Paper No. 62, Training Policies Branch (Geneva, ILO, 1990), p. 8.

[40] See Mairin B. Brennan: "Women chemists reconsidering careers at research universities", in *Chemical and Engineering News* (Washington, DC), Vol. 74, No. 24, p. 8.

[41] Lie et al., op. cit., p. 174.

[42] ibid., p. 187.

[43] ibid., p. 174.

[44] J. Singh: *Women graduates and the labour market: The Commonwealth experience*, Working paper of the Commonwealth Secretariat for the 5th UNESCO/NGO Collective Consultation on Higher Education, 1996, pp. 6-8.

[45] ILO: *World Employment Report 1998-99: Employability in the global economy – How training matters* (Geneva, 1995), p. 155.

AT THE WORKPLACE: CAREER DEVELOPMENT IN PRACTICE

4

INTRODUCTION

The recruitment, full development and retention of qualified women are increasingly recognized as being essential to the economic success and competitiveness of firms. Accordingly, one of the main objectives of equal opportunity programmes is to remove the invisible cloak that often shrouds women and their contributions.

Many women enter the workforce at the same level as men, only to see their careers progress more slowly. They are often more qualified than their male counterparts and must work harder and perform better to obtain top jobs. A Chilean study estimated that women earning the equivalent of men had an additional four years of formal education.[1] A German survey published in 1997 found that 34 per cent of female managers had masters' degrees compared with 25 per cent of male managers and 46 per cent held doctoral degrees compared with 36 per cent of men.[2] A large-scale study of bank employees in Canada found that women equalled or surpassed male colleagues on all important human resources measurements such as education, length of service, dedication and job performance.[3] The National Committee on Pay Equity in the United States reports that, in 1998, men with a primary degree earned US$49,982 per annum compared with US$35,408 earned by women, and men with a master's degree earned around US$18,000 more than women (US$60,000 against US$42,000). Similarly, at doctoral level, men earned US$69,188 compared with the US$51,662 earned by women.[4] Therefore, "educational segregation" only partially explains the braking effect on women's careers. Even women with similar qualifications and experience to men encounter greater difficulty than men in reaching top jobs.

Three theories have been advanced to explain women's under-representation in senior management.[5] The first claims that "feminine" characteristics handicap women in the male corporate environment. Most research, however, shows little or no difference between the capacity, qualifications and motivation of professional and managerial women and men. The second theory holds that women are blocked by the prejudices and stereotypes that men have of women: the word "manager" is usually identified with so-called "masculine" traits. The third theory focuses on the inherent discrimination in the policies and practices of organizations, including denial of access for women to the kinds of challenging assignments that are important for career development and promotion.

A detailed analysis of the various steps and requirements involved in the recruitment and promotion processes of organizations is necessary to identify and rectify the mechanisms contributing to differential treatment. For instance, perceptions of the social and occupational roles of men and women often overly influence appointment decisions. Selection criteria and procedures may also be insufficiently developed to ensure an objective and fair assessment of candidates. Above all, many decision-making structures are wholly or mostly composed of men, contributing to a general condition of gender blindness and an incapacity to recognize the presence of qualified women. However, women with family responsibilities can face very real constraints in meeting the seniority or mobility criteria often required for promotion.

This chapter examines how and why career paths for men and women differ. It looks at the various obstacles women confront throughout their careers and the measures adopted by organizations to recruit, retain and promote women in professional and managerial jobs. As will be seen, this not only involves specific action to advance women's careers, but also increasingly implies creating workplaces that are more flexible, which value diversity and which are more people-oriented and family-friendly.

Why close the gender gap?

"Because not only is it the right thing to do, it's also good for business."

Source: Royal Bank of Canada: *Making the differences work: Closing the gender gap* (Toronto, 1995), p. 5.

GENDER DIFFERENCES IN CAREER PATHS

Men's and women's career paths differ significantly. A survey of 17 major corporations in the United States that focused on age and sex found that younger men followed a career trajectory similar to that of older, successful male executives, while both older and younger women moved upwards more slowly than men did.[6] Women surveyed in Thailand reported that they have fewer career opportunities than men. They believed that, except in finance and commerce, women were discouraged from investing in a career because in senior positions they received less social recognition than men.[7] As mentioned earlier, slowness in the progress of women's careers is also related to the fact that they tend to move typically into support functions rather than into the "line management" functions that lead to more senior positions.

The persistent stereotype associating managers with being male is a key obstacle in introducing more gender equality into career paths.[8] Characteristics considered to be "masculine" rather than "feminine" are generally regarded as traits required for management (box 4.1). As a result, women often try to adapt themselves to work environments and expectations created by men. However, management styles are evolving towards valuing a certain mix of so-called "masculine" and "feminine" characteristics. A study of women managers in the United Kingdom reported that the characteristics most highly valued by their organizations were being competitive, cooperative and decisive, while the least valued were being emotional, manipulative and forceful.[9]

Box 4.1.   Some typical characteristics of the sexes

Male	*Female*
Forceful	Intuitive
Independent	Spontaneous
Logical	Caring
Manipulative	Cooperative
Competitive	Flexible
Resilient	Emotional
Decisive	Thorough

Source: G. Morgan: *Images of organisation*, cited in Traves, op. cit., p. 145.

Social perceptions of what constitutes suitable work for men and women often mean that they are assigned different tasks and responsibilities from the outset and receive different compensation. Subsequently, they tend to be streamed into different career tracks. In Japan, where large companies often employ a two-track system for recruiting university graduates (figure 4.1), men are mostly recruited for the managerial track (*sógó*), which assigns employees complex tasks, requires job rotation and transfers, and has no limit on promotion. Women, however, are mostly recruited for the clerical track (*ippanshoku*), which involves less complex jobs, limited job rotation and transfers, and promotion opportunities only to lower-level or local management positions. In the 1980s, the banking and financial sectors in Japan opened up formal promotion chances for women by introducing a career conversion system, thereby allowing women in clerical positions to apply for conversion to the managerial career track at a certain stage (30 usually being the minimum age) in their careers. However, only a limited number of women succeeded in entering the managerial track, as mobility remained a major obstacle. When they did, they had to start again at the junior supervisory level because they lacked the training and job experience gained by men recruited for that track.[10] Some companies have introduced a midway track that does not require geographical mobility, thus enabling selected women to take up more responsible jobs. Progress is illustrated in a report of a Japanese bank which planned to hire more female than male graduates in 1998. Of the 410 graduates to be hired for general managerial and professional posts, 230 were to be women and the bank intends to increase this figure fivefold in the coming years.[11]

Figure 4.1.   Percentage distribution of men and women by career track, Japan
(survey of 40 firms with career-tracking systems)

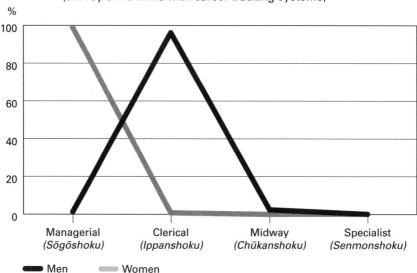

Source: Japan Institute of Women's Employment (JIWE): "A survey report on career tracking" (1990), cited in Lam, op. cit., p. 215.

In the bid to attract and retain qualified and talented employees, organizations are increasingly concerned about providing opportunities for women to enable them to reach management positions and are taking a hard look at workplace practices that block women's chances. Attitudinal factors play an important role (box 4.2). A survey in Singapore identified common reservations about hiring women. Many respondents felt that married women were unsuitable for jobs requiring frequent travel and there was a reluctance to hire women to head departments staffed by men. As is the case with men, there was a preference for promoting women who had a proven track record within the organization, rather than recruiting women externally. There were doubts that women (especially working mothers) would take their careers seriously and be willing or able to work the long hours necessary to succeed. In addition, it was feared that women would have more difficulty in gaining the trust and respect of customers.[12]

These attitudes are also reflected in another survey on perceptions and stereotypes of women.[13] Again, there was a belief that women would not be as committed to their careers as men. However, this survey showed that only a third of the women involved had ever taken leave of absence and most of the time it was taken for family reasons, predominantly on account of maternity. If these breaks were excluded from the figures, then men in fact took more leave of absence than women did. Fears that women would not work the long hours required were also refuted by the survey. The women who were interviewed worked 56 hours a week on average, which was the same as had been reported

Box 4.2. Myths associated with women in business and common reservations about hiring/promoting women

- Women switch jobs more frequently than men. This "fact" has not been statistically proven. One legitimate explanation for why people move is that they are no longer challenged or given an opportunity for advancement.

- Women take jobs away from the family breadwinner. Viewing males as the primary breadwinner is no longer the rule. Single, widowed and divorced women are also the main breadwinners.

- Women would not work if economic reasons did not force them into the labour market.

- Training of women is wasteful when they leave work for marriage or children. This attitude appears to be more of a scapegoat reason than a valid reason to discriminate. Men leave companies at a comparable rate to women.

- Neither men nor women prefer to work for a woman.

- Women fall apart in a crisis.

- Women are too concerned with the social aspects of their jobs and cannot be trusted with important matters.

- Women are more concerned than men about working conditions. This attitude, though thought of as negative, is theoretically beneficial to the working environment and can promote motivation.

- Women, in contrast to men, do not require their jobs to be self-actualizing.

- Women are less concerned with getting ahead, with success and with power. These attitudes are changing as women become more educated and look at their work as an important part of their existence.

- Women cannot take executive jobs because they must be available to relocate with their executive husbands.

- Women are not prepared to travel extensively for a company.

Source: *Public Personnel Management*, Vol. 28, No. 1, 1999, p. 88.

for their male counterparts in a similar survey in 1989. Only 14.1 per cent of the women covered by the 1992 survey refused relocation, while 20 per cent of men had refused relocation according to the 1989 survey. Women also matched men in quantitative skills. Of the women interviewed, 23 per cent had spent most of their corporate careers in finance; this was true for 27 per cent of the men. Only 16 per cent of the men were in commercial banking or diversified financial sectors compared with 26 per cent of the women.

A survey of the Canadian civil service in 1996 concluded that, "resistance to women's entry into non-traditional and mainstream line management positions continues".[14] Women continue not only to dominate the administrative support categories, but they are disproportionately compressed in lower levels of virtually every other occupation. The study also found that both female and male respondents tended to agree that higher standards of performance were

Figure 4.2.   Why is female representation so low? (opinions of chief executive officers, in percentages)

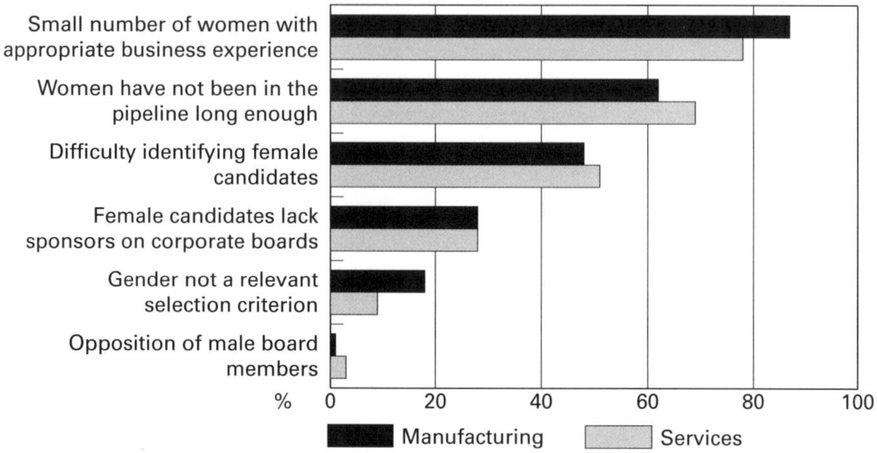

Source: Survey of Chief Executive Officers, in Catalyst: *Women in corporate leadership: Progress and prospects* (New York, 1996).

applied to women than to men. Men acknowledged being tougher on women in their appraisals. The study also referred to a "faith phenomenon". This meant that a woman had to demonstrate her competence to do a particular job while a man, whether within or from outside the organization, could be offered a position based on "faith" in his potential. This made it difficult for women to gain access to positions in fields that are traditionally male dominated, including line management and executive positions.

A lack of adequate planning and identification of future managers combined with a lack of training, support and coaching can lead to deficient management later on, and thus negatively affect the quality of service and products. Therefore, the systematic identification of potential managers and the structuring of their career paths are often considered crucial for both men and women and for the firm or organization itself. Rendering procedures for recruitment, job assignment and promotion more objective and making these processes more structured and transparent can give women a better chance. Restricting the reliance on informal networks for decisions about promotions makes such decisions more visible and more accurately perceived.

Along with attitudinal hurdles, various other obstacles faced by women in their careers have been identified and often point to institutional and structural barriers. Figure 4.2 shows the factors which chief executives view as explaining gender differences in career patterns.

Gender differences in career paths are evolving in response to the new management structures and work roles that are linked to the restructuring, "downsizing", decentralizing and "delayering" which organizations are

Table 4.1.   Factors suggested by women in Europe for improving women's recruitment at different management levels (opinions expressed as percentages)[1]

Factor	Junior management	Middle management	Senior management
Equal opportunity programmes directed at all employees	40.5	38.5	29.1
Company childcare provisions	43.9	35.8	23.6
Special courses to support women in management[2]	77.7	68.2	43.2
Public advertisement of positions	35.1	35.1	38.5
Revised selection/promotion procedures	24.3	33.1	41.2
Mentoring[3]	39.2	47.3	45.9
Quotas for female representation	12.8	14.2	22.3
Reduce workload of individual managers	10.1	16.2	12.8
Number of responses	452	462	398
Number of valid cases	148	148	148
Average number of answers[4]	3.1	3.1	2.7

[1] Each group of respondents was asked to choose the three most important factors.   [2] Includes answer categories "special training courses" and "self-awareness training".   [3] "Official mentoring programmes" and "informal mentoring by female managers".   [4] Calculated on the basis of the ten original answer categories.

Source: S. Quack and B. Hancké: *Women in decision-making in finance*, Report prepared for the use of the European Commission, Directorate General V, Industrial Relations, Employment and Social Affairs (Wissenschaftszentrum Berlin für Sozialforschung, Berlin, 1997), p. 53.

undergoing in order to remain competitive in the global environment. A recent study in the United Kingdom identified several new barriers to women's careers. It noted that "decentralization of central support functions, most notably personnel, to business units resulted in a demand for a broader range of skills and general management experience than that normally held by women who had followed highly specialized and narrowly focussed careers".[15] It also found that with changes in both specialist and general management roles, broad organizational experience was essential for career success. However, women were not able to gain access to key developmental experiences such as job rotation, lateral moves, assignments to special development projects or secondments. This was mainly due to their lack of exposure to sponsorship, networking and visibility. Another problem the study identified was that the increased time and work pressures involved in switching from general management to middle management support functions was particularly discouraging to women with family responsibilities. Careful monitoring and adaptation is needed if changes in organizational structures and the breakdown of traditional hierarchies are to provide opportunities for women rather than create new obstacles. Management development training, career planning and equal opportunities policies for assisting women in their careers need to be adapted accordingly. Table 4.1 shows factors suggested by women in Europe for boosting women's recruitment at higher levels.

In interviewing top company directors (CEOs), lack of general management or line experience was cited as the greatest impediment to women's advancement. Women executives, however, were more than twice as likely as CEOs to consider factors intrinsic to the work environment – male stereotyping and preconceptions, exclusion from informal networks – as significant barriers to their advancement.

This gap is central to the issue of women's advancement. Because women are subject to stereotypes regarding their ability or willingness to accept highly visible or international assignments, they are often not considered for the revenue-generating or "line" positions which are often necessary for promotion to and through the ranks of senior management.

Source: Statement of Donna Dillon Manning, Vice-President, Catalyst, to 41st Session of the United Nations Commission on the Status of Women, Panel on Women and the Economy, Mar. 1997.

GETTING OVER THE RECRUITMENT HURDLE

Occupational segregation sets the stage for in-built gender bias in prospecting, recruiting and hiring patterns even if discrimination is formally prohibited. Figure 4.3 shows executives' perceptions of women's opportunities in entry-level jobs for selected Asian countries. While men and women may have similar qualifications and the possibility to apply for all jobs, the selection process often favours men or women for certain jobs. Objective criteria are not always applied to either job content or applicants' qualifications. This is reinforced by applicants themselves, who frequently prepare and apply for jobs along gender lines. Furthermore, in job interviews, certain questions may be asked of women and not of men such as whether they plan to marry or have children, and these bear no relation to the job to be performed.

A major source of gender bias is the definition or understanding of the profile of an effective manager. While some studies find little difference between the leadership styles of men and women, others reveal important differences. For example, one study found that men tend to adopt an approach which relies more on the power of position and formal authority, whereas women are more likely to adopt a more participative style, share information and power, and promote people's self-esteem.[16] It follows that if there are different views of what constitutes an effective manager, then techniques and methods for recruitment and selection are likely to test for certain skills and qualities considered essential for the successful manager. In cases where a "male view" of managerial qualities is the norm, women can be disadvantaged in assessment procedures.

Establishing goals and setting targets for recruiting and promoting women help overcome bias in prospecting and recruitment. When a Canadian bank realized that 75 per cent of its employees were women but that they comprised only 9 per cent of executives and 13 per cent of senior managers, it set up a task force to remove barriers to women's advancement, put action plans into place and assigned deadlines for meeting targets. By 1996, women constituted 20 per cent of senior executives and 22 per cent of senior managers.[17] A chemical firm plans that its hiring and promotion of women will mirror the graduate female/male profile in the college recruitment pool by 2001, when it also expects women to make up 34 per cent of its managers.[18] To bridge the gap, the firm

Figure 4.3.   Executives' perceptions of women's opportunities in entry-level
jobs in selected Asian countries and territories, 1997
*(Question: "Are women in your country given the same opportu-
nity as men in entry-level jobs?")*

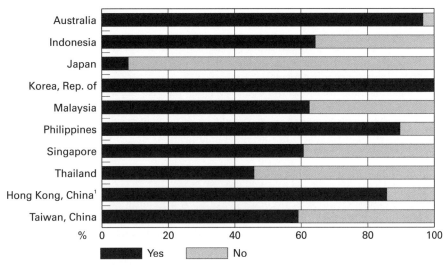

[1] Prior to July 1997.
Source: "Asian Executives Poll", in *Far Eastern Economic Review*, 1977.

started by raising the proportion of women (and minorities) at entry-level management from the then current 37 per cent to 43 per cent. In 1994, the TD Bank Financial Group in the United States expressed concern at the lack of female corporate officers. To deal with this problem, a task force was created to design an initiative comprising several programmes, including those on career development, succession planning, respect and flexibility. This has become an integral part of the human resources mission of the TD Bank Financial Group. An executive development programme and a "targeted development" programme for women were launched in 1996 with the objective of providing equal development opportunities for all employees. The project resulted in an increase in women officers from 8 per cent to 19.2 per cent. Even more encouraging is the fact that the proportion of women at senior vice-president level had reached 12 per cent in 1999, up from zero in 1994. The company was awarded a 1999 Catalyst Award for its initiative.

Job prospecting in a wide variety of feeder environments (schools, universities, training institutions) should not just make it clear that women are encouraged to apply for jobs by avoiding suggestions that jobs are for men only or omitting irrelevant job requirements which may discourage women. A more proactive approach should increase women's opportunities and provide organizations with a wider choice of qualified candidates. If a company is committed to remedying biased hiring practices, then recruitment officers and agencies can be instructed to make special efforts to find women candidates.

Selection on the basis of competence or merit can help prevent bias against women, although too heavy a reliance on technical qualifications may exclude many capable women. Selection criteria can be broadened so that analytical, communication and management skills are given more value. A computer company operating in Australia that made such changes saw women candidates increase by 75 per cent.[19]

As mentioned earlier, making recruitment procedures clearer, more transparent and better structured helps ensure fairness and gives women a better chance. In more specific terms:

> Qualifications for a position should be based on a current job description which accurately identifies the nature, purpose and functions of the job, without regard to any preconceived notions of who should be performing it. Job descriptions:
>
> • should not be adapted to meet the qualifications of any particular individual whose application is anticipated;
>
> • should be made available to all potential applicants and to staff members involved in the recruitment and selection process.[20]

Interviewers can also be instructed to ask all candidates a set of specific questions and to carefully rank candidates according to their actual replies, qualifications and experience. This way, subjective impressions interfere less with assessment, and decisions cannot be made for or against a person on the spot in just a few minutes. Making it mandatory for all personnel asked to interview candidates to be trained in interview techniques and gender-sensitivity issues also helps.

The careful monitoring of selection tests is necessary to ensure that their content and results are job related and free from any bias against sex. Men also experience the glass-ceiling effect when promotions rely heavily on informal networks and stereotyped perceptions of characteristics considered necessary for management. Often, men also do not possess the so-called "masculine" attributes commonly viewed as essential for good management. More men are also increasingly committed to spending more time with their families and so are not prepared to put in the long hours expected in traditional management. Therefore, many men also stand to benefit from the opportunities being created by the increasing priority being given to the strategic value of feminine attributes for effective modern management, where teamwork, good communication skills, intuition and emotional intelligence are critical for acquiring a competitive edge. Objective recruitment and promotion systems can also ensure that men who may otherwise be overlooked have a better chance to compete.

PROMOTION OPPORTUNITIES

First assignments can be crucial for future career movement and women given lower-level entry jobs than men may be handicapped throughout their careers. In the equal opportunity policies of organizations and firms, therefore, special attention needs to be given to men's and women's initial placement in order to correct such gender-based differences.

Certain career advancement requirements such as mobility and seniority may be more difficult for women to meet. Transfers to distant locations are often required to broaden experience and knowledge in preparation for management positions. These transfers may be relatively frequent and can pose serious problems for women who are married or who have children or elderly relatives to care for. Several companies in Turkey have indicated that mobility is a problem for women in a society that assigns them the main responsibility for childcare. This directly contributes to the preference for male employees in terms of promotion and career development opportunities.[21] But even for a woman without a partner or dependants, it is often assumed that by virtue of being a woman she is not suited or prepared to undertake a transfer.

A large bank in Canada has recognized that both men and women are now struggling to balance work, family and life demands and that many employees, not just women, are less interested in relocation. Its policy of requiring an annually declared willingness to relocate appeared to be a barrier for many employees, with the result that some even declared themselves "fully mobile" so as to receive job options, even if they then declined these due to personal circumstances. The bank thus decided to introduce more flexible mobility choices and to better advertise opportunities. References to mobility were removed from annual performance appraisals and this made mobility an opportunity rather than a strict requirement. The same bank also instituted a "JobLine" system that advertises all jobs up to executive level on a 24-hour telephone line. Widely disseminating clearer information on job opportunities is another useful tool to eliminate bias in candidate selection, and to identify candidates who might be missed in traditional selection methods.[22]

Length of work experience can be another obstacle for women who may have taken some time off or worked part time for family reasons. Women reintegrating into the workforce cannot always return to their previous job level; many must accept lower-level jobs or start over again and this limits their career prospects.

Strict seniority criteria for promotion are another hurdle for women. Remedies suggested by a Canadian study include the following:[23]

- revising all seniority units and barriers in order to merge units not reflecting significant differences in employee skills;
- abolishing irrelevant barriers such as tests or other requirements which prevent movement between remaining units;
- abolishing lines of progression where skills acquired in lower-level jobs are not necessary to perform higher-level ones;
- calculating seniority on a plant-wide basis; and
- taking affirmative action measures to increase women's seniority. This means using the concept of "constructive seniority" (for example, attributing a number of seniority years based on age), allowing seniority to accumulate during maternity or parental leave, or suspending all seniority rules for women until employment equity targets for the various occupations have been reached.

Formal assessment schemes can be another important tool for improving women's careers. Performance assessments based on a normative profile of skills and personal characteristics inevitably involve subjective judgements about what is acceptable. Open and accessible performance assessment procedures, using neutral and measurable criteria, are instrumental in ensuring greater equality of opportunity. They can be particularly useful if they provide avenues for discussing difficulties encountered in meeting achievement targets and for offering possible remedies.

Identifying potential career paths, establishing long-term career goals and involving employees in their own career development plans also help ensure that potential women managers are kept in mind. Kraft Food's management development programmes include succession planning as well as mentoring and diversity training, the aim being to increase workforce diversity through hiring and promotion and thereby helping women managers to shatter the glass ceiling. In 1989, 4.7 per cent of Kraft's managers were female. By 1994, this figure had risen to 30.4 per cent in spite of a 4.5 per cent overall reduction in the company's managerial workforce.[24] Naturally, women's presence on panels where career paths are sketched and promotions considered is of great importance.

A critical step in preventing gender bias is ensuring that procedures and techniques for recruitment and promotion are gender neutral. A Canadian bank has developed measures to avoid gender bias which, while fairer for all employees, address the issue of advancing women (box 4.3).

Box 4.3.   Making procedures gender neutral:
Measures selected by Toronto–Dominion Bank

- A clearly stated employment equity policy, underlining a commitment to a fair and non-discriminatory work environment.

- Accountability frameworks and competency models for key job families, to help managers base their appraisal and development of individuals on an objective assessment of performance.

- A recruitment policy using objective behavioural training techniques to isolate skills and competency requirements for jobs.

- A placement philosophy emphasizing internal recruitment and promotion.

- A corporate succession planning programme identifying key positions and resources. In conjunction with this programme, an executive development programme targeted career-pathing, education and profiling of individuals. Senior positions were filled through a competency rating system allowing objective identification and assessment of candidates.

- All compensation policies to be gender neutral and designed to foster pay for performance.

- Managers to be trained on the practical application of policies and annual audits conducted to ensure appropriate implementation of policies.

Source: Information provided to the ILO by the Canadian Employers' Council on Toronto–Dominion Bank (Apr. 1997).

RECRUITING FOR TOP JOBS

Companies often use external recruitment (of men) for hiring into senior executive positions. When a firm realizes the strategic importance of hiring women into senior positions, there can be difficulties in identifying qualified women. Looking within the company may result in identifying the need to overhaul career development systems and review training programmes to enlarge the pool of potential women candidates. This, however, may not solve what may be immediate goals to fill vacant executive posts with women. Women often complain that they are overlooked for senior positions as men, who because of peer pressure may be reluctant to appoint women from within the firm, usually dominate selection processes. In fact, they may find it easier to resort to external recruitment.

A number of initiatives have been taken by governments and women's associations to track successful women managers and include them on rosters for potential recruitment. Catalyst, an organization founded in the United States to assist women in business and professional work, has developed a "corporate board placement service", whose database contains over 2,000 carefully screened and well-qualified women. It helps companies find suitable women for their boards of directors. The European Women's Management Development Network also puts its members in touch with potential employers. There are many other networks of women managers and women in business throughout the world that provide support, advice, training and contacts. In 1998, the Australian Government initiated an "executive search pilot programme" and an "early warning system" aimed at encouraging an increase in the number of women appointed to federal government boards and bodies. The latter aims to ensure that female candidates are considered early in the appointment process. Details of suitably qualified women are provided by the Office for the Status of Women to ministers' offices well ahead of the deadlines for such vacancies. With the increasing interest of firms in attracting women, recruitment agencies are also under pressure to prospect for young women candidates from academic and training institutions in their pre-graduation year, and also from the pool of more experienced women managers.

THE RIGHT TRAINING

Appropriate training not only propels women towards management positions; it also contributes to their effectiveness once in them. Identifying potential women managers and ensuring that they receive "cross training" (i.e. training in different areas to gain broader experience) can help increase their presence in the pool of future managers and equip them with the skills for successful and higher-level management.

Factors limiting women's access to training need to be identified and remedied. A survey of companies in Germany found that women comprised only 14 per cent of on-the-job training programmes for managers. This figure was higher (29 per cent) in the service sector. As childcare was identified as an obstacle, steps were taken to incorporate childcare arrangements in training programmes.[25]

A United States insurance company ensures that women are included in its accelerated development programme. During an intensive three-month training and orientation period at the company's headquarters, information on a variety of company functions is given and detailed career plans are formulated. An average plan includes three to five assignments, each of 12 to 24 months' duration, including at least one geographical relocation. Experience includes staff, line, home, office, field, project and management positions, with the intention that participants develop broad-based backgrounds. An adviser, programme manager and supervisor are also assigned to every participant for coaching, providing feedback and developing career plans.[26]

Tailoring training to potential women managers may also be needed as their scarcity in organizations poses additional challenges. Once appointed, they become very visible and have to deal with curiosity, concern or even resentment. Also, they face gender-related difficulties that include being "less exposed to informal networks where critical information is shared, or being judged against different standards, with a narrower range of acceptable behaviour".[27] Developing assertiveness and better presentation skills, building confidence and encouraging risk-taking, learning how to understand and cope with stressful and often hostile environments, and learning how to balance home and work may then be important components of training programmes for women. Deutsche Telekom in Germany has several training programmes to attract and promote women employees. "Fair is more advantageous" is a programme designed to develop better collaboration based on partnership. Another programme consists of a one-year coaching (especially in management tasks) programme for women, which is taken in parallel with their professional work. A special programme for women only, entitled, "Being a manager: between aspirations and requirements", trains women on issues of presentation, behaviour and work relations.[28]

Mainstreaming training opportunities or integrating gender concerns into ongoing training programmes is another means of addressing gender bias. Training in managing people, management skills, induction, performance appraisal, discipline, selection, coaching skills and so forth can be made more gender sensitive through appropriate pedagogical approaches and training materials.

Training can be a critical complement to a policy giving preference to internal over external recruitment for management positions. In a cosmetics company in Belgium for example, 75 per cent of employees were women, yet none of them were managers. The company decided to limit the external recruitment of male candidates and focused on further training for women who already had organization-specific qualifications. Eight years later, half of the management jobs were held by women as a result.[29]

WORKING TIME

Working extremely long hours is commonly viewed in organizations as an expression of commitment and loyalty. With stiffening global competition, employees in the financial and professional services in particular are feeling growing pressure to work longer hours and managers are often exempt from national legislation limiting working hours. Important meetings may take place at the end of the working day and socializing after work may be expected or required for advancement. This can pose particular problems for women, to whom society assigns the main responsibility for household maintenance and family care. Many women have a strong commitment to their jobs, but do not necessarily wish to sacrifice their family life to such an extent.

In the United Kingdom, one in four workers are part-time workers, but this is true of less than one in seven professionals and one in ten managers.[30] Lack of opportunity for part-time work contributes greatly to gender imbalance in management. Moreover, it is more difficult to climb up the career ladder as a part-timer. A perception of less commitment and availability results in women receiving fewer challenging assignments and responsibilities, while less contact with colleagues limits their access to information and networking. Addressing these issues and opening up opportunities for part-time work in management careers is critical to furthering gender equality.

Differences in working hours are central to explaining men's faster career progression and gender differences in managers' salaries. A 1992 survey of managers in Germany found that 16 per cent of women and 4 per cent of men worked up to 40 hours per week; about 52 per cent of women and 45 per cent of men worked 41-50 hours per week; 25 per cent of women and 41 per cent of men worked 51-60 hours; and 7 per cent of women and 10 per cent of men worked over 60 hours.[31]

JOB DESIGN AND WORK ORGANIZATION

Job design can affect the type of assignments given to men and women and their subsequent career tracks. Jobs that provide scope for innovation and development can give the relevant jobholders higher profiles. Often, more complex and attractive functions are required for some jobs while others, although fundamental to the success of an organization, are more routine and less likely to lead to promotion. Men are more likely to be assigned the more challenging jobs and thus receive greater opportunities and attention. A British study of men's and women's perceptions of their job content indicated differences in the types and levels of skills perceived to be necessary for their jobs. Men's and women's jobs were found to involve different skills or attributes, and men's jobs were thought to be higher skilled. Women placed more stress on the personal and social relationships essential in service-type occupations. A major problem was that these "female" attributes were usually given a lower value than "male" attributes in job evaluations.[32]

New forms of work organization that involve more participatory decision-making structures and emphasize teamwork and cooperation can provide women with more opportunities than traditional work settings based on hierarchical structures and individual competition. Women tend to progress faster in modern, more dynamically organized firms as they are exposed to more diversity and complexity in their work. Teamwork and job rotation also increase employees' skills and prepare them better for management positions.[33]

BALANCING PROFESSIONAL AND FAMILY RESPONSIBILITIES

Severe constraints are placed on all workers with responsibility for caring for children, the elderly or sick relatives. Tradition allocates the main responsibility to women in these areas, which logically implies that they usually have less time to devote to their careers. Lack of flexibility in working hours and work combined with inadequate care services, whether at home, in the community or at the workplace, can seriously hamper workers' efforts to balance their work and family life and can be particularly discouraging for women aspiring to and capable of holding management jobs.

Small children have a marked effect on women's participation in the labour force. Nonetheless, the more qualified women are, the more they will keep working throughout their childbearing years. Yet even the most qualified women often take time off, work part time or drop out altogether. While the growth in women's employment has been mainly through part-time jobs, working part time is usually regarded as an impediment to career advancement. Promoting a positive view of the concept of the part-time manager could definitely enhance women's career possibilities. It could also give men the option of spending more time with their families.

Career interruption for family reasons often implies losses in seniority, less likelihood of receiving training and depreciation of job skills. Moreover, employers may view interruptions as a signal that women may leave again and so assign them less important positions. A clear outcome of this is that managerial women's salaries usually lag behind those of men when they return to the labour force.[34]

Planning the timing of training, job assignments and promotions at the same time as starting a family is crucial if women are to compete alongside men for top management positions and lead a balanced family life. Women more than men are caught having to push back the "biological clock" owing to the increasing duration of education, and the need to gain work experience and move a few notches up the managerial ladder before they take time out to have children. Given the difficulties encountered trying to advance after a so-called "career break", many women opt for establishing their careers before starting a family. In this respect, the age at which firms and organizations award first promotions is far more critical for women than men.

A 1998 survey in the United Kingdom reveals how women's advancement into managerial positions slows down compared with men's advancement from

Figure 4.4. Balancing career and personal life, United States: How women executives do it (percentages)

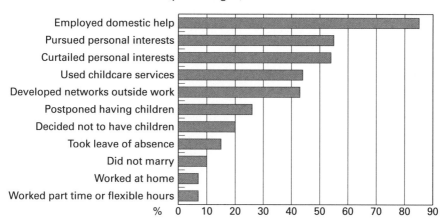

Source: Catalyst: "Women in corporate leadership: Progress and prospects", Executive Summary (New York, 1996), p.2.

age 35 onwards. In the age group 25-34, there was little difference between the percentage of male and female employees who were managers (28.4 per cent and 26.6 per cent respectively). In the age brackets 35-44 and 45-54, the percentage for men jumped to 45.4 per cent and 49.1 per cent respectively, while the figures for women were 27.1 per cent and 29.9 per cent respectively.[35]

Figure 4.4 shows survey results on how women balance their careers and family life in the United States. But balancing work and family life is also increasingly important for men. A recent survey of managers in the United Kingdom found that nearly two-thirds of both male and female managers consider that work and home life are equally important.[36] This trend is mirrored in a 1998 survey on the views of women and men regarding careers and family life.[37] A commentator noted that: "This report isn't about what women want. This is about what 45 per cent of the workforce wants. And men's attitudes on these issues are far more similar to women's than has been assumed to now."[38]

According to the US Bureau of Labor Statistics, 60 per cent of all marriages are dual-career marriages. This constitutes 45 per cent of the workforce.[39] The number of single fathers in 1998 had risen to 2.1 million. In 1997, only 17 per cent of all families conformed to the previously traditional model of a wage-earning father with the mother staying at home with one or more children. A 1986 survey of *Fortune 500* chief executive officers and human resource directors found that 63 per cent of the respondents "felt that it was not 'reasonable' for men to take any parental leave". By 1997, a similar survey found that only 22 per cent of the respondents agreed that for men, part-time arrangements were not acceptable options.[40] This reflects the fact that such attitudes are slowly but surely changing.

"The struggle to have both a good family life (or personal life) and a good career arises from a dominant societal image of the ideal worker as 'career-primary', the person who is able and willing to put work first and for whom work time is infinitely expandable."[41] Managerial jobs have been traditionally structured to suit someone with a full-time support system backing them up from home, that is, someone to shop, cook, wash, clean and maintain personal and family relations (Christmas and birthday cards, organizing social occasions and so forth) – in other words, someone to take care of everything outside work.[42] Thus, it comes as no surprise to learn that, in spite of attitudinal changes, a Swedish survey from 1998 shows that women still do 82 per cent of all housework. In only 10 per cent of families with children do men and women share the housework and 69 per cent of fathers take no paternity leave.[43]

In a survey in Australia, 40 per cent of men compared with 28 per cent of women felt that work interfered with family life. Thirty-five per cent of women felt that their partner's work added to family tension while only 28 per cent of men felt this way. Only 10 per cent overall considered that family life interfered with work.[44]

There is growing consensus that programmes to help employees balance work and family should be available for both men and women. This encourages the sharing of family responsibilities and men too can benefit from a better family life. Figure 4.4 shows how women executives cope. Achieving cultural change within companies implies that management and employee training should promote the idea that men too have family responsibilities. Otherwise, work and family programmes will be viewed as being only for women, and women using them may see their chances for promotion diminish. Thus, if parental leave and part-time work options are available, men should also be encouraged to take them. Work and family programmes are normally tailored to the needs of both the employees and the organization, and can be worked out between management and workers. They often include flexible working time and workplace arrangements (e.g. teleworking); various kinds of leave (maternity, paternity, parental, career breaks, and so forth); short-term leave for family emergencies; and assistance with childcare or care of the elderly (sponsoring places in community centres, referral information services, workplace crèches, breastfeeding rooms and so forth).

The value of work and family programmes has increasingly been recognized in the light of broad demographic changes, the need to recruit and retain women workers, and the awareness of the effects of unresolved work and family conflicts on work performance and productivity. On the other hand, pressure on organizations to restructure and downsize can make workers with family responsibilities hesitant to solicit more flexible arrangements for fear of jeopardizing their careers or even their jobs. Women in management positions may be particularly affected by this. It is important that companies ensure the viability of their work and family programmes by bearing in mind that the most effective and efficient employees and managers are often those who are confident of managing responsibilities in all spheres of their lives.

COMBATING SEXUAL HARASSMENT

Sexual harassment is generally defined as unwelcome physical, verbal or non-verbal conduct of a sexual nature.[45] Sexual harassment has also been recognized as a form of bullying or exertion of power over others rather than an attempt to initiate sexual relations. This has been particularly observed when the victim is in a subordinate position at the workplace, or is working in a non-traditional job. While women managers may be directing others, their presence in what has been a predominantly male occupation may be resented by male subordinates, peers and higher-level managers. A study of women executives in Argentina noted that many employees cannot accept a woman in a senior position and, as a result, she becomes the target of unpleasant sexual comments and is accused of having sexual relations to obtain her position.[46]

Other research suggests that women's entry into non-traditional management jobs seems to intensify the nature and extent of sexual harassment. A study in the United Kingdom found that the few women who succeeded in obtaining management positions in the insurance sales division of one company were subjected to continuing sexual harassment by supervisors, colleagues and clients.[47] Regardless of the strategy adopted, they failed to achieve further promotion despite the fact that they had top sales records. Protesting and complaining earned the label of "feminist" and "whinger". Trying to be "one of the men" only invited further harassment. Attempts to ignore the situation and detach themselves led to high levels of stress and eventually to voluntary transfer to another area. Lack of recognition of the true problem and failure to deal with it, translated into women being viewed as unsuitable for insurance sales, the company's loss of highly performing women, and discouragement to women from entering this "non-traditional" field.

Sexual harassment can cause emotional and physical stress and lead to stress-related diseases. This reduces the individual's efficiency and results in costs to employers. The Royal Bank of Canada notes the effects of harassment on victims and the work environment: "Harassment involves conduct which tends to interfere with a climate of understanding and mutual respect for the dignity and worth of each person. It undermines morale, interferes with the productivity of its victims and their co-workers and undermines the integrity of the employment relationship."[48] There appears to be growing consensus among researchers that organizational contexts (structures, organizational climate and culture) play a significant role in the perception and incidence of sexual harassment.[49]

Sexual harassment in the workplace is not easy to quantify. However, most surveys reveal that a considerable number of women are affected. Figure 4.5 shows that in most countries surveyed, many executives consider that it is indeed a problem.

Firms and organizations throughout the world have developed policies and measures to prevent sexual harassment at work, often to comply with legal obligations (see box 4.4 for a sample policy statement). In some cases, measures

117

Figure 4.5.   To what extent is sexual harassment in the workplace a problem in your country/territory? (selected Asian countries/territories, 1997)

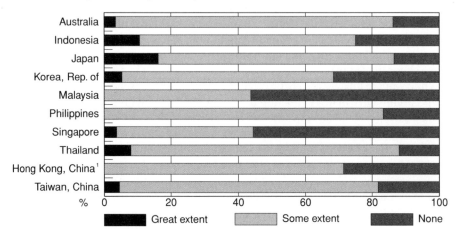

¹ Prior to July 1997.
Source: "Asian Executives Poll", in *Far Eastern Economic Review*, 1977.

Box 4.4.   Sexual harassment policy statement of the Prudential Insurance Company of America

The statement notes that sexual harassment affects both men and women, but women are still most often the victims. Just like other forms of discrimination, sexual harassment hurts more than the obvious victim. It directly impacts on all those working for the company and can lead to low morale, poor productivity or the loss of a valued employee. Thus the company would not tolerate sexual harassment in any form or at any rank.

To address this problem, the company set up three advisory committees composed of women, at senior management, middle management and non-management levels.

Any employee who feels that he or she has been subjected to sexual harassment should bring the matter to light as soon as possible. Given the sensitivity of the issue, employees can discuss the situation with human resource professionals, or anyone in their reporting chain. Employees are assured that all allegations will be investigated. Complaints will be handled confidentially, with steps taken to prevent retaliation against any person filing a complaint or participating in the investigation of a complaint. Disciplinary action for offenders may include dismissal.

Source: ILO: *Conditions of Work Digest: Combating sexual harassment at work*, Vol. 11, No. 2 (Geneva, 1992), p. 226.

---

have been introduced through collective bargaining. Most company policy statements indicate that sexual harassment will not be tolerated and that disciplinary action will be taken against offenders. They usually define sexual harassment, distinguishing it from mutual attraction and consensual relationships. Complaint procedures are often foreseen and, given the sensitivity of the problem, frequently provide for special informal and formal procedures. Complainants may also be assisted by nominated counsellors or advisers. A difficulty for many organizations is how to apply their policy to acts of sexual harassment perpetrated by contractors, clients, customers or other people on their premises.

HUMAN RESOURCE MANAGEMENT TO ADVANCE WOMEN

Various approaches have been developed to tackle discrimination and prejudice in the workplace. These include initiatives such as establishing an equal employment opportunity policy, positive action programmes, diversity management programmes and linking equality and quality goals. While there are differences and similarities in these approaches, the actual approach that is adopted and the way it is implemented depends on the situation in the organization and the wider social and economic contexts. Experimentation with such approaches has paralleled developments in human resource management in general. However, there is a need for more comparative information within and across countries on the results obtained.

Equal employment opportunity policies

An important step for companies to ensure that more women reach management positions is the development of a policy and practical measures that broadly promote equality. By establishing such a policy, senior management demonstrates interest and commitment and sends a powerful message to all managers and employees. Deciding on what specific measures and programmes to implement usually requires an assessment of the employment skills, qualifications, age and family profiles of employees. It is clearly essential to involve women managers and employee representatives in all stages of this process. Measures may include training, the introduction of more flexibility into working time and work organization, and assistance with the care of children and the elderly. The measures largely depend on the actual needs of the employees, the situation of men compared with that of women, and the available resources inside and outside the organization.

Companies and organizations worldwide have developed equal employment opportunity policies either to comply with national legislation or in recognition of their importance for business and the recruitment and retention of women. In the Caribbean, approximately half of the 65 employers that responded to an ILO survey indicated they had established such a policy, and one-quarter had policies addressing sexual harassment in place.[50]

> An equal employment opportunity policy is a commitment to engage in employment practices and procedures which do not discriminate, and which provide equality between individuals of different groups or sex to achieve full, productive and freely chosen employment.
> Source: Lim, op. cit., p. 110.

119

Achieving targets: Positive action

Positive or affirmative action often forms part of an overall equality policy:

> It entails a systematic approach to achieve specific targets according to an established order of priorities and a fixed timetable, with a system of monitoring and an evaluation of the results. A positive action programme is intended to be temporary; once the consequences of past discrimination have been rectified, positive action should be removed.[51]

On the other hand, equal employment opportunity should be a permanent part of an employer's personnel policy.

Positive action has generally been viewed as a means of levelling the "playing field" so that everyone has an equal chance. Another interpretation sees it as a compensation for past wrongs or discrimination. A wide variety of measures are involved. Some of them are broadly acceptable to employers and workers alike, such as that of providing women with additional or remedial help in order to help them "catch up". These include special training courses or assistance with dependants' care. Other measures, such as quota systems or numerical targets for the recruitment and promotion of women, are more controversial as these can be interpreted as "reverse discrimination" and sometimes may result in the appointment of unqualified women. This can be detrimental both for the job at hand and the woman herself. But while quotas can be too rigid, targets are a more flexible instrument for both helping employers recruit and promote qualified women and for monitoring progress.

> The adoption of an affirmative action programme stems from the observation that the banning of discrimination is not in itself enough to eliminate it in actual practice … The concept of 'positive action programmes' encompasses measures which set out to eliminate and make good any de facto inequalities, by enabling members of groups suffering from discrimination to enjoy comparable opportunities for education and training and the means to participate on an equal footing in occupational life in all sectors of activity and occupations and at all levels of responsibility. Like the special measures of protection or assistance, which are not considered as discrimination because they seek to protect certain vulnerable groups, the concept of 'affirmative action' views these measures as the means to promote equality of opportunity of certain social groups which are subject to recognized discrimination, and which are applicable as long as the target social groups are not in a position to exercise their rights to equality in practice.
>
> Source: ILO: *Equality in employment and occupation*, Report III (Part 4B), International Labour Conference, 83rd Session, Geneva, 1996, p. 117.

One of the largest voluntary positive action schemes is "Opportunity 2000" in the United Kingdom. Its members comprise over 300 organizations including banks, building societies, government departments, the police, educational establishments and most of the recently privatized large employers. Members agree to increase the number of women in key business areas through positive action measures, including numerical targets. Launched in 1991, its campaign is firmly based on the business case for equal opportunities. By the year 2000, the aim was to have markedly improved women's opportunities. Measures have been introduced in three main areas: balancing work and home commitments; increasing women's self-confidence; and encouraging women to consider "non-traditional" fields of work. Many of the organizations are trying to bring about cultural change, as in the case of the "long hours" culture which makes many employees fear that they will be seen to be uncommitted if they choose flexible work options. The companies involved in the programme have achieved increasing levels of female participation in management. Between 1994 and 1995, women's share of management positions in these companies rose from 25 per cent to 31 per cent. Among senior managers, this increase was from 12 per cent to 17 per cent, and among directors, from 8 per cent to 16 per cent.[52]

> "The principles of affirmative action are fundamental to Lend Lease's future".
>
> Managing Director, Lend Lease (an Australian finance and property group)
>
> Source: Affirmative Action Agency: *Best employers in affirmative action: Case studies* (Sydney, Australian Government Publishing Service, 1996), p. 7.

In recent years, affirmative or positive action has been questioned not only on the grounds of possible reverse discrimination, but also in terms of its effectiveness in promoting equality. One study of corporations in the United States found that it resulted in women being pushed to the top fairly rapidly, and finding themselves, "more often in non-vital 'window-dressing' capacities, such as vice-president of public relations or affirmative action, rather than in the key positions necessary to the success of their organizations".[53]

Another problem that has emerged as a result of women gaining positions through additional support, coaching and so forth has been men's belief that these women do not earn their promotions on merit. To counter possible antagonism, some companies are routinely opening up network and support groups to all employees, and encouraging men to participate. Thus, the US Labor Department invites men to apply for the women's executive leadership programme.

In general, it can be argued that "affirmative action can do what it is supposed to do when there is an unambiguous guarantee of equal opportunity, clear standards of performance and a commitment to raise people to meet those standards".[54] An example of this is Procter & Gamble's initiative to attract women and minority candidates through internship and other outreach programmes.[55]

Diversity management

In contrast to positive action and equal employment opportunity policies that focus on a particular group (usually women or a given race), diversity management responds to the different needs, career aspirations, contributions and lifestyles of workforce participants. This management approach recognizes that employees are not all the same and that their very differences and potential entail a variety of benefits and productivity improvements. Diversity can be seen to "consist of visible and non-visible differences that include factors such as sex, age, background, race, disability, personality and work style".[56] By its very definition, diversity management involves a range of initiatives and measures as it addresses the many varying needs of employers and their employees.

There is a debate, however, surrounding the approach of diversity management. For example, some practitioners believe in a purely individual approach while others recognize social group differences. In practice, most initiatives embrace both approaches.[57] Much of the literature on diversity management emphasizes the fact that diversity management initiatives have to be individually tailored to meet the needs of each individual company.

Since a diversity management approach involves targeting needs such as management or assertiveness training rather than groups, two crucial concerns need to be addressed: first, how to meet the needs of specific groups; and second, how to ensure that groups have access to programmes designed to meet the needs of a range of individuals. As mentioned earlier, objective and fair processes, including recruitment, selection, training and appraisals, can benefit women. Objectivity and equality are also central to successful diversity management. This concept, however, goes further and strives to provide all employees with a package of benefits from which individuals choose those best suited to their situation. The ongoing transition from "work/family" to "work/life" programmes provides an example. A Canadian bank has a work and lifestyle programme which gives employees access to alternative work arrangements such as flexible working time, reduced working hours, teleworking and job sharing. These work options, conducive to balancing work and family, are available to all employees.[58] Another example is Northern Trust Corporation, a multibank holding company in the United States. The company launched a diversity initiative in 1988, which included diversity training, enhanced communication, career development, employee retention and also the building of a childcare centre. By 1995, the number of women with the position of senior vice-president or higher had increased from 3 to 17.[59]

Practising diversity management requires managers to be responsible for continually developing themselves and their employees. This involves upward appraisals, where managers receive feedback on their performance not only from their superiors, but also from their subordinates and peers. Their duty is to make everyone feel valued and ensure that their full potential is realized. To be successful, the approach and its various features must be supported by a company-wide culture that promotes the empowerment of individuals, has decentralized decision-making, participation and consultation, and values experimentation.

Equal opportunities and diversity management approaches illustrate different ways of achieving change (table 4.2). The equal opportunities approach focuses more on positive action and on monitoring the numbers trained, employed or promoted in certain under-represented groups. External factors such as pressure groups and legislation often play a considerable role in influencing organizations to develop equal opportunities policies, which are mainly administered by human resources departments. Diversity management, however, emphasizes an organizational culture where all employees, and

Table 4.2.   Diversity management and equal opportunities: Different approaches

Diversity management	Equal opportunities
Ensures all employees maximize their potential and their contribution to the organization	Concentrates on issues of discrimination
Embraces a broad range of people: no one is excluded	Focuses mainly on women, ethnic minorities and people with disabilities
Concentrates on issues of movement within an organization, the culture of the organization, and meeting business objectives	Places less emphasis on cultural change and meeting business objectives
Is the concern of all employees, especially managers	Concerns mainly personnel and human resource practitioners
Does not rely on positive/affirmative action	Relies on positive action

Source: Kandola and Fullerton, op. cit., p. 49.

especially managers, are responsible. It is driven by "an internal need for change as a response to external economic and business needs which result from the increased representation of women in the workforce and the need to utilize all skill areas in the search for organizational survival and effectiveness".[60] Diversity management does not seek to address the imbalances in the labour force. It focuses on the "presumed" diverse workforce already working in the company and the diverse pool of potential employees in the labour market.[61]

The creation of a diverse workforce may be more of an issue for countries which have a homogeneous workforce but which are experiencing increasing migration pressures and the need to integrate long-term migrants or ethnic groups. For example, India, partly due to its size, is an extremely diverse country both culturally and socially. Differences can exist in religion, social position (caste) and language, to give but a few examples. These differences often result in gaps in income, education and access to resources. Some companies operating there have begun to use diversity management to create improved working environments. One example of this is a United States electronics company that initiated a three-stage diversity programme. Initially the programme was viewed as a foreign issue and not something that concerned the local workforce. Over a two-year period, however, attitudes changed and the contribution of diversity to business success was acknowledged.[62]

The literature does not provide clear evidence of the results of diversity management, either as an effective management tool or as a model approach for eliminating discrimination. More and more companies, however, seem to have confidence in diversity management for improving their competitive edge. They are increasingly adopting this approach and providing diversity management training for their employees, particularly in such countries as Australia, Canada, South Africa, the United Kingdom and the United States (including American subsidiaries operating in Europe and many other parts of the world). In terms of whether diversity management can contribute to reducing gender inequalities, opinion is divided and the jury still out. Participants at the 1997 ILO tripartite

Figure 4.6. Awareness-based diversity-training model

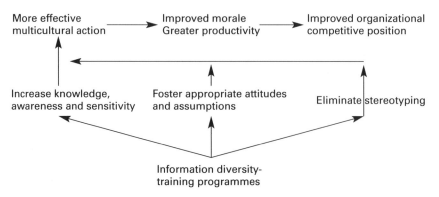

Source: A.P. Carnevale and S.C. Stone: "Diversity beyond the golden rule", in *Training and Development,* Oct. 1994, p. 30.

meeting expressed the need for caution and monitoring before advocating the rolling back of equal opportunity policies which have already proved effective in reducing discrimination and promoting more women into management. According to one author:

> Dealing with diversity is not about civil rights or women's rights; it is not about levelling the playing field or making amends for past wrongs; it is not about eliminating racism or sexism; and it is not about doing something special for minorities and women. Rather it is about enhancing the manager's ability to tap the potential of a diverse group of employees ... the focus is not on how the company is doing with improving relationships or eliminating racism or sexism, but rather how it is doing with creating managerial capability that will lead to the development of an organizational environment that works naturally for everyone.[63]

In training for diversity, both awareness-based training and skill-based training are recommended. On the one hand, awareness-based training focuses on increasing the knowledge, awareness and sensitivity to diversity issues within the company at a cognitive level. Skill-based training, on the other, addresses behaviour, providing tools to encourage efficient communication and interaction within the company.[64]

Diversity training for managers and staff usually aims at creating awareness of individual differences and emphasizes that competitiveness requires that all employees reach their full potential (figure 4.6). Not only must management, career planning systems and practices be adapted accordingly, but organizational culture and structures must likewise be adapted. Companies often make such training mandatory for all managers and employees. Role-playing and video presentations are essential instruments as they help to reveal, acknowledge and deal with existing prejudices. Such awareness training is critical so that gender issues are not lost in the general search for valuing all aspects of difference. For those organizations that have already developed equal opportunities structures and initiatives, it has been recommended that these be built on to develop managers towards the wider perspective of managing diversity.[65]

Total E-Quality

Another interesting approach that has been gaining ground makes gender equality a precondition for the delivery of quality products and services. The "Total Quality Management" (TQM) concept, which has been practised for some time, focuses organizational strategies on improving quality through solving problems caused by processes and work organization. It is based on the principle that quality can and must be managed: in short, problems must be prevented, not just fixed. TQM regards processes and not people as the problem and considers every employee responsible for quality. Management must be involved and must take the lead, and quality improvements can be planned and organized. They must also be measured and be continuous. Combining TQM with equality for women (Total E-Quality) encourages a greater contribution of women and a better recognition, use and development of their aptitudes, which may differ from those of men. Total E-Quality[66] aims at identifying, promoting and putting to optimum use the talents, skills and qualities of women in the corporate setting by letting women share in responsibility, information, and initial and further training, and also in remuneration and bonus schemes according to their performance and on an equal rights basis. This presupposes a corporate culture that pursues an equal opportunities policy and measures for its implementation. Total E-Quality starts from the premise that equality of opportunity for women and men gives the employer a competitive edge and is indispensable for an innovative and future-oriented personnel management policy.

To encourage this approach in Germany, a system has been devised to award companies a certificate and Total E-Quality logo, which can then be used for marketing and public relations purposes over a three-year period. It is a distinction for companies whose personnel management policy is guided by the tenets of equal opportunities. Thus, the award is evidence of the fact that equality of opportunity leads to a more efficient use of human resources, which in turn boosts the quality of the company's input and output; this in turn guarantees competitiveness. Application for the Total E-Quality's certificate is voluntary and based on companies' self-appraisal. Eligible companies can be of all types and sizes so long as they employ more than 25 staff and have an annual turnover of DM1 million. The awards are decided by a jury of representatives from employers' and workers' organizations, the federal employment office and a government training institution. Companies applying for the label must submit a checklist (box 4.5) and show how their personnel policies are oriented towards equal employment opportunities. In addition, they must give priority to male and female collaborators and promote measures to further their potential.[67]

A project to undertake a cost-benefit analysis of Total E-Quality during 1999 was jointly funded by the German Federal Ministry for Women and the Commission of the European Union. All previous holders of the award were

---

Box 4.5.   Checklist for Total E-Quality label

- Employment situation of women in the company
- Staff recruitment, promotion of junior staff members
- Personnel development and further training
- Reconciliation of family life and professional activity
- Partnership-based behaviour at the workplace
- Institutionalization of equal opportunities
- Equality of opportunity as corporate policy and objective of innovative management strategies

Source: Total E-Quality Association. http://www.total-e-quality.de/english/ application. htm.

---

interviewed on their experience with equal opportunity policies. Based on those interviews, the subsequent evaluation phase determined criteria for the benefits that personnel policies oriented toward equal opportunity have brought to companies. The results and recommendations were presented at an international conference in the year 2000. In consultation with project partners from Austria, Denmark and Italy, the various points of departure in the individual countries will be discussed and joint measures and strategies for the implementation of corporate equal opportunity policies will be developed, including the implementation of Total E-Quality in the European context.

A pilot project on gender-related management, jointly funded by the European Commission and the Austrian Government, has built on the concept of Total E-Quality developed in Germany to design training on "Managing E-Quality". In contrast to the Total E-Quality focus on the needs of women employees and customers, Managing E-Quality considers senior private and public management – predominantly male – as the primary target. This stems from the recognition that all segments of society and all social actors need to be addressed by measures on work and family reconciliation. A sensitivity training process is intended to supply key decision-makers with the skills to initiate top-down development. Rethinking corporate culture and work organization is no less important than issues such as management style, corporate strategy and personnel development. The project organizes leadership seminars for the target group and has developed an extensive curriculum. A training manual for equality-oriented management was published in 1998.[68]

Human resources information: The need for benchmarking

Relevant comparative information on personnel policies, strategies and career-planning systems of organizations is instrumental in making human resources management more effective. Systematizing this kind of data has been described as "benchmarking". This concept was originally defined by Rank Xerox as a continuous process of measuring products, services and practices against leading competitors or those recognized as foremost in a particular field in order to help identify areas of improvement and thus enable the company to remain competitive in the global environment.[69]

Benchmarking in human resources is still being developed. One initiative is the setting up in 1992 of a national human resources database in South Africa called the Breakwater Monitor. The database is managed by the Cape Town Graduate School of Business in partnership with 130 leading private- and public-sector organizations. It provides company-specific data which compare a company to others in its industrial sector and to the national sample, and evaluates staff composition, recruitment, promotions and terminations by race, job grade and sex. Rankings are provided on training and development expenditure as a percentage of remuneration, average training expenditure per employee and the number of human resource staff per 1,000 employees. Data across occupational levels are collected and analysed by race and sex.[70]

This type of data is instrumental for organizations to plan and decide on their human resource strategies, and to increase their organizational efficiency. Such information is critical for monitoring gender equality, assessing progress, and developing positive action or other measures to advance women in organizations. Furthermore, it allows cost-benefit analyses of investment in training and women's promotion to be carried out.

KEY CAREER-BUILDING STRATEGIES

A number of strategies have proved effective in helping to promote women to management jobs. These include networking, career tracking, mentoring, succession planning and, above all, the adoption of a comprehensive approach.

Networking

Even when women overcome the initial obstacles in their careers and secure training and job assignments leading to advancement, they are often prevented or deterred from reaching higher levels of responsibility by (mostly male) networking, which is particularly powerful at higher levels. Networking arrangements provide invaluable information, visibility and support. When more senior positions become vacant, the "network" typically suggests suitable candidates drawn from its own circles and who are practically always men. In some countries, women who are selected are often closely linked to informal male networks, such as through certain elite families or social groups in a country.[71]

Another example of this type of exclusion can be found in "old boy" or "school tie" networks, often linked to prestigious or exclusive educational institutions. A survey in the United Kingdom found that the "old boy" network is regarded as the most important career barrier, not only for women (38 per cent) but also for men (23 per cent).[72]

Women also often lack access to "head-hunting" agencies that specialize in recruiting senior management. In Finland, for example, even though women qualify for access to recruitment pools, until recently such agencies, consultancies and recruitment firms have paid little attention to them.[73]

Broadening networking functions throughout an organization and opening up networks to women could improve opportunities for women. A study of women managers in Nicaragua and Costa Rica found that most of them had heard about their jobs through informal networks and personal contacts, and were selected without any formal competitive process. This applied to both the public and private sectors.[74] Often companies promote the development of women-only networks, mainly to provide support and to identify strategies targeting them. In one Australian city, 11 major firms are involved in an inter-company network to encourage women in their personal and professional development.[75] Women's networks for support and sharing information on strategies and techniques are often critical for women to learn how to move up the ladder in organizations.

Career tracking

A strategy pursued by some companies is to "career track" women upwards in the organization. This involves identifying female employees of high potential, and helping them gain visibility and experience through challenging and high-profile assignments. Special training may be offered in addition to mentoring by high-level managers who provide advice and contacts. Career tracking already exists for men, but women tend to remain invisible unless there is a special effort and commitment by senior management to systematically and consciously career track them in the same way. Monitoring and reporting on women's progress in the organization and the accountability of managers on this issue are important ways of making this strategy successful.

Mentoring

Mentoring involves the pairing of younger potential managers (sometimes referred to as "high flyers" or "fast trackers") with older, experienced and more senior managers who provide coaching, support, advice and visibility. The word "mentor" comes from the Greek legend of Odysseus, who entrusted the tutelage of his son Telemachus to the goddess Athene. She transformed herself into the human form as Mentor, a wise counsellor and helper to Telemachus while Odysseus was away on his travels. In short, the first recorded mentor was a woman.[76]

Mentoring has often been conducted on an informal and ad hoc basis and, as such, has tended to favour men mentoring men. In recent years, a Canadian bank has introduced mentoring on a systematic, formal basis as a strategy to develop individuals and thus its human resource potential. Mentoring relationships are based on the individual's desire to develop new skills or gain additional competencies. A written agreement between the mentor and protégé spells out the skills areas to be developed, the duration of the relationship and other modalities. Designated coordinators serve as primary resources for both protégés and mentors, and they review periodic reports from each mentoring pair in order to track and evaluate progress.[77]

In an effort to promote women, some companies are now pairing female "fast trackers" with senior-executive mentors (usually men), within or even outside their own companies. The Swedish Government helped a company develop a mentorship programme to give women extra support in job development. First, the jobs, age, education, training and ambitions of all female employees were reviewed. This revealed that they had far more ambition, education and training than they were able to utilize in their current jobs. That was true at all levels: in the office, on the shop floor and among managers. Around 200 women were then asked to suggest possible mentors, and subsequently to select one of them. Each pair (protégé and mentor) met at least once a month over a 12-month period. The results were mutually beneficial. Women gained much greater visibility and a better understanding of how the organization worked and how (mostly male) managers thought. Mentors (mostly men) came to understand differences in how women and men think and express themselves in an organization. They learned about listening and appreciated that the female approach can enrich the entrenched male approach.[78]

Mentoring is just one tool to promote better management and is usually part of a broader career planning system. It provides a framework for dialogue to take place between higher levels of management and other employees. This leads to mutual learning about different levels of an organization, as well as reflection on and identification of the actual strategies employed by the mentor to attain high-level management jobs. Women benefit particularly from mentoring as it can increase their visibility, bestow greater legitimacy and allow access to key male executives. Women being mentored by men in senior positions influences the informal and formal structures of organizations, and the close relationships that are formed help break down sexual prejudices and stereotypes. This, however, engenders certain risks as it is often considered suspect for a man to share power and information with a woman. Factors making a mentoring programme successful are listed in box 4.6.

Box 4.6. Making a mentoring programme successful

- Enlist support from senior management
- Make it part of a larger human resources development effort
- Involve voluntary participants only
- Make it time-limited
- Carefully select mentors and protégés
- Achieve the right balance between a structured and flexible relationship
- Ensure that everyone is aware of potential problems
- Pilot the scheme before launching it on a large scale
- Orient mentors and protégés before starting the relationship
- Monitor effectively

Source: Norton and Tivey, op. cit., p. 47.

Succession planning

Planning correctly for the filling of managerial posts is a key factor in preparing women for such jobs and guaranteeing a more even gender balance in management. Some companies are devising novel succession strategies. For example, senior managers may be requested to indicate the three people most likely to replace them: the first should be a manager who would fill the job in an emergency; the second should be someone who could be groomed for the job over three to five years; the third must be a woman or member of an ethnic minority group. Managers are then expected to give that third person opportunities to gain the experience needed to merit the promotion.

Box 4.7.   Retaining women: A checklist

- Employ more than one woman at a time, especially in areas which are isolated or where there are few or no women.

- Undertake exit interviews to establish why women leave the company or survey them after they have left.

- Make sure that there is a sexual harassment prevention policy and that all staff are aware of the policy and associated procedures, and know what is acceptable behaviour and what is not.

Source: Affirmative Action Agency, Australia: *Action News*, Newsletter No. 32, Apr. 1997, p. 2.

Differences in the types of discrimination experienced by women are reflected in the preferences indicated for different types of policies (table 4.1 on page 105). Those in junior and middle management prioritized special courses to support women in management, childcare provision by the company, and company programmes for equal opportunity. Middle management also referred to mentoring programmes as an effective strategy. Senior management favoured mentoring by experienced management colleagues, special courses to support women in management, revised selection and promotion procedures, and the public advertising of positions. While the women managers who were interviewed stated that the obstacles increased with management level, on average they suggested fewer measures for senior than for junior management. This may indicate that the measures put forward are only partially appropriate for senior management and that new approaches in dealing with the problems at this level may need to be developed.[79]

A comprehensive approach

Strategies to improve women's career opportunities only work if fully integrated into a sustained and wide-reaching initiative adapted to the culture of each firm or organization. As mentioned earlier, women often have to work harder than men do to achieve the same levels of responsibility. Organizational structures, policies and procedures, often unconsciously based on socially constructed "masculine" attributes, should be critically examined to identify the invisible barriers hindering women. Examining the situation and devising and implementing remedies depends very much on senior management's commitment to examine obstacles created by the organization's culture and social attitudes. Remedies may involve such actions as the following:

- sensitivity training of managers to gender and family issues;
- exit interviews to find out why women leave (box 4.7);
- the development of strategies and programmes which value diversity in recruiting and developing employees;
- introducing more flexibility in working-time arrangements and places of work (e.g. teleworking);
- identifying different management styles, and valuing attributes that women may bring to management;
- developing more open communication styles;
- creating opportunities for lateral mobility and for horizontal working relationships;
- introducing more objective procedures for recruitment, hiring and promotion (basing promotion on merit rather than seniority or counting periods of leave or calendar years of part-time work for seniority purposes);
- devising job mobility that does not necessarily involve geographical transfers or providing optional shorter transfer periods;
- providing families relocating with assistance packages (relocation grants, education grants and childcare, spousal employment and so forth);
- devising a policy and programme to prevent sexual harassment at work;
- including women in training programmes; and
- establishing part-time management positions, to enable women with family responsibilities to take the management route.

The range of options is thus wide indeed. The appropriate package will vary between firms, according to the barriers to women's advancement specific to each unique culture and work environment. Box 4.8 gives an example of a comprehensive affirmative action programme.

Box 4.8. Example of a comprehensive affirmative action programme

Westpac, a major Australian bank, was one of the winners of the Best Affirmative Action Award given by the Australian Government Affirmative Action Agency in 1995-96. The bank is attempting to change the traditional structure of a predominantly female (62 per cent) workforce, with most women concentrated at lower levels and part-time jobs. To this end it has been working closely with the Finance Sector Union in a variety of programmes. Workplace changes include the decentralization of much of the data processing, resulting in over 60 per cent of team leaders being women.

Box 4.8 (cont.)

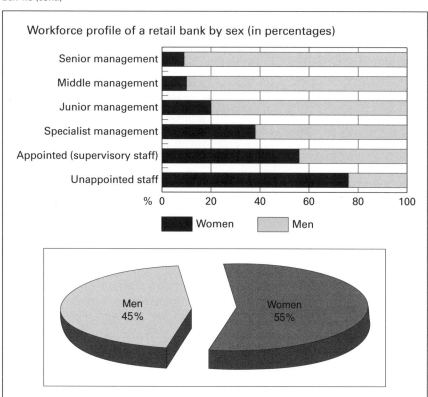

Workforce profile of a retail bank by sex (in percentages)

Source: Affirmative Action Agency, Australia: *Annual Report 1995-96*, op. cit., p. 3.

The bank identified the lack of women in management as one of the most critical issues. Its research showed that a glass ceiling existed between the supervisory and management grades (see the figure above); that the promotion rates of women with comparable performance levels and educational qualifications to their male colleagues were lower; and that women's separation rates were relatively high, particularly in supervisory jobs. Westpac changed its recruitment, training and assessment procedures; established a Women in Management programme focused on mentoring; and addressed work and family issues, including the improvement of part-timers' career prospects.

On recruitment, the bank requested recruitment firms to search actively for women candidates and required that at least one woman candidate be short-listed; it organized briefings on equal employment opportunities and affirmative action for the recruitment agencies it used; and it briefed external suppliers, including advertising consultants, on sexual harassment and diversity.

As part of its drive to create a merit-based culture, Westpac developed assessment schemes to select managers. Selections are based on merit, using psychometric tests, role plays and group exercises to assess a range of "hard" and "soft" skills, such as counselling, communication and problem solving. Affirmative action principles have been integrated into selection processes. Peer and 360-degree appraisals for promotion, internal advertising of positions with self-nomination, and targeted selection interviews are now the norm.

The bank recognizes that development for management roles cannot just rely on formal training, but also needs a range of suitable on-the-job experiences. To give high-potential women a wider business exposure, Westpac established a Women in Management programme. Group meetings and focus groups are conducted to seek women's views on business issues, and include guest speakers for various topics, including women in management. In 1994, 776 women participated in the programme, all sponsored by zone chiefs and regional managers. In addition, the General Manager Branch of Banking personally sponsors a small group of women and actively seeks their views on business issues. The General Manager is involved in approving remuneration reviews, transfers and promotions for this group. Results have been tangible, such as an increase of nearly 4 per cent of women moving into management positions between 1994 and 1995.

To raise awareness on equal employment opportunities and affirmative action throughout the organization, in 1994-95 Westpac began an intensive programme of training workshops on affirmative action and workforce diversity. In addition, briefings to all executives and managers highlight managers' responsibilities for achieving acceptable affirmative action outcomes. By the end of 1997, it was planned that all employees would have received training on the bank's sexual harassment policy and procedures. Its affirmative action policy is also communicated to employees via the Westpac Employee Guidelines, the staff magazine and the induction programme.

Source: Affirmative Action Agency, Australia: *Annual Report* 1995-96, op. cit., pp. 4-6.

ENSURING EFFECTIVENESS

Sensitization

Formal policies and measures can only succeed if staff are educated about the gains these entail for individuals and the organization. Sensitization programmes typically focus on making managers gender sensitive and convincing them of the value of gender equality for the very future of the firm or organization (box 4.9).

Box 4.9.   Key actions for genuine commitment

- Top-down support clearly communicated to all employees
- Managers educated and motivated in implementing and disseminating the policy
- Managers held accountable for women's advancement

Evaluation

Companies need to develop mechanisms to measure change, evaluate strategies and assess their own progress in eliminating glass ceilings. Some countries have introduced laws obliging companies to systematically monitor progress and have devised methodologies to help them in this task. Employers may consider that this entails costs and constitutes an administrative burden. However, the economic advantages of promoting women, and thus developing and using their resources to the fullest, warrants such an effort and can be viewed as an investment, rather than a cost.

Commitment and accountability

Real change in organizations, especially in terms of social perceptions, requires conviction and a determined commitment from the very top. Few companies so far have regarded dismantling of the glass ceiling as a priority in terms of meeting business objectives or compliance with equality principles or laws. The introduction of a few measures (flexible working schedules, assistance with childcare, work/family programmes and so forth) to give women more opportunities to work and advance, albeit only to certain levels, is often inadequate. In order to take a hard look at recruitment and promotion systems and to identify and implement strategies to ensure that women reach the top, it is vital that executive directors of companies appreciate the importance of capitalizing on the full potential of their female staff. This involves recognizing women's capacity to provide invaluable input for creating products and services appreciated by women and keeping in mind the image their company presents to consumers.

Ways of promoting change among managers have included linking their pay or bonuses to their performance on gender equality and diversity issues, and making it mandatory for male managers to participate in company-sponsored groups on gender issues.

CONCLUSION

Dismantling the glass ceiling requires understanding it as:

> a series of events in the careers of female managers and professionals, rather than a fixed point beyond which advancement is impossible. Even women may fail to recognize the glass ceiling for what it is – a cumulative outcome of attitudinal, cultural and organizational biases that are at work in corporations.[80]

Once understood, a systematic organization-level approach addressing all existing barriers is essential for women to break through the glass ceiling.

Although policies are more advanced in industrialized countries, promoting women in management should not be viewed as a "luxury". Rather, it is indispensable to enable firms worldwide to use and develop women's talents and potential to the fullest.

Notes

[1] See E. M. Pollack: "Mujeres y mercado de trabajo: Desafíos para una participación con equidad", in M. E. Valenzuela (ed.): *Igualdad de oportunidades para la mujer en el trabajo* (Santiago, Servicio Nacional de la Mujer, 1996), p. 393.

[2] *Führungskräfte in Politik, Wirtschaft und Gesellschaft*, results of a survey by the Union die Leitenden Angestellten (Managerial Union of Employees in Germany), Mar. 1997, p. 45.

[3] The study concerns the Bank of Montreal task force on the advancement of women. See M. C. Mattis: "Organizational initiatives in the USA for advancing managerial women", in M. J. Davidson and R. J. Burke (eds.): *Women in management: Current research issues* (London, Paul Chapman, 1994), p. 271.

[4] National Committee on Pay Equity: "The wage gap by education: 1999", Fact Sheet. http://www.feminist.com/fairpay/f_education.htm.

[5] R. J. Burke and C. A. McKeen: "Career development among managerial and professional women", in Davidson and Burke, op. cit., pp. 65-66.

[6] L. Larwood: "Career paths of successful executives: Do they differ by sex?", in D. M. Saunders (ed.): *Fairness in employee selection, Vol. 1: New approaches to employment management* (Greenwich, Ct., Jai Press, 1992), p. 102.

[7] S. Siengthai and O. Leelakulthanit: "Women in management in Thailand", in N. J. Adler and D. N. Izraeli (eds.): *Competitive frontiers: Women managers in a global economy* (Cambridge, Mass., Basil Blackwell, 1994), p. 168.

[8] A. B. Antal and D. N. Izraeli: "A global comparison of women in management: Women managers in their homelands and as expatriates", in E. A. Fagenson (ed.): *Women and work, Vol. 4: Women in management – Trends, issues and challenges in managerial diversity* (Newbury Park, Ca., Sage Publications, 1993), p. 63.

[9] J. Traves et al.: "Careers of women managers in the retail industry", in *Service Industries Journal* (London), Vol. 17, No. 1, 1997, p. 145.

[10] A. Lam: "Equal employment opportunities for Japanese women: Changing company practice", in J. Hunter (ed.): *Japanese women working* (London and New York, Routledge, 1993), pp. 197-223.

[11] "Dai-Icho Kanyo to recruit more female graduates", in *Daily Yomiuri*, 26 Mar. 1997.

[12] A. Chan and J. Lee: "Women executives in a newly industrialized economy: The Singapore scenario", in Adler and Izraeli, op. cit., p. 134.

[13] : "Reality Check: Women", *In Motion* Fact Sheet. http://www.inmotionmagazine.com/ stereo. For the full article, see R. Redwood: "The glass ceiling", published in In Motion. http://www.inmotionmagazine.com/glass.html.

[14] Canadian Human Rights Commission (CHRC): *Annual Report 1996* (Ottawa, 1996).

[15] C. Edwards et al.: *Organizational change and women managers' careers: The restructuring of disadvantage?*, Working paper (Kingston, United Kingdom, Kingston University, 1996), p. 18.

[16] J. Rosener: "Ways women lead", in *Harvard Business Review*, Nov./Dec. 1990.

[17] Information provided to the ILO by the Canadian Employers' Council, Apr. 1997.

[18] Catalyst: "1999 Catalyst award winners move women up", Press Release. http:// www.catalystwomen.org/press/release010799.html. The award winners were Baxter Healthcare, Corning Incorporated and the TD Bank Financial Group.

[19] The company involved was Hewlett-Packard. Reported in J. Teicher and K. Speritt: "From equal opportunity to diversity management: The Australian experience", in *International Journal of Manpower* (Bradford), Vol. 17, No. 4/5, 1996, p. 125.

[20] L. L. Lim: *More and better jobs for women: An action guide* (Geneva, ILO, 1996), p. 97.

[21] Information provided to the ILO by the Turkish Confederation of Employer Associations, 7 Apr. 1997.

[22] See Royal Bank of Canada: *The Diversity Factor*, Vol. 4, No. 1, Fall 1995.

[23] L. Dulude: *Seniority and employment equity for women* (Kingston, Ontario, IRC Press, 1995), p. 137.

[24] National Partnership for Women and Families: "Affirmative action programs help women shatter the glass ceiling". http://www.nationalpartnership.org/workandfamily/affirmact/aa_glass. htm, p. 4.

[25] *Gleichbehandlung von Männern und Frauen im Arbeitsleben: Umfrage der Bundesvereinigung der Deutschen Arbeitgeberverbände*, Survey conducted by the Confederation of German Employers' Associations, Bonn, 1992.

[26] See Mattis, op. cit., p. 273.

[27] M. Wiig: *Women in the bank group: A review of progress, issues and future actions* (Washington, DC, World Bank, 1994), p.16.

[28] *Trojaner Forum für Lernen*, Vol. 4, No. 1, p. 24.

[29] Federal Ministry for Education and Science Research and Technology and Commission of the European Communities: *Total E-Quality: Chancengleichheit im Unternehmen Paradigmenwechsel in der Personalpolitik* (Brussels, European Commission, 1997), p. 37.

[30] Trades Union Congress (TUC): *Professional and managerial staffs – trends and prospects* (London, Feb. 1997), p. 16.

[31] Survey concluded by the Confederation of German Employers' Associations, op. cit.

[32] See S. Horrell et al: "Gender and skills", in *Work, Employment and Society* (Cambridge), Vol. 4, No. 2, 1990, pp. 189-216.

[33] Lim, op. cit., p. 117.

[34] J. P. Jacobsen and L. M. Levin: "Effects of intermittent labour force attachment on women's earnings", in *Monthly Labor Review* (Washington, DC), Vol. 118, No. 9, 1995, pp. 14-19.

[35] Institute of Management: *Labour market trends* (London, 1998), p. 279.

[36] K. Charlesworth: *A question of balance? A survey of managers' changing professional and personal roles* (London, Institute of Management, 1997), p. 52.

[37] Catalyst: "Two careers, one marriage: Making it work in the workplace", Fact Sheet. http://www.catalystwomen.org/press/facts2c.html.

[38] R. Bellinger: "Dual-career couples want flexible hours and jobs, study finds", in *EE Times Online*, 30 Sep. 1998.

[39] Catalyst: "Two careers, one marriage...", op. cit.

[40] Catalyst: "Father's Day 1999", Fact Sheet. http://www.catalystwomen.org/press/factsfathers99.html.

[41] H. Glezer and I. Wolcott: *Work and family life: Reciprocal effects*, Paper presented at the Sixth Australian Institute of Family Studies Conference on Changing Families, Challenging Futures, Melbourne, 25-27 Nov. 1998. Published by Australian Institute of Family Studies. http://www.aifs.org.au/institute/afrc6papers/glezer.html.

[42] ibid.

[43] U. Koch: "Equality issue lands on the manager's desk", in *Nordic Labour Journal*, Vol. 2, 1998.

[44] Glezer and Wolcott, op. cit.

[45] See ILO: *Conditions of Work Digest: Combating sexual harassment at work*, Vol. 11, No. 1 (Geneva, 1992), pp. 10-12.

[46] L. Heller: *Porqué llegan las que llegan?* (Buenos Aires, Feminaria Editoria, 1996), p. 86.

[47] M. Collinson: "It's only Dick: The sexual harassment of women managers in insurance sales", in *Work, Employment and Society* (London), Vol. 10, No. 1, 1996, pp. 29-56.

[48] Royal Bank of Canada, *Employee Rules JO-61-11*, cited in a flier on sexual harassment, "Maintaining a professional environment: Harassment, don't let it happen!".

[49] G. Timmerman and C. Bajema: "Sexual harassment in the European workforce", research project commissioned by the European Commission and conducted by the University of Groningen, Netherlands. It is referred to in *News from NIKK* (Oslo), No. 1, 1997. *The Nordisk Institutt for Kvinne-og Kjønnsforskning* (Nordic Institute for Women's Studies and Gender Research) is an interdisciplinary Nordic research institution financed by the Nordic Council of Ministers. It is a forum for gender and equality research and activities in the Nordic countries.

[50] Information collected and provided by employers' organizations in the Caribbean, May, 1997.

[51] Lim, op. cit., p. 114.

[52] Incomes Data Services Ltd: *Study 597* (London, Opportunity 2000, 1996), pp. 1-2.

[53] Larwood, op. cit., p 102.

⁵⁴ C. Moskos: "Affirmative action: The army's success…", cited in A. M. Joseph and H. A. Coleman: "Affirmative action and economics: A framework for analysis", in *Public Productivity and Management Review* (Thousand Oaks, New Delhi, and London), Vol. 20, No. 3, 1997, p. 269.

⁵⁵ Work and Family Institute, Australia: "Affirmative action programs help women shatter the glass ceiling". http://www.nationalpartnership.org/workandfamily/affirmact/aa_glass.htm, p. 3.

⁵⁶ R. Kandola and J. Fullerton: "Diversity: More than just an empty slogan", in *Personnel management* (London), Vol. 26, No. 4, 1994, p. 46.

⁵⁷ See D. Mahnke: *Diversity management: What is it?*, unpublished working paper (Geneva, ILO, 1999), p. 4.

⁵⁸ Information provided to the ILO by the Canadian Employers' Council, Apr. 1997. The bank in question is the Canadian Imperial Bank of Commerce.

⁵⁹ Work and Family Institute, Australia, op. cit., p. 4.

⁶⁰ M. McDougall: "Equal opportunities versus managing diversity: Another challenge for public sector management?", in *International Journal of Public Management* (Glasgow), Vol. 9, No. 5/6, 1996, p. 71.

⁶¹ Mahnke, op. cit.

⁶² C. S. Venkata Ratman and V. Chandra: "Sources of diversity and the challenge before human resource management in India", in *International Journal of Manpower* (Bradford), Vol. 17, No. 4/5, 1996, p. 98.

⁶³ R. T. Roosevelt: "Managing diversity: A conceptual framework", cited in Mahnke, op. cit.

⁶⁴ P. Carnevale and S. C. Stone: "Diversity beyond the golden rule", in *Training and Development*, Oct. 1994, pp. 22-39.

⁶⁵ McDougall, op. cit., p. 71.

⁶⁶ "Total E-Quality" is an initiative from trade and industry. It dates back to a conference of the network, "Positive Action", of the European Commission held in May 1994 in Como (Italy). Co-founders of "Total E-Quality" Deutschland were staff of the companies Bayer AG, DT Bad Kissingen Technische Vertrieb GmbH, Deutsche Telekom AG, Hoechst AG, Albert Mühlenberg OHG, Philips GmbH, VW AG, the social partners including Deutscher Gewerkschaftsbund (German Trade Union Federation), Bundesvereinigung der Arbeitgeberverbände (Confederation of German Employer Associations), the Federal Ministries of Education and Science, Research and Technology and Family Affairs, Senior Citizens, Women and Youth, as well as the Institute for Employment Research of the Federal Employment Agency and the Bildungswerk der Hessischen Wirtschaft e. V. While "Total E-Quality" has been initiated by trade and industry, membership is not restricted to representatives of the economy.

⁶⁷ Federal Ministry for Education and Science Research and Technology and Commission of the European Communities: *Total E-Quality: Chancengleichheit im Unternehmen Paradigmenwechsel in der Personalpolitik* (Brussels, European Commission, 1997), pp. 11 and 46.

⁶⁸ E. Pircher et al.: *Managing E-Quality: Manual on executive training for equality oriented management*, published by the Policy Division for Women's Affairs of the Austrian Federal Ministry of Labour, Health and Social Affairs, the Federal Minister of Women's Affairs and Consumer Protection, the Austrian Federal Employment Service, and the Municipal Department for the Promotion and Co-ordination of Women's Affairs (Vienna, 1998).

⁶⁹ F. M. Horowitz et al.: "Human resource development and managing diversity in South Africa", in *International Journal of Manpower* (Bradford), Vol. 17, No. 4/5, 1996, p. 143.

⁷⁰ ibid.

⁷¹ N. Mansor: "Women managers in Malaysia: Their mobility and challenges", in Adler and Izraeli, op. cit., p. 107.

⁷² Charlesworth, op. cit., p. 29.

⁷³ E. Hänninen-Salmelin and T. Petäjäniemi: "Women managers, the challenge to management? The case of Finland", in Adler and Izraeli, op. cit., p. 179.

⁷⁴ M. M. Snyder et al.: "Personnel practice in careers of women at the top in government and business in Nicaragua and Costa Rica", in *Public Administration and Development* (Chichester, United Kingdom), 1995, Vol. 15, No. 4, p. 146.

⁷⁵ Teicher and Speritt, op. cit., p. 127.

⁷⁶ B. Norton and J. Tivey: *Management directions, Vol. 8: Mentoring* (Corby, United Kingdom, Institute of Management, 1995), p. 1.

[77] Royal Bank of Canada, *The diversity factor*, op. cit.

[78] J. F. Fletcher: *Men and women working together: The KOM Programme* (Uppsala, Ord & Form AB, 1994), pp. 27-28.

[79] Quack and Hancké, op. cit., p. 54.

[80] Mattis, op. cit., p. 264.

POLICIES FOR PROMOTING WOMEN IN MANAGEMENT

5

INTRODUCTION

Empowering women to break through the glass ceiling requires action on many fronts. The right qualifications and training are central, as are policies and practices in the workplace to eradicate discrimination at all levels. Governments also play a fundamental role in regulating the social, political and economic environments and, ultimately, in making these receptive to gender equality and the guarantee of equal rights.

National policies and programmes promoting equality between men and women are usually broadly based and cover all walks of life. While these do not always directly address the issue of women in decision-making, they do provide an important framework and a basis for specific action in that area. Employers' and workers' organizations, together with a range of women's organizations, are also key actors in raising awareness, implementing national policies and developing innovative measures that enable women to attain and perform well in management positions.

NATIONAL POLICIES AND PROGRAMMES

Almost every country in the world has adopted legislation prohibiting discrimination or guaranteeing equal rights for men and women. The ILO's Discrimination (Employment and Occupation) Convention, 1958 (No. 111), and Equal Remuneration Convention, 1951 (No. 100), are amongst the most highly ratified of all international labour Conventions, with 145 and 149 ratifications respectively as of December 2000. Equality clauses are also increasingly included in collective agreements. Nonetheless, efforts are still necessary to achieve gender equality in the labour market.

In many cases, employment legislation has been quite effective in eliminating formal legal and institutional discrimination. However, enforcement mechanisms such as penalties or positive action measures have not always been adequate enough to ensure equality in practice. A number of countries have pursued three types of positive action with some success: the development of non-discriminatory recruitment, training and promotion procedures; the monitoring of the distribution of the sexes across functions and grades; and the setting of goals and targets. The results, though, have been mixed. Commitment to equality in the public sector has indeed improved the situation of women, but this has occurred at a slow pace because of insufficient resources or restructuring within the public service. In the private sector, positive action initiatives are usually voluntary and have so far been fairly limited.

This situation has prompted governments to re-examine their legislative provisions and to amend them. In 1995 for example, the Government of Ghana with the support of the United Kingdom Department for International Development, initiated a project, "Women in Public Life" (WIPL), with a view to examining the position and status of Ghanaian women in the civil service. The research phase of the project is complete; and the results are being analysed and will be used as a basis for creating appropriate measures. In some countries in East Africa, and in Bangladesh and the United Kingdom, there have been similar projects. The initiatives in these countries have resulted in a wide range of policies and activities including training for both men and women, new human resource management policies, and organizational restructuring.[1] In Argentina, the National Congress has passed legislation (Act No. 24.465). Section 3 of this Act establishes a special method of hiring to promote the employment of women, young people and older people.[2] In both Poland and Lithuania,[3] gender equality Acts are currently under discussion in the respective parliaments.

Several significant international initiatives are under way. One is the implementation of commitments made in 1995 during the United Nations Fourth World Conference on Women in Beijing. By September of 1997, 110 of the participating countries had prepared national action plans and 21 more had completed drafts. This represents 70 per cent of the 187 delegations that attended the Conference. However, there were less successful outcomes in 20 per cent of the countries, where little progress has been made through a lack of implementation mechanisms and resources, or because of economic and political conditions which work against women's interests. Four per cent of participating countries reported negative developments for the same reasons.[4]

National action plans submitted by European Union member States for 1999 referred to the creation and expansion of childcare facilities. Reintegration into the labour market was also a common concern in most of the action plans. That equal opportunities should be considered as one of the pillars in a nation's employment strategy, to be reviewed and revised annually, is a significant achievement in itself.[5]

Another initiative of the United Nations Economic Commission for Latin America and the Caribbean (ECLAC) is under way in Latin America and the Caribbean. The "Regional Programme of Action for the Women of Latin America and the Caribbean, 1995-2001" was reviewed in 1997. One of the conclusions was that women's participation in decision-making had not increased to the extent that could be expected given developments in other areas. However, it is suggested that if appropriate initiatives such as legislation, affirmative action and equal opportunities are taken, more gender equality could still be achieved.[6]

The greatest challenge, however, remains the enforcement of rights and legal obligations. An ILO study has noted that "most mechanisms of enforcement are not meeting their potential to help redress direct and indirect discrimination in employment".[7] At the same time, the study highlighted a number of approaches which could effectively remedy that situation, such as trade union representative action in discrimination cases, or placing the burden of proof on employers to show that they do not engage in discriminatory employment practices.

Promoting positive action

A shift in emphasis from opposing discrimination to actively promoting equality has resulted in an increase in positive or affirmative action programmes. As in the case of organization-level action, these include measures to increase the proportion of women in certain sectors or in training programmes. To achieve this, quotas or targets are often applied. However, there are important differences between quotas and targets, and employers tend to prefer targets because they allow for more flexibility in reaching a certain goal. Quotas can restrict the recruitment or promotion of men until a certain percentage of jobs are held by women. This may result in the best candidates not being appointed and lead to charges of reverse discrimination. Positive action measures also cover wide-ranging actions such as awareness-raising to counter stereotyping, advocacy with employers, adjustments in working time and work organization, and vocational training, retraining and counselling. Advocates of positive action measures stress that they:

> should be part of a plan, with numerical goals and a fixed time frame, and with provisions for reporting and monitoring. This reinforces the principle that affirmative action is a temporary "catch-up" strategy whilst equal opportunities in general are a universal right and as such have a permanent place in employment policy at all levels.[8]

Governments have often promoted positive action programmes by introducing them in the public sector (box 5.1)

In the private sector, positive action measures are usually undertaken on a voluntary basis. However, there are sometimes legal obligations upon firms to develop positive action programmes, as is the case in Australia, Canada, Italy and Norway. In France, all companies and organizations with more than 50 employees are required to report on the situation of men and women in relation to recruitment, training, promotion and working conditions. Their reports serve as guidelines for occupational equality plans, which set out specific measures to accelerate the advancement of women.

In Australia, the 1986 Affirmative Action Act requires businesses with 100 or more employees to report annually to the Government on their affirmative action programmes. Organizations which do not comply are named in a report to Parliament and become ineligible for government contracts and specified industry awards. To help companies comply with this legislation, the Affirmative Action Agency provides them with a strategic planning model, pre-designed

---

Box 5.1.   The Berlin Anti-Discrimination (Public Sector) Act, 1991

- Six-year promotion plan for women with two-year binding targets
- All vacancies to be advertised internally and externally
- Where no women apply, repeat external advertisements
- Each group of candidates to contain an equal number of qualified women and men
- Selection committees to contain equal numbers of men and women
- Fifty per cent of apprenticeship places are to be reserved for women where they are under-represented
- Women to be given priority for jobs if trained in an occupation with less than 20 per cent women
- Preferential recruitment of qualified women until women make up 50 per cent of an occupation and 50 per cent of the earning brackets within the occupation
- Training on equal opportunity policies for personnel managers
- Regular reporting on meeting targets

---

report forms and a five-level assessment scale. These instruments and the overall procedure aim at providing organizations with better feedback on their programmes and facilitating benchmarking on an industry-wide basis. As mentioned earlier, companies also receive encouragement through the granting of "best affirmative action employer awards".[9] In 1999, a possible revision of the Affirmative Action Act was under discussion, with the preparation of an Equal Opportunity for Women in the Workplace Amendment Bill 1999. The Government has promoted this bill as a vehicle for minimizing paperwork required from employers and for creating a more flexible framework within which employers can operate to meet the requirements of the Act.[10]

In Zimbabwe in the early 1990s, the Government developed positive action plans for the public service and for education and training. In the former case, the preparation of a report highlighting gender imbalances resulted in the implementation of wide-ranging measures, such as the systematic compiling of lists of women candidates, the revision of assessment criteria, and the identification of women with managerial potential. Some positive results were achieved and, though difficulties remain, the Government is pressing ahead with the positive action plan.[11]

Convinced of the need to overcome persistent discrimination despite legislation and awareness-raising programmes, in 1987 the Belgian Government adopted legislation to promote positive action plans in the private sector. The law spells out in detail the nature and content of such plans. As a result, a growing number of businesses, together with trade unions and government institutions, have been developing such plans. Since 1993, businesses with more than 300 employees are required to submit an annual report on equality of opportunity for men and women in their organizations. A 1992 law also requires that any plans for organizational restructuring should be accompanied by a positive action plan (*Cellules Action Positive*) for working women.

In Canada, the Employment Equity Act was amended in 1995 to empower the Canadian Human Rights Commission (CHRC) and the appropriate federal authorities to monitor which employers' initiatives comply with the new Act. These officials can monitor, for example, how businesses identify pools of qualified women candidates for available jobs or how they eliminate bias in recruitment and promotion procedures. Under the new law, federal employers continue to submit annual reports on the representation of four designated groups in their organizations: women, indigenous peoples, visible minorities and workers with disabilities. They must also continue to review their workforce and employment systems, and develop appropriate action plans accordingly. What is significantly novel about the Act is the authority given to the Commission to check both public- and private-sector employers for their success in systematically achieving the kind of diversity that exists in Canadian society and in the Canadian labour force at large. Compliance officers operate on the basis of persuasion and negotiation with employers, but the Commission is empowered to issue orders should this process fail. Either party may then appeal to specific tribunals to resolve contentious issues. The Act makes clear, however, that Parliament is more interested in bringing about an enlightened and purposeful commitment to change than in generating lingering disputes. Thus, for instance, the contentious notion of determining whether discrimination has taken place has been replaced by an obligation on employers to take specific steps to bring about appropriate representation of the four designated groups in their workforce.[12]

As mentioned earlier, there has been some criticism of positive action programmes in recent years, namely that they constitute a form of reverse discrimination. In 1995, the European Court of Justice ruled that the European Union's Directive on Equal Treatment should exclude measures guaranteeing women absolute and unconditional priority. The decision makes it clear that automatic and rigid quotas are not permissible under the Directive. This has provoked considerable debate, as positive action had been considered necessary to correct imbalances in sectors where women were under-represented. Proposals were made that the European Commission should modify the Directive so that it would specifically authorize positive action measures which had not been called into question by the ruling; in particular, the preferential treatment of the under-represented sex – either men or women as the case might be.[13] For example, in a February 1999 report, the European Union Committee for Women's Rights calls for an inter-institutional working party to be set up in order to promote equality between all women and men using all means, including positive action.[14]

Programmes addressing the glass ceiling

Some governments are developing specific actions to tackle the problem of the glass ceiling directly. In Mexico, a "National Plan for Women, 1995-2000" contains a chapter on the rights of women and their participation in decision-making. The chapter contains a lengthy and detailed list of priorities for action, including the promotion of women to management positions in the private and public sectors. It also calls for research into the factors hampering the full participation of women in decision-making at all levels. In addition, it proposes an information system to regularly monitor the proportion of men and women in management positions in the public and private sectors, and also in academic and social life.[15]

The US Department of Labor launched a programme in 1991 to dismantle the glass ceiling. It was designed to promote a high-quality, all-inclusive and diverse workforce capable of meeting the challenges of global competition. The programme involves an internal educational effort for the Department's officials, encouragement of voluntary efforts in the corporate community, and public recognition and reward for companies with creative and effective programmes aimed at ensuring equal opportunity. The programme also conducts compliance reviews of federal contractors to ensure that there is no discrimination, and that they actively recruit qualified workers from all segments of the labour force and offer training and advancement opportunities equally to all employees.[16]

In 1995, the Spanish Government launched the "Optima" programme to promote equal opportunities in business. This aimed to establish a group of companies with model programmes that could be replicated by others and widely publicized. One of the main objectives has been to promote women to managerial positions. The programme also provides for the production of teaching materials such as a catalogue of positive action, a guide on positive action, and a practical guide to analysing equal opportunities between men and women in organizations. Participating companies are required to submit their positive action plans to the Government's *Instituto de la Mujer* (Women's Institute). Once approved, a management and technical team accompanies firms in the implementation and follow-up of the action plans. The *Instituto de la Mujer* has also published a detailed guide on the non-sexist selection of personnel.

THE ROLE OF THE SOCIAL PARTNERS

Both employers' and workers' organizations are actively involved in the promotion of gender equality in general. They also have programmes specifically addressing professional and managerial women. Yet, one difficulty can be determining to what extent and in what circumstances a manager is an employee or a representative of the employer. A survey of women managers conducted by a Belgian national managerial employees' organization found that half of the respondents were unionized. It noted that the rate of unionization decreased as one moved up the hierarchical ladder.[17]

An Argentine employers' organization, *Unión Industrial Argentina* (UIA), has created a subcommittee on women and work to formulate and implement strategies to promote, stimulate and strengthen the position of women executives and entrepreneurs in the economic and productive process. The subcommittee's objectives include building up the executive, entrepreneurial and leadership capacity of women, increasing their self-esteem and confidence, and promoting an appreciation of their aptitudes and interests. Various training programmes have been set up to attain these objectives. The subcommittee also aims to provide opportunities for contacts and exchanges of information and experience, and to conduct research on the situation of managerial women. A general plan of action provides for a variety of activities:

- the setting up of a database of people and institutions concerned with issues of women and work;
- the identification of foundations and businesses which could finance projects for women in management;
- the establishment of a list of companies created in the last five years which are headed by women, both in Argentina and in other countries, to track their experiences;
- the publication of an information bulletin;
- the inclusion of "Women and Work" in the web site of the UIA;
- the organization of training activities, workshops and so forth; and
- the provision of a consultancy service and network for information needed to develop projects for the integration of women in business.

In 1997, the subcommittee conducted a survey of men and women in businesses which were members of the UIA. The purpose of the survey was to examine the changes brought about by the growing proportion of women managers, to analyse women's career paths and their participation in workers' and employers' organizations, and to examine their work and personal situations. This activity aims to stimulate further research and action to improve women's situation in business.

In the United States, the Chicago Area Partnerships (CAPS), a consortium of corporations, advocacy groups and federal agencies working on a range of human resources projects, has produced a report providing the business community with examples of the best affirmative action and equal opportunity policies and practices available. These practices simultaneously enhance diversity, competitiveness and profitability. According to CAPS, corporate case studies confirm that proactive, affirmative actions are also pro-business.[18]

In Europe, the Council of European Professional and Managerial Staff organized a symposium in 1995 entitled, "Career and family life: Can professional and managerial staff strike the right balance?", which involved participants from 17 European countries. Responding to the key question of whether senior leadership will remain in the hands of individuals without family responsibilities, the symposium stressed the need for the manifold values that men and women with family responsibilities can bring to the creation of new cultures in leadership.

That same year, the European Trade Union Confederation launched an action plan to improve women's presence in trade union decision-making processes. It advocates that both unions and employers adopt policies and programmes to eliminate direct and indirect discrimination and guarantee the protection of dignity. In addition, they should publish and monitor information on employment and hiring, promotions, salaries and so forth desegregated by sex. Where women are found to be under-represented, the organization should set definite objectives to remedy the imbalance. The plan points out the need to ensure women's participation in joint committees where collective agreements are negotiated and concluded so that positive action is implemented in business.[19]

The International Co-operative Alliance (ICA) emphasizes that the worldwide cooperative movement, as a people's organization, supports a move towards gender equality in decision-making, not least within its own organization. The ICA has adopted a resolution on gender equality in cooperatives and has asked its members to provide gender-disaggregated data on membership and employees. Special education and training programmes for women have also been initiated.[20]

WOMEN NETWORKING

Men have traditionally networked amongst themselves, especially socially outside working hours. Women are willing to join in mixed social functions, but are often less keen or have less time to take part in such gatherings. This means that they have less opportunity to network informally. In addition, women often rely on family and friends for career advice rather than approaching colleagues or more senior people in their organization, and this contributes to a certain amount of "invisibility". Nevertheless, in recent years there is evidence that women themselves have been forming networks, locally, nationally and internationally.

In New York as early as 1962, a national non-profit research and advisory organization called Catalyst was founded both to enable women in business and professional jobs to achieve their maximum potential and to help employers capitalize on the talents of their female employees. Over the decades, Catalyst has tracked the careers of qualified women who often work outside traditional board-of-director circles. Catalyst's research work combines the publication of national studies with the provision of internal organizational assessments for corporations and professional firms. The organization produces an annual *Census of Female Directors*, which is a complete list of women on the boards of *Fortune 500* companies.

Catalyst's research and advisory services focus on analysing workplace barriers and opportunities for women and on helping companies and professional firms to develop successful strategies to retain, develop and advance women. In 1993, Catalyst was commissioned by the US Department of Labor's glass ceiling commission to produce a report on successful corporate initiatives for breaking the glass ceiling for minorities and women. Catalyst also gives short-term assistance such as advice on human resource policy changes and coaching on how to establish a mentoring programme and women's workplace networks. It provides information on best practices in such areas as work/life supports, women's leadership development, sexual harassment and managing diversity. Catalyst's information centre represents an important resource on women's workplace issues for corporate contributors and the media. Each year, the "Catalyst Award" is presented to three corporations or professional firms that have demonstrated outstanding achievement in promoting women's careers and their development as leaders.

The European Women's Management Development network (EWMD), based in Brussels, was created in 1984 under the auspices of the European Foundation for Management Development and has members in over 30 countries around the world. The EWMD hopes to contribute to improving management quality by developing and promoting women's full potential as managers. Achieving this involves the following:

- identifying and encouraging best practices for women's management development;
- facilitating communication between those who work to promote women in management;
- publicizing women's achievements in management;
- encouraging women to seek opportunities; and
- providing a forum for collecting and exchanging information about women's management development in Europe and internationally.

Members are encouraged to find ways to help men and women work together in greater harmony and to achieve a better balance between their professional and private lives. It encourages organizations to adopt flexible approaches that respect and respond to individual needs, including work patterns and career paths. It promotes different and non-traditional ways of working as a means of tapping the full potential of employees and of achieving greater creativity and improved productivity. The services provided by EWMD to its members include:

- a directory of members including information on professional qualifications, languages spoken, and relevant experience;
- regular national and international newsletters and a programme of local conferences;
- training and development activities organized by the national networks;
- an annual international research symposium; and
- an annual international conference at which participants can share experiences and access the latest research findings on women in management.

The European Network of Resource Centres has as its goal the creation of a network of resource centres for women in Europe. An example of one of these resource centres is the *ResursCentra* for women in western Sweden. Based in Gothenburg, this organization offers a wide range of services to the women in surrounding areas, including information and advice on careers, starting up companies and developing projects. In addition, the centre provides information about other resources available to women in the area. *ResursCentra* can also provide details on current development projects, gender research and women's networks. At the organization's office, newspapers, literature and copying facilities are made available. It is also possible to borrow conference rooms, use computers and have access to the Internet.

In Uruguay, a network of professionals, *Mujeres en Carrera* (Career Women), brings together managerial, professional and entrepreneurial women to help them in their personal and professional development. The network provides support, contacts and information on cultural, economic and social issues. It also encourages women who have already achieved high-level positions to share their experiences with other women, for instance on how they have managed to balance family and professional responsibilities. The network also seeks to increase organizational awareness of the great potential offered by talented and qualified women, who are assuming new roles in the country's economy. *Mujeres en Carrera* organizes workshops, courses, conferences and meetings, and conducts research on women's situation. It thus promotes a positive view of a career as a form of economic, personal and professional development.

The Women's Institute of Management (WIM), based in Malaysia, reaches out to the whole Association of Southeast Asian Nations (ASEAN) region and beyond to promote the leadership of women in all sectors. Since it was launched in 1994, WIM has organized close to 100 training courses and events in all states of Malaysia, reaching around 6,000 women from 123 women's organizations. It has produced six training manuals and a finance handbook for entrepreneurs, professionals and social workers. WIM's training courses are targeted at the advancement of women, especially those in lower income groups. In particular, it is reaching out to help provide business skills to women who are single parents.[21]

Also worth mentioning in this context is the example of the South African Federation of Business and Professional women, which organizes seminars on business topics for its members, thereby expanding their local and international business networks and promoting equal opportunities. To that end, it has created a prestigious "Gold Award" for companies that:

- appoint women to senior management positions in non-traditional areas;
- provide absolute parity in salary and all fringe benefits;
- are leaders in innovative benefit policies such as extended maternity leave and day care for employees' children;
- nominate all deserving women candidates for supervisory and management training; and
- base promotions on merit while providing career development plans.[22]

CONCLUSION

Women are undoubtedly making significant inroads into management. Changing social attitudes towards women's roles in the labour market and at home have been central to this process and anti-discrimination legislation has encouraged women to obtain qualifications and seek jobs in new fields. However, the job market remains highly segregated both horizontally (in terms of occupations) and vertically (in terms of hierarchical levels). Despite improvements, there is often frustration with the slow pace of change, especially considering how much women have caught up with men in terms of education.

Strategies to speed up the advancement of women have generally focused on the following areas:

- enacting equality laws and rendering complaint procedures more effective;
- providing family care assistance;
- revaluing "feminine" occupations;
- moving women into more scientific areas;
- insisting on objective criteria in recruitment and promotion;
- questioning organizational structures in terms of their efficiency and treatment of both men and women;
- building networks; and
- raising awareness and changing social attitudes.

Progress in these areas is, however, dependent on labour market trends and available economic opportunities. A negative employment outlook tends to dampen efforts to improve women's situation. Predicted labour shortages may benefit women if companies use the right strategies. Nonetheless, even when economic opportunities are poor because of recessions, economic downturns and the like, it is certain that women's presence in the labour force will continue to grow, both numerically and qualitatively. As the proportion of professional women reaches a critical mass, the contribution of qualified women will increasingly be perceived as a bottom-line requirement, and thus the position of women will be less subject to the vagaries of the market-place.

Increased competition and economic globalization, which are promoting new forms of flexible organization and new management styles, can further boost women's labour market position, as these new forms put more emphasis on organizations and attitudes that are flexible, non-hierarchical, cooperative and holistic. Such environments de-emphasize the old rigidities which have been restrictive to women and allow a more positive appreciation of so-called "feminine" management qualities and styles: being less combative, being more consensus and solution oriented, being more practical and supportive of other staff and so forth.

As women catch up with men in many areas, one key issue that emerges is the gap between the small proportion of women with secure, well-paid jobs and the bulk of women remaining in low-skilled positions, often on a part-time, temporary or other precarious basis, not to mention the vast majority of the world's women who work in the informal economy. Thus, it should be kept in perspective that, for the majority of women to improve their occupational and employment status, broad-based measures have to be pursued in tandem with specific strategies to promote women in management. The latter could perhaps aspire to junior or middle management, if not the very top, and could indeed serve as role models for future generations.

Notes

[1] P. M. Amos-Wilson: "Some issues concerning women in senior management: A case study from Ghana", in *Public Administration and Development* (London), Vol. 19, No. 3, 1999, pp. 217 and 227.

[2] A. M. Mass et al.: *Rompiendo el techo de cristal: Las mujeres en el management en Argentina*, Working paper (Geneva, ILO, 1998), pp. 2-3.

[3] The Women's Rights Center, Lithuania: *Women's rights in the constitution*, Women's Rights Center Report. http://free.ngo.pl/temida/legis.htm.

[4] Monitoring UN Conference Agreements: "Moving ahead with national action plans". http://www.igc.org/wedo/monitor/plans.htm.

[5] European Commission, DGV: *National action plans on employment 1999, Europa*. http://www.europa.eu.int/comm/dg05/empl&esf/news/nap_en.

[6] "Access to power and participation in decision-making in Latin America and the Caribbean: Policies for gender equity looking to the year 2000", Seventh Session of the Regional Conference on the Integration of Women into the Economic and Social Development of Latin America and the Caribbean, Chile, Nov. 1997. See http://www.eclac.org/English/Meetings/confwomen/l-1063-i.htm, pp. 1-2.

[7] C. Thomas and R. Taylor: *Enforcement of equality provisions for women workers*, Working Paper No. 20, Equality for Women in Employment Interdepartmental Project (Geneva, ILO, 1994), pp. 35-36.

[8] S. Bullock: *Women and work* (London, Zed Books, 1994), p. 104.

[9] Affirmative Action Agency, Australia: *Annual Report* (Sydney, 1996).

[10] Parliament of the Commonwealth of Australia, House of Representatives: "Equal Opportunity for Women in the Workplace Amendment Bill 1999: Explanatory Memorandum", Circulated by authority of the Minister for Employment, Workplace Relations and Small Businesses, the Honourable Peter Reith MP, 1998-99, p. 2.

[11] U. A. Chari: *Positive action measures to promote the equality of women in employment in Zimbabwe*, Working Paper No. 16, Equality for Women in Employment Interdepartmental Project (Geneva, ILO, 1993).

[12] CHRC: *Annual Report 1996* (Ottawa, 1996).

[13] European Commission, Employment and Social Affairs: *The Magazine* (Brussels), No. 1, p. 15, 1997. See also ILO: *Equality in employment and occupation*, Special Survey by the Committee of Experts on the Application of Conventions and Recommendations, Report III (Par 4B), International Labour Conference, 83rd Session, Geneva, 1996, p. 117.

[14] M. Eriksson: *Report 1999-2004*, Committee on Women's Rights and Equal Opportunities (Strasbourg, European Parliament, 1999), para. 21.

[15] *Diario Oficial*, 21 Aug. 1996.

[16] US Department of Labor, Office of Information: *News* (Washington, DC), 8 Aug. 1991.

[17] Union des Ingènieurs et Cadres – Confédération Française Démocratique du Travail (UIC-CFDT): *Cadres Plus*, No. 55, Feb. 1997 (Supplement to *CADRES-CFDT*, No. 375-376), p. 9. See http://francenet.fr/~ucc-cfdt/333b.htm.

[18] Chicago Area Partnerships: *Pathways and progress: Corporate best practices to shatter the glass ceiling* (Chicago, 1996). This consortium includes participants from the Labor

Department's Office of Federal Contract Compliance Programs, the Chicago Urban League, the Mexican American Legal Defense and Education Fund, Women Employed, the Chicago Jobs Council and ten major corporations.

[19] Positive Action Coordination Group of the European Commission: *Actions Positives*, Bulletin No. 2, Aug. 1995 (Brussels, European Commission, 1995).

[20] The International Co-operative Alliance (ICA): "ICA president recognizes International Women's Day", press release, Geneva, 8 Mar. 1999.

[21] See WIM web site. http://ngo.asiapac.net/wim/wim.html.

[22] R. Erwee: "South African women: Changing career patterns", in N. J. Adler and D. N. Izraeli (eds.): *Competitive frontiers: Women managers in a global economy* (Cambridge, Mass., Basil Blackwell, 1994), p. 338.

INTERNATIONAL ACTION TO PROMOTE EQUAL EMPLOYMENT OPPORTUNITIES

6

INTRODUCTION

> *We take a decisive step towards globalizing social progress each time we champion gender equality as a matter of human rights, social justice, economic efficiency and sustainable development.*

(Message by the Director-General of the ILO to the President of the Beijing+5 Conference, 2000)

The coming together of countries within the United Nations and the pooling of their concerns, resources, strategies and activities have produced over the decades a formidable array of legal instruments and programmes to further the cause of gender equality and equality of opportunity. The number of clear mandates and commitments has been multiplying in an attempt to address the myriad forms of discrimination in social, political, cultural and economic life, which ultimately hamper women's employment and career prospects. International action is a powerful stimulus in promoting professional and managerial women, and is all the more necessary since increasing women's participation in decision-making remains one of the areas most resistant to change. This chapter summarizes the ILO's standard-setting activities in relation to women and workers and, within the context of recent actions taken within the United Nations system, discusses its policies and programmes for gender equality and for advancing women in professional and managerial careers.

INTERNATIONAL LABOUR STANDARDS ON WOMEN WORKERS

By the end of the year 2000, the ILO had adopted 183 Conventions (and 191 accompanying Recommendations), covering a broad range of labour matters. Most of these instruments apply equally to women and men. Women should thus enjoy the same rights as men in the various fields covered, such as fundamental human rights, employment and training, working conditions, and occupational health and safety. In addition, a number of ILO standards specifically target women workers.

Two predominant trends may be distinguished in the ILO's standard-setting activity on equality of opportunity and treatment between women and men.

From the ILO's foundation in 1919 to the 1950s, the emphasis was on protecting women workers from exceedingly arduous conditions of work. A primary objective was to safeguard women's health, with special reference to childbearing and child rearing. Accordingly, minimum standards on maternity leave and benefits were among the first to be adopted by the ILO's annual sessions of the International Labour Conference. By the beginning of the 1950s, the emphasis was shifting towards eliminating discrimination against women in employment and towards more positively promoting equality of opportunity and treatment for women workers. More recently, there has been a movement towards insisting that gender equality means according women and men equal opportunities in every respect, including coverage by protective legislation. Such protection may vary according to the different needs of men and women, as for example the protection of reproductive organs from hazardous substances in the workplace. Positive action measures for women or men may also be required on a temporary basis to redress particular inequalities.

ILO standards on gender equality

Many international labour standards have contained provisions promoting equal opportunity, identifying a variety of grounds on which distinctions should not be made between people in their work, livelihood, education and training. In 1944, the ILO's Constitution and mandate were renewed and strengthened with the adoption of the Declaration of Philadelphia. Among other things, this affirmed that "all human beings, irrespective of race, creed or sex, have the right to pursue both their material well-being and their spiritual development in conditions of freedom and dignity, of economic security and equal opportunity".[1] In 1998, the ILO again recognized the continuing importance of these principles by including the Discrimination (Employment and Occupation) Convention, 1958 (No. 111), and the Equal Remuneration Convention, 1951 (No. 100), in the adoption of the Declaration on Fundamental Rights and Principles at Work and its Follow-up at the 86th Session of the International Labour Conference in 1998.

Discrimination in employment and occupation

The most comprehensive standards are contained in Convention No. 111 and Recommendation No. 111, both adopted in 1958 to deal with the overall problem of discrimination based on race, colour, sex, religion, political opinion, national extraction or social origin. The Convention defines discrimination as "any distinction, exclusion or preference [on any of the grounds specified] ... which has the effect of nullifying or impairing equality of opportunity or treatment in employment or occupation".[2] However, distinctions, exclusions or preferences based on the inherent requirements of a particular job are not considered to be discrimination. Also excluded are the special measures of protection or assistance provided for in other ILO Conventions or Recommendations.

As would be expected from instruments dealing with fundamental human rights, both of the above apply to all individuals and all forms of employment, whether they occur in the private or the public sector and whether they are salaried or independent. The Convention defines the terms "employment" and " occupation" as including "access to vocational training, access to employment and to particular occupations, and terms and conditions of employment".[3]

Recommendation No. 111 spells out the matters covered by these different fields:

- access to vocational guidance and placement services;
- access to training and employment of choice on the basis of individual suitability for such training or employment;
- advancement in accordance with individual character, experience, ability and diligence;
- security of employment tenure;
- equal remuneration for work of equal value; and
- conditions of work, including hours of work, rest periods, annual holidays with pay, occupational safety and occupational health measures, and also including social security measures and welfare facilities and benefits provided in connection with employment.

ILO member States that have ratified Convention No. 111 undertake to declare and pursue a national policy aimed at eliminating all forms of discrimination in respect of employment and occupation. They are bound to repeal any statutory provisions and modify any administrative instructions or practices inconsistent with this policy and, in cooperation with employers' and workers' organizations, to enact legislation and promote educational pro-grammes that favour its acceptance and implementation. The policy is to be implemented under the direct control of a national authority or of vocational guidance, training and placement services under the direction of such an authority.

Recommendation No. 111 spells out in more detail the measures that should be taken to implement the policy. It suggests that appropriate agencies should be set up, in particular to foster public understanding and acceptance of the principles of non-discrimination, and also to examine complaints that the policy is not being observed.

Both instruments have had a significant impact on the promotion of equality of opportunity and treatment. Over the years, the Committee of Experts on the Application of Conventions and Recommendations – a key element in the ILO's supervisory machinery – has noted a great variety of legislative and practical measures taken worldwide to eliminate discrimination and promote equality of opportunity and treatment, particularly for women workers. Such measures have included the following:

- achieving equality for women through education, and vocational training and guidance, including programmes aimed at stimulating access to jobs traditionally held by men;
- launching public advertising and information campaigns;

- developing measures to relieve women from the principal responsibility for childcare by ensuring that male and female employees are entitled to leave for family reasons;
- creating administrative bodies to advise on women's rights, formulate government policy and action, and determine cases of alleged discrimination; and
- designing measures to establish equality of treatment in the areas of social security payments, pensions, income tax, and family and civil law, and in access to the necessary resources to sustain employment (credit, land, tools and so forth).

As discrimination on the grounds of sex is a universal problem, it received particular attention both in the 1988 General Survey of the ILO Committee of Experts on the Application of Conventions and Recommendations and in the Committee's 1996 Special Survey on Convention No. 111.[4] These surveys underlined the progress made in countries that had established machinery to ensure the actual implementation of their national policy promoting gender equality of opportunity and treatment.

Indirect discrimination, which seriously affects equality of opportunity and treatment, was also studied and particular attention was given to gender-based occupational segregation. Archaic attitudes and stereotypes on the distribution of "male" and "female" tasks were found still to be prevalent in many countries, even though some progress had been noticeable over the years. The surveys also confirmed that sexual harassment is a threat, both to women workers and to companies and organizations. The Committee observed that affirmative action measures, sometimes called "positive discrimination", are often extremely useful in the first stages of eliminating discrimination and achieving real equality. It also noted that merely banning discrimination is not sufficient to eliminate it in practice. In general, the surveys stressed the need for governments to take a comprehensive approach, involving legislative and practical measures to address all sources of discrimination and to encourage understanding and acceptance of the principle of equality.

Equal remuneration

The Equal Remuneration Convention (No. 100), and Recommendation (No. 90), both adopted in 1951, relate specifically to the elimination of discrimination between male and female workers in terms of remuneration: they call for equal pay for men and women for work of equal value.

Convention No. 100 lays down the general principle that ratifying member States are to promote and, in so far as is consistent with the existing methods in operation for determining rates of remuneration, ensure the application to all workers of the principle of equal remuneration for work of equal value. Under the Convention, "the term 'remuneration' includes the ordinary, basic or minimum wage or salary and any additional emoluments whatsoever payable directly or indirectly, whether in cash or in kind, by the employer to the worker and arising out of the worker's employment".[5] The Convention and Recommendation advocate the establishment of methods for an objective appraisal of the work to be performed, whether by job analysis or other procedures, with a view to providing a classification of jobs without regard to sex.

A General Survey on equal remuneration was undertaken by the Committee of Experts in 1986 to review the law and practice relevant to these instruments in ILO member States.[6] While noting some encouraging progress made throughout the world in the application of the principle of equal pay, particularly the accelerating trend to enact legislation and create specialized bodies to assist in its implementation, the Committee expressed concern about persistent problems in giving practical effect to the requirements of the equal pay instruments. For instance, the definitions and criteria used in national legislation for comparing jobs are often more restrictive than those set out in the Convention, and hence can lead to narrow interpretations. The Committee also noted the importance of establishing easy methods and readily accessible procedures for comparing the value of different jobs without taking into account, either directly or indirectly, the sex of workers. Particular difficulties for job evaluation exist in areas where men and women are segregated into different occupations, industries and specific jobs within organizations as a result of strongly entrenched historical and social attitudes. Therefore, to ensure equal pay in an industry employing mostly women, the basis of comparison should not be confined to the establishment or business concerned.

Whatever the means adopted to achieve equal pay, it is essential that the social partners (employers' and workers' organizations) be fully committed to that goal. Much depends on their determination to eliminate traces of discrimination from collective agreements and pay scales. More generally, the Committee observed that many of the difficulties in achieving equal remuneration are intimately linked to the general status of men and women in employment and society: equal evaluation of work and equal rights with regard to all components of remuneration cannot be achieved in a general context of inequality. Given the multiple causes of unequal remuneration, the most effective results have been obtained in countries that have taken action to tackle all aspects of the problem simultaneously. Nowhere, however, has discrimination been completely eliminated in this area.

Maternity protection

The Maternity Protection Convention, 1919 (No. 3), was among the first ILO instruments to be adopted. Applicable to all women in industry and commerce, it provides for 12 weeks' maternity leave in two equal parts: six weeks preceding childbirth and a compulsory six-week period following it. It also lays down a right to benefits sufficient for the maintenance of the mother and her child, which should be provided either out of public funds or through a system of insurance. Furthermore, it specifies the right to free attendance by a doctor or midwife. The Convention prohibits the dismissal of a woman during maternity leave or during an illness arising out of pregnancy or confinement, and provides that breaks shall be granted during working hours for nursing the baby.

The provisions of Convention No. 3 are taken up in more detail in the Maternity Protection Convention (Revised), 1952 (No. 103), which is also wider in scope. This Convention applies to women employed in industrial undertakings and in non-industrial and agricultural occupations, including domestic workers and women wage earners working at home. In terms of the benefits sufficient for the maintenance of a woman and her child, Convention No. 103 fixes the rate of cash benefits, where these are provided under compulsory social insurance and based on previous earnings, at not less than two-thirds of these earnings.

Recommendation No. 95, supplementing Convention No. 103, suggests extending maternity leave to 14 weeks, and increasing cash benefits to 100 per cent of previous earnings plus the granting of certain additional benefits. It recommends more medical care, the guaranteeing of employment security for a longer period, the establishment of nursing facilities and the adoption of measures to protect the health of pregnant and nursing women. The latter includes the prohibition of forms of work harmful to the health of the woman or her child, and the woman's right to be transferred to work not harmful to her health.

In 2000, the Maternity Protection Convention (No. 183) was adopted. It strengthens the provisions in a number of areas, notably regarding health protection and non-discrimination, and it significantly broadens the scope of coverage. Convention No. 183 applies to all employed women, "including those in atypical forms of dependent work".[7] The length of maternity leave is extended from 12 to 14 weeks, and additional leave shall be provided before or after the maternity leave period in the case of illness, complications or risk of complications arising out of pregnancy or childbirth. The new Convention sets a more uniform minimum level of benefits, which is independent of the funding source, and provides greater flexibility to member States to finance benefits through compulsory social insurance funds or public funds, or in a manner to be determined by national law and practice.

The period of employment protection is greatly extended under Convention No. 183 to include the pregnancy, absence on leave and a period following the woman's return to work. However, the protection is no longer absolute. Termination of employment on grounds related to the pregnancy or birth of the child and its consequences for nursing is prohibited, and the burden of proof is placed on the employer. The new Convention also provides the right to one or more daily breaks or a daily reduction of hours of work for the woman to breastfeed her child. The breaks or the reduction of daily hours of work are to be counted as working time and remunerated accordingly.

The accompanying Recommendation (No. 191) provides more detailed guidance regarding maternity leave, benefits, the financing of benefits, employment protection and non-discrimination, health protection, breastfeeding and related types of leave.

Workers with family responsibilities

Recognizing that changes in the traditional roles of men and women in society are necessary to achieve full equality between the sexes, in 1981 the International Labour Conference adopted the Workers with Family Responsibilities Convention (No. 156), and Recommendation (No. 165). These instruments provide that men and women workers must be enabled to exercise their right to obtain or engage in employment without experiencing discrimination because of their family responsibilities and, to the greatest extent possible, "without conflict between their employment and family responsibilities".[8] Convention No. 156 provides that ratifying member States will take account of the particular needs of workers with family responsibilities in regard to vocational guidance and training, terms and conditions of employment and social security, and also through the development or promotion of public or private community services such as childcare and family services and facilities. Moreover, appropriate measures are to be taken to promote information and education aimed at engendering broader public understanding of the principle of equality of opportunity and treatment for men and women workers, and of the problems confronting workers with family responsibilities. Family responsibilities as such should not constitute a valid reason for termination of employment.

Recommendation No. 165 suggests concrete measures for creating employment and working conditions which meet the needs of such workers, for example reduced working hours, flexible schedules, parental leave, childcare, family services and facilities, social security benefits and tax relief, and so forth.

FROM PROTECTION TO EQUAL TREATMENT

As mentioned earlier, there has been a marked shift in emphasis from special protection to the promotion of equality in ILO standard-setting activities on women, particularly since 1975. In the ILO and in its member States, standards that establish special protective measures for reasons not directly connected with maternity and women's reproductive function have been undergoing a critical review. These are increasingly seen as an obstacle to the full integration of women into economic life and as a means of perpetuating traditional notions about women's roles and abilities.

A review was called for in the Declaration on Equality of Opportunity and Treatment for Women Workers, adopted by the 1975 International Labour Conference, on the occasion of International Women's Year. Article 9 of that Declaration reiterates that the protection of women at work should be an integral part of efforts aimed at continuous promotion and improvement of living and working conditions of all employees. It states that women should be protected, on the same basis and with the same standards of protection as men, that studies and research should be undertaken into processes which might have a harmful effect on women and men from the standpoint of their reproductive function, and that measures should be taken to extend special protection to women for types of work proved to be harmful in this respect.

A 1985 ILO resolution on equal opportunities and equal treatment for men and women in employment recommended that all protective legislation applying to women should be reviewed in the light of up-to-date scientific knowledge and technical changes, and that it should be revised, supplemented, extended, retained or repealed, according to national circumstances. It also requested that protective ILO standards be reviewed periodically to determine whether their provisions remain adequate and appropriate in the light of experience acquired since their adoption, and also in the light of scientific and technical information and social progress.

It becomes clear then that ILO instruments setting special standards for women (other than maternity protection) are few, and that the rationale for most of them is to protect women from safety and health conditions potentially harmful to their reproductive capacity or to non-notified pregnancy. Examples include the prohibition in industry from employing women in painting work involving the use of white lead, laid down in the White Lead (Painting) Convention, 1921 (No. 13), and restrictions on loads to be carried by women, as covered in the Maximum Weight Convention (No. 127), and Recommendation (No. 128), of 1967.

In 1989, an ILO Meeting of Experts on Special Protective Measures for Women and Equality of Opportunity and Treatment stressed that the review of protective measures for women workers is but one means of action to ensure equal opportunity and treatment between men and women in employment, and that this objective will not be achieved until some basic attitudes and practices in society are changed. As many employed women have multiple roles which create additional burdens, there is a need to provide structures to alleviate these burdens and to allow men to share more fully in family responsibilities.

The adoption of standards on night work, part-time work and home work in recent years reflects the evolving debate on special protective measures for women. They are of particular relevance to women because of the predominance of women in these forms of work. The main purpose of the Night Work (Women) Convention (Revised), 1948 (No. 89), was to protect women by prohibiting their employment at night in industries, although women in managerial positions were exempted. In 1990, a Protocol to Convention No. 89 was adopted which added flexibility to that prohibition, by allowing variations in the duration of the night period and by including additional possibilities of night work for women. This Protocol was accompanied by the adoption of the Night Work Convention (No. 171), and Recommendation (No. 178), of 1990. These new instruments apply to both men and women workers in most sectors and provide for a wide range of measures to protect the working conditions of night workers. Convention No. 171 makes an exception to equal treatment in that it provides that an alternative to night work be available to women workers before and after childbirth, for a period of 16 weeks of which at least eight weeks should be taken before the expected date of childbirth.

In 1994, the International Labour Conference adopted the Part-Time Work Convention (No. 175), and Recommendation (No. 182). This was the first time that standards were adopted specifically addressing the protection of workers who do not work full time. Their aim is to protect part-time workers so that their working conditions are at least equivalent to those of comparable full-time workers, and to facilitate access to freely chosen part-time work to meet the needs and interests of both workers and employers. In 1996, the Home Work Convention (No. 177), and Recommendation (No. 184), were adopted to protect the employment and working conditions of home workers.

GLOBAL ACTIONS TAKEN WITHIN THE UNITED NATIONS SYSTEM

Several ground-breaking instruments and activities undertaken within the United Nations system over the past two decades have set the scene for mobilization of the international community on gender equality issues.

The United Nations Convention on the Elimination of All Forms of Discrimination against Women

The adoption in 1979 of the United Nations Convention on the Elimination of All Forms of Discrimination against Women demonstrated the wide international consensus on removing obstacles to women's full participation in the political, social, economic and cultural life of their countries. States that were party to the Convention agreed to pursue by all appropriate means and without delay a policy of eliminating discrimination against women, by embodying equality between men and women in their national constitutions or other relevant legislation. They also agreed to establish legal protection of women's rights and to take all appropriate measures to modify or abolish existing laws, regulations, customs and practices that discriminate against women. Article 4 states that the adoption of temporary special measures aimed at accelerating de facto equality between men and women shall not be considered discrimination, and shall in no way entail the maintenance of unequal or separate standards.

Articles 10 and 11 include provisions fundamental to professional and managerial women, as they ensure equality of rights with regard to education and employment. Article 10 urges member States to eliminate discrimination against women in education. States are to ensure the same conditions for career and vocational guidance and the elimination of stereotyped concepts of gender roles. Access to studies at all levels is to be ensured on the basis of equality.

Article 11 of the Convention ensures the same rights for men and women in employment, including the application of the same selection criteria, free choice of profession, and the right to promotion, job security and all benefits and conditions of service. It also covers the right to receive training and retraining, equal remuneration and equality of treatment.

The 1995 Fourth World Conference on Women

The Fourth World Conference on Women, held in Beijing in 1995, was the best attended United Nations conference in history. The 189 governments present unanimously affirmed that achieving gender equality was a matter of fundamental human rights and a prerequisite for social justice. The Platform for Action, adopted by the Conference, contained a series of strategic objectives to guide countries in their efforts to achieve equality. First among these was the full implementation of the United Nations Convention on the Elimination of All Forms of Discrimination against Women, so as to insure equality and non-discrimination under the law and in practice. Other strategic objectives included promoting women's economic rights and independence, eliminating occupational segregation and all forms of employment discrimination, and harmonizing work and family responsibilities for both women and men.

Great attention was paid to ensuring women's equal access to and full participation in power structures and decision-making. The Platform for Action specifically called upon governments to:

- monitor and evaluate progress on women's representation at all decision-making levels, in both the public and private sectors;
- take positive action for building a critical mass of women leaders, executives and managers in strategic decision-making positions;
- restructure recruitment and career development programmes so as to ensure women's equal access to managerial, entrepreneurial, technical and leadership training, including on-the-job training; and
- develop career development programmes for women of all ages that include career planning, tracking, mentoring, coaching, training and retraining.

Beijing+5: Global High-level Plenary Review of the Beijing Platform for Action

The Beijing+5 Special Session of the General Assembly, "Women 2000: Gender Equality, Development and Peace for the Twenty-First Century", was held in New York in June 2000. The main aim was to speed up the full implementation of the 1995 Platform for Action and the 1985 Nairobi Forward-looking Strategies for the Advancement of Women (NFLS). Beijing+5 reviewed and assessed progress in the implementation of both the NFLS and the Platform for Action. NGOs, including women's groups and other civil organizations, were invited to contribute to the preparations, particularly regarding suggestions for further actions or initiatives which might be necessary in order to successfully and fully implement the Platform for Action beyond the year 2000.[9]

The Beijing+5 Conference showed that progress, although uneven, has been made towards gender equality. The discussion on gender issues has deepened, and gender has become part of the political agenda in almost all countries. New initiatives for action that came out of the Conference include combating the trafficking of women and violence against women, ensuring women's full enjoyment of their rights to health and related services, the empowerment of women economically and politically, and the encouragement of their full participation in conflict prevention and resolution.

ILO POLICIES AND PROGRAMMES TO PROMOTE EQUALITY IN EMPLOYMENT

Reflecting the global initiatives described above, ILO activities on gender issues have been stepped up over the past two decades. The focus has been placed on various key issues for women's work and careers, including:

- promoting the ratification and implementation of international labour standards of special relevance to women;
- gender-based policies and programmes for employers' organizations;
- gender equality in trade unions, including the increased incorporation of women workers' concerns in collective bargaining;
- women's presence in private-sector activities, including small businesses;
- women in management;
- increased equal opportunity for women in vocational training and technical education;
- greater harmony between work and family responsibilities; and
- social protection, especially for vulnerable groups of women.

These concerns are reflected in the ILO programmes and projects described below.

Women workers' rights

An interregional project, launched in 1994-95 in nine countries,[10] disseminates information and conducts training on women workers' rights. The publication of a multimedia training package and information kit forms the basis for the national training activities in those countries. Project activities include national "train-the-trainer" workshops and the setting up of national steering committees with representatives from government, and employers' and workers' organizations. The mandate of each national committee is to draw up national plans of action on the dissemination of information on women workers' rights. A guide entitled *ABC of women workers' rights and gender equality*[11] explains the legal frameworks and socio-economic developments surrounding gender equality and women workers' rights.

"More and Better Jobs for Women"

The ILO's long-term global programme, "More and Better Jobs for Women", is intended to enhance national capacities and to strengthen legal and institutional frameworks for improving the quantity and quality of women's employment. The programme supports and complements national efforts through the preparation and dissemination of information and guidelines on policies, programmes and best practices. Internationally, it aims to sharpen global concern for women's employment issues and promote a comprehensive and integrated approach to creating more and better jobs for women. Member States' ratification and implementation of core ILO standards on human rights is an important element of the programme.

The programme recognizes that while some women have made inroads into previously male-dominated occupations and have breached the glass ceiling, most of them remain disadvantaged relative to men in terms of their opportunities and treatment in the labour market, their participation in economic decision-making, their access to training and productive resources, and their vulnerability to retrenchment and unemployment. Its strategy therefore involves many components:

- equal pay for work of equal value;
- improved occupational safety and health measures;
- family-friendly workplaces;
- better employment security and working conditions for those in part-time, temporary and home-based work;
- the elimination of occupational segregation which perpetuates "good" jobs for men and "bad" jobs for women;
- the creation of productive and remunerative employment opportunities;
- the promotion of education and training for women and girls;
- entrepreneurship development; and
- improved access to productive resources (including credit, technology and marketing).

Mainstreaming gender issues

In the ILO's budget for 2000-01, and in the Director-General's report to the 87th Session of the International Labour Conference in 1999,[12] gender was identified as cutting across the four strategic objectives: promoting fundamental principles and rights at work; creating greater employment and income opportunities for women and men; enhancing the coverage and effectiveness of social protection; and strengthening social dialogue.

In a speech on International Women's Day, 8 March 1999, the Director-General declared a strong commitment to gender equality and expressed his intention to give high priority "to ensuring that the ILO is counted among the most progressive organizations in the field of gender equality". In the light of this strong commitment, efforts are being reinforced in the following areas:

- **Structure:** All programmes are developing and strengthening institutional arrangements to effectively mainstream gender. Gender issues are being integrated into new and/or existing mechanisms for programming, implementing, monitoring and evaluation.
- **Substance:** Efforts are being made to internalize gender equality in all ILO technical work, support and operational activities. This is expected

to create new analytical frameworks, enrich the knowledge base and improve the quality of products, services and information. All programmes are required to apply gender analysis and take explicit action, including gender-specific interventions, to promote gender equality.

- **Representation:** To improve the gender balance of professional staff within the organization, a target of 50-50 to be reached by the year 2010 has been set. Career development opportunities for support staff will be improved and specific measures taken to create a family-friendly work environment.

This process of policy formulation and strategic planning was visibly strengthened by the approval in 1999 of the Action Plan on Gender Equality and Mainstreaming in the International Labour Office. Mainstreaming gender into technical work, operational activities and support services is expected to improve the ILO's competence on gender issues regarding knowledge and information, products and services and also lead to the development of indicators and tools to support gender mainstreaming.

Training courses on gender issues in the world of work are organized for ILO staff and constituents to enable them to enhance their capacity for gender analysis and gender planning and thus enable them to better integrate gender concerns into all ILO programmes and projects.

Women in management

An ILO project has developed training materials for management development institutions to use in the training of trainers and women managers in Africa, and it is planned to adapt and use these for other regions. The aim was to develop effective methods of training women managers and to provide skills in policy analysis while implementing and evaluating the integration of gender concerns into development planning and management. This has involved designing training programmes to sensitize policy-makers and employers about women in management and gender issues, creating "women in management units" in management development institutes, and preparing staff to teach gender-related issues and conduct research on women in management. The *General trainers guide*, jointly produced by the ILO and the University of Alberta in Canada, contains seven modules on gender issues for policy-makers and women managers in Africa.

The Women's Entrepreneurship Development and Gender in Enterprise (WEDGE) unit has been established within the ILO's InFocus Programme on Boosting Employment through Small Enterprise Development. It concentrates on improving the incomes, employment conditions and prospects of women engaged in SMEs, and places particular emphasis on poor women and their households in least developed countries. It also addresses key gender issues within enterprises of all sizes, including factors limiting the growth and expansion of women-owned enterprises.

WEDGE comprises three major interrelated elements: expanding the knowledge base, promoting advocacy, and developing appropriate services and products to support the needs of women entrepreneurs. It is essential to gain knowledge about women entrepreneurs and their enterprises, as well as the factors influencing their development, because without knowledge, little can be done in relation to advocacy and services. Studies have recently been completed in Bangladesh, Bulgaria and Senegal, and others are under way in the Caribbean and Thailand. It is also necessary to develop knowledge about good-practice policies and programmes from around the world to promote and support women entrepreneurs.

The ILO's support for women entrepreneurs includes projects and programmes to develop business knowledge and skills, as well as access to credit and finance. WEDGE is working closely with the national organization of Chinese employers to develop a resource centre for women entrepreneurs' associations. It is supporting the Ministry of Women's and Veterans' Affairs in Cambodia to help it convert traditional skills training centres into centres for the economic empowerment of women.

The major strategies adopted by the WEDGE programme involve the development of information exchanges, networking and the creation of strategic alliances, both within the ILO and with other key development partners. The ILO is ideally placed to promote the interests and development of women entrepreneurs through the constituents in its member States. Strategic importance is given to the key role that representative, member-based associations can play in promoting and supporting small enterprises. This also applies to associations of women entrepreneurs, who can become more effective advocates for their own causes by developing a "voice" with policy-makers and the business community.

GENDER EQUALITY AND EMPLOYERS' ORGANIZATIONS

Employers' organizations are well positioned for advocacy work on promoting women in management. Even though there has been a considerable increase in the proportion of businesses owned or operated by women, these often make up only a small proportion of the membership of employers' organizations. Table 6.1 illustrates the situation in Latin America. The case of Colombia, where women make up 35.3 per cent of the positions on the governing body of the National Association of Industrialists, shows that it is possible to have a greater gender balance in such bodies. A key challenge for employers' organizations is to encourage equality in employment, and to promote the participation of more women managers and women entrepreneurs in their organizations. Expanding the access of women entrepreneurs to training and services offered by employers' organizations is fundamental to integrating women into the mainstream of business.

The ILO's Bureau for Employers' Activities has been active in promoting gender equality in employment, as well as mainstreaming women in management and entrepreneurship. Gender-based projects and guidelines have been designed for implementation through employers' organizations with the

Table 6.1.   Women on the governing bodies of selected business or employers'
organizations, latest year available (selected Latin American countries)

Country	Year	Business or employers' organization	Total	Women	Women as % of total
Bolivia	1993	Bolivian Private Employers' Confederation	10	0	0
Brazil	1990	National Industry Confederation (CNI)	15	0	0
		National Trade Confederation	33	0	0
		Rio de Janeiro Industry Federation	26	0	0
		State of São Paulo Industry Federation	28	0	0
Chile	1998	National Agricultural Society	11	0	0
		Banking Association	9	0	0
		Industrial Development Society	13	0	0
		Chilean Construction Chamber	11	0	0
		National Society of Mining	4	0	0
Colombia	1997	National Association of Industrialists (ANDI)	355	18	5.1
El Salvador	1994	National Private Enterprise Association[1]	74	2	2.7
Mexico	1994	Confederation of National Chambers of Industry	74	2	2.7
		Confederation of National Chambers of Commerce	305	11	3.6
Nicaragua	1993	Higher Council of Private Enterprise	20	1	5.0
		Nicaraguan Chamber of Commerce	12	2	16.7
Paraguay	1998	Federation of Producers, Industry and Commerce	16	0	0
		Rural Association of Paraguay	37	0	0
		Chamber of Exporters	9	0	0
		Paraguayan Industrial Union	14	0	0
		Christian Employers' Association	13	1	7.7
Peru	1994	Association of Exporters	37	2	5.4
Uruguay	1998	Chamber of Industry	16	1	6.3
Venezuela	1991	FEDECAMARAS[2]	301	14	4.7

[1] Represents 37 associations.   [2] Presidents of chambers.
Source: ECLAC: *Participation and leadership in Latin America and the Caribbean: Gender indicators* (Santiago, Chile, 1999).

aim of promoting sensitization, changes of attitude, and the recognition and value of integrating gender equality into business.

ILO projects have engaged the participation of employers' organizations around the world to raise awareness and promote equality. Several regional and interregional projects have developed activities by employers' organizations to integrate women into the mainstream of business. One such project, involving 22 employers' organizations in Latin America, promoted the integration of women in the private and public sectors. Another initiative, Promotion of Women in the Private Sector: Activities through Employers' Organizations, was intended to help participating employers' organizations design policies and conduct programmes to promote gender equality in employment, and to increase the number of women managers and business entrepreneurs so as to fully utilize human resources for economic and social development.[13] Workshops organized in Africa were designed to improve the capacity of participants to analyse their current situation regarding gender equality in employment and to equip them better to promote equal opportunity policies for men and women. Yet another project is the provision of ILO assistance to the Chinese Enterprise Directors' Association (CEDA) and the Chinese Employers' Confederation (CEC) in developing a women entrepreneurs' resource centre.

These projects have provided the basis for the ILO's Bureau for Employers' Activities to formulate a series of indicators to help ILO staff members around the world measure positive change as they assist employers' organizations in promoting gender equality. There are two main indicators: first, the number of employers' organizations engaged in activities that encourage equal opportunity and treatment for men and women at work; and second, the level of increased participation of women in management, as business entrepreneurs, and/or in employer representational functions, as reported by employers' organizations. The Bureau has published a brochure entitled, "As one employer to another: What's all this about EQUALITY?", in English, French and Spanish. This is a guide to equitable employment and provides concrete information about promoting equal opportunity policies and practices in the workplace.

The next section highlights a number of recommendations that employers wishing to promote gender equality should consider.

How employers and their organizations can promote gender equality in the workplace

An important step for employers is to recognize that, from an economic efficiency perspective, discrimination in the workplace can be counterproductive as it can prevent particular groups of either sex from realizing their full development potential and usefulness within the workforce. Equal employment opportunity policies can help ensure the availability of a wider and more diverse range of potential applicants, thus improving the chances for employers to obtain the best person for the job. In addition, they can increase the likelihood of increased productivity and efficiency. By having equal opportunity programmes that are properly implemented and closely monitored, employers' policies and practices can help promote gender equality in the workplace. It is critical that these be adequately reflected in personnel policies and outline the intentions and measures to be taken for equal participation and treatment.

Equal opportunity policies and programmes which employers can adopt include the following:

- policies creating a positive environment of working conditions and welfare for all individuals;
- the adoption and implementation of policies and programmes to combat gender-based job segregation. These may include affirmative action programmes designed to increase opportunities for women to move into managerial positions and into skilled and non-traditional jobs through, for example, leadership and skills training;

- the enforcement of strict policies to prevent sexual harassment and discrimination; and
- family-friendly policies, such as family leave and health care for both men and women.

Employers' organizations can promote equal opportunity policies and programmes by:

- supporting tripartite and bipartite consultations and negotiations leading to the reinforcement of equal opportunity at all levels;
- designing and implementing leadership and skills training programmes as tools to enhance the managerial skills of women managers and entrepreneurs;
- collecting and analysing qualitative and quantitative data on women's participation at various levels in the workplace; and
- improving the networking capability of employers' organizations with other institutions and associations, particularly in the design and implementation of programmes to promote gender equality in employment and the role of women in the socio-economic development of society.

GENDER EQUALITY AND TRADE UNIONS

Trade unions are an important and effective vehicle for organizing women workers and promoting gender equality in the world of work. Too often, however, they first have to face the challenge of implementing gender equality within their own organizations, particularly in leadership positions, as shown in table 6.2 for Latin America.

The ILO's Bureau for Workers' Activities provides training and advisory services, in addition to executing projects to strengthen women's participation in trade unions and workers' organizations. For example, a project in Asia on workers' education assistance has aimed at strengthening trade union action on women workers in relation to child labour in Indonesia, Thailand and Viet Nam. In Africa, a project on workers' education covering Ghana, Uganda, Zambia and Zimbabwe has worked towards integrating women members into rural workers' organizations.

The Bureau has also published a guide to gender equality bargaining for use in seminars, workshops and other promotional activities. It addresses such issues as working conditions, maternity and family responsibilities, the rights of non-permanent and vulnerable workers, dignity at work and giving a voice to women.

In general, ILO programmes for workers seek to maximize the active involvement and participation of women workers and to include gender and equality concerns in all their activities. Efforts include requiring trade unions involved in the programmes to ensure that women constitute a certain percentage of participants, and the organization of specific gender awareness-raising

Table 6.2. Women on the national governing bodies of national unions and union confederations, latest year available (selected Latin American countries)

Country	Year	Organization	Leadership level	Total	Women	Women as % of total
Argentina	1994	General Labour Confederation	National governing council	24	0	0
Aruba	1998	Trade union	Executives	11	1	9.1
Barbados	1998	Congress of Trade Unions and Staff Associations of Barbados	Executives	65	19	29.2
Bolivia	1997	Bolivian Workers' Federation	Executive committee	40	1	2.5
Brazil	1998	United Workers' Confederation	Executives	–	–	30.0
Chile[1]	1998	Amalgamated Workers' Confederation	National executive board	7	2	28.6
		National Countryside Commission	Presidency	1	0	0
Colombia	1997	Colombian Workers' Confederation	National executive board	87	6	6.9
		Amalgamated Workers' Confederation	Executive committee and national board	90	8	8.9
Cuba	1996	Cuban Workers' Confederation	Secretariat of the 17th Congress	20	5	25.0
Dominica	1997	Civil Service Association	Executives	13	7	53.8
		Waterfront and Allied Workers' Union	Executives	11	2	18.2
		Dominica Trade Union	Executives	13	2	15.4
		Dominica Teachers' Association	Executives	28	8	28.6
		Dominica Amalgamated Workers' Union	Executives	10	6	60.0
Dominican Rep.[2]	1991	Amalgamated Workers' Confederation	Executive bureau	11	2	18.2
Mexico	1991	Mexican Workers' Confederation	National executive bureau	47	2	4.3
Nicaragua[3]	1993	National Workers' Confederation	National executive board	12	3	25.0
Panama	1997	Alliance of seven confederations	Governing boards	88	12	13.6
Paraguay	1997	Combined Workers' Confederation	National executive board	19	2	10.5
		National Workers' Confederation	National executive board	25	0	0
		Paraguayan Workers' Confederation	National executive board	27	3	11.1
		State Union Confederation	National executive board	14	2	14.3
Peru	1994	General Confederation of Peruvian Workers	Executives	53	2	3.8
		Peruvian Workers' Confederation	Executives	16	5	31.3
		Peruvian Farmers' Confederation	Executives	23	3	13.0

Table 6.2. (cont.)

Country	Year	Organization	Leadership level	Total	Women	Women as % of total
Saint Lucia	1997	St. Lucia Civil Service Association	Executives	10	4	40.0
		St. Lucia Teachers' Union	Executives	7	3	42.8
		National Workers' Union	Executives	22	5	22.7
Uruguay	1998	Inter-Union Workers' Assembly	Executive secretariat	13	6	7.6
Venezuela[4]	1998	Venezuelan Workers' Confederation	National executives	17	1	35.3
		General Confederation of Workers	National executives	24	2	8.3
		Venezuela Amalgamated Workers' Confederation	National executives	15	3	20.0
		CODESA	National executives	11	1	9.0

[1] Largest confederation. [2] There are other confederations in the country. [3] Confederation of longest standing. [4] Confederation with the most members.

Source: ECLAC: *Participation and leadership in Latin America and the Caribbean: Gender indicators* (Santiago, Chile, 1999).

activities. Detailed statistics are maintained on women's involvement in all ILO projects intended for workers.

SOCIAL DIALOGUE ON GENDER EQUALITY

The inadequate representation of women, particularly at the decision-making level in labour administrations, employers' organizations and trade unions, and the scarcity of gender concerns being dealt with by tripartite social dialogue institutions or being brought to the collective bargaining table, are interconnected. The fewer the number of women involved, the more difficult it often is for their voices to be heard in what are essentially male-constructed institutions. Yet, with the continued growth of women's labour force participation and their essential contribution to household income, their potential for strengthening the role and relevance of the social partners and tripartism cannot afford to remain underdeveloped. Women's current disadvantageous position in many aspects of the labour market makes overcoming the obstacles to their participation in social dialogue institutions a considerable challenge.

A combination of creative and innovative approaches and political commitment are needed to transform the structures of employers' organizations, trade unions and tripartite bodies to make them gender sensitive and responsible. Box 6.1 shows a good example.

Box 6.1. Strengthening social dialogue on gender issues
in the Southern Cone

During the 1990s, the ILO launched a programme to promote and strengthen social dialogue on gender issues in the labour market for the four MERCOSUR countries (Common Market of the Southern Cone, comprising Argentina, Brazil, Paraguay and Uruguay), with Chile as an associate member. Action plans for national follow-up activities were elaborated. A follow-up programme at national and regional level has been actively promoted by the ILO. In each country, a working group was set up to supervise the adaptation of an ILO training module on women workers' rights to the national situation. A tripartite workshop was organized to present and discuss the findings of the national modules and to develop a work plan adapted to each country. The ILO provided technical input and organized study tours, and regional monitoring and evaluation seminars. In 1998, a course on international labour standards and women workers' rights for participants from the tripartite commissions created in the five countries was held at the ILO Training Centre in Turin, Italy.

As a result of this programme, tripartite commissions on gender equality were created for the first time in all the countries involved or, as in the case in Chile, a commission was strengthened. In Argentina, Paraguay and Uruguay, this happened as a direct effect of programme implementation; in Brazil, it was also the product of another ILO initiative to improve the application of Convention No. 111.

The tripartite commissions play an advocacy and advisory role in relation to national policy-making concerning the promotion of equality of opportunity

---

for women in the world of work. This includes identifying areas of priority concern to all parties involved, formulating recommendations for policy-making and programming, and coordinating certain strategic projects and actions. They also play an advocacy role towards the wider public and within other governmental bodies. In each country, the commission focuses on specific issues: in Brazil, on race and gender discrimination; in Chile, on maternity protection, sexual harassment and the promotion of gender equality clauses in legal texts; in Uruguay, on gender gaps in vocational training, for example. Within this framework, data collection and research were sponsored and the findings were disseminated through seminars and workshops. In Brazil and Chile, the national commissions have been successful in launching similar tripartite bodies at regional, state and provincial level.

The results of these major outputs of the programme can be summarized as follows:

- greater political visibility of gender equality issues at national level, including gender discrimination cases in the labour market;
- social dialogue strengthened at national level; coordination and cooperation mechanisms set up to define and implement programmes and activities for promoting gender equality; networking relationships initiated or strengthened;
- increased commitment and technical capacity of individuals to actively mainstream a gender perspective in their respective institutions and organizations;
- more attention to women's issues at the sectoral level; women's committees strengthened within the employers' and workers' organizations, as a direct consequence of the growing importance attached to equality issues at the national policy level; and
- a regional network among tripartite committees in the four Southern Cone countries, set up under the umbrella of MERCOSUR.

The tripartite commissions described in box 6.1 have proved to be good-practice examples for social dialogue in general and an effective vehicle for including gender issues in the political arena. Gender is a topic on which the different social partners can easily and efficiently share an interest, set up common goals and strategies, and implement joint action. The intensive cooperation among different ILO units for launching and monitoring the process was clearly an important factor in the success of the programme. Key elements of this process include the following:

- the stimulating effect of regular regional and international tripartite meetings;
- the investment in training of individuals as gender advocates;
- the focus on building networks at the national and regional levels;
- the reference to a broader integration framework such as MERCOSUR; and

• the combination of a demand with a supply-driven approach to gender equality as part of sectoral and national labour policies.

However, the challenge remains to institutionalize the systematic mainstreaming of gender in national employment policies and programmes. This includes proposing a change of agenda in order to meet the specific needs of disadvantaged groups of women or men. Whether the tripartite commissions on gender equality are able to strengthen their potential will depend on the political, technical and financial commitment of national policy-makers.

CONCLUSION

International labour standards on gender issues are key to attaining equality of opportunity and treatment for all women, and for enabling women to realize their potential in management and decision-making. Moreover, ILO programmes and projects developed and implemented since 1995 approach gender equality in the world of work as a matter of human rights, but also as critical for sustainable development, the effective use of human resources, and family and child welfare. Both the quantitative and qualitative dimensions of employment are addressed, as is women's empowerment. Current targeted assistance focuses on employment creation and poverty alleviation, and covers the promotion of job equality and the provision of social protection to specific groups of women workers. Activities related to women workers' rights are given importance, as is the fight against the trafficking of women and children.

Increasingly, a gender perspective is being systematically incorporated or mainstreamed into all ILO programmes and projects, and many interventions take a holistic approach and relate simultaneously to the various critical areas of the Beijing Platform for Action.

The ILO attached great importance to Beijing+5. A preparatory symposium organized by the ILO's Governing Body in March 2000 addressed ways in which the ILO's global objective of decent work for men and women could help accelerate the implementation of the Platform for Action. The primary goal of the ILO today is to promote opportunities for women and men to obtain decent and productive work in conditions of freedom, equity, security and human dignity. All those who work have rights at work. This applies not only to wage workers in registered companies, but also to self-employed and casual workers in the informal economy and to the hidden, predominately female workers of the "care" economy.

Decent work means meeting or exceeding core labour standards, in other words, setting a threshold for work and employment which embodies universal rights and which, for a given society, is consistent with its values and goals. Achieving decent work involves ensuring respect for fundamental principles and rights at work, promoting employment creation, providing social protection, and engaging in social dialogue. At the heart of the ILO's decent work agenda are the issues of gender equality and development. Enhancing women's role in decision-making and mangement is key to successfully addressing inequalities in the labour market.

Notes

[1] Part II *(a)*.

[2] Article 1, 1*(a)*.

[3] Article 1, 3.

[4] ILO: *Equality in employment and occupation*, General Survey by the Committee of Experts on the Application of Conventions and Recommendations, Report III (Part 4B), International Labour Conference, 75th Session, Geneva, 1988; idem: *Equality in employment and occupation*, Special Survey by the Committee of Experts on the Application of Conventions and Recommendations, Report III (Part 4B), International Labour Conference, 83rd Session, Geneva, 1996.

[5] Article 1*(a)*.

[6] ILO: *Equal remuneration*, General Survey by the Committee of Experts on the Application of Conventions and Recommendations, Report III (Part 4B), International Labour Conference, 72nd Session, Geneva, 1986.

[7] Article 2(1).

[8] Article 3.

[9] Women Watch: "Beijing+5: What and when". http://www.un.org/womenwatch/followup/beijing5/index.html; UN News: "5 Year Review: Beijing+5". http://www.un.org/womenwatch/followup.

[10] China, Egypt, El Salvador, Hungary, India, Mali, Suriname, Viet Nam and Zimbabwe.

[11] Geneva, ILO, 2000.

[12] ILO: *Decent work*, Report of the Director-General, International Labour Conference, 87th Session, Geneva, 1999.

[13] ILO, Bureau for Employers' Activities: *National workshops on women and gender issues through employers' organizations*. http://ILO.org/public/english/dialogue/actemp/conf/1998/recent.htm#r20.

SELECT BIBLIOGRAPHY

Adler, N. J.; Izraeli, D. N. (eds.): *Competitive frontiers: Women managers in a global economy* (Cambridge, Mass., Basil Blackwell, 1994).

Affirmative Action Agency, Australia: *Annual Report 1995-96* (Sydney, 1996).

Amos-Wilson, P. M.: "Some issues concerning women in senior management: A case study from Ghana", in *Public Administration and Development* (London), Vol. 19, No. 3, 1999, pp. 217-219.

Anker, R.: *Gender and jobs: Sex segregation of occupations in the world* (Geneva, ILO, 1998).

de Avelar, S.: *Women in economic decision-making in Brazil: A glass ceiling report*, Working paper prepared for an Expert Group Meeting on Women and Economic Decision-Making organized by the United Nations' Division for the Advancement of Women, New York, Nov. 1994.

Bertino, D.; Silvera, S.; Ulshoefer, P.: *Reorientación profesional para la mujer*, Working paper, Equality for Women in Employment Departmental Project (Geneva, ILO, 1994).

Brennan, M. B.: "Women chemists reconsidering careers at research universities", in *Chemical and Engineering News* (Washington, DC), Vol. 74, No. 24, June 1996, pp. 8-15.

Bruegel, I.: "Globalization, feminization and pay inequalities in London and the UK", in J. Gregory, R. Sales and A. Hegewish (eds.): *Women, work and inequality: The challenge of equal pay in a deregulated labour market* (New York, St. Martins Press, 1999).

Brush, C.: "Women's entrepreneurship", in ILO Enterprise Forum: *A new spirit of enterprise: Articles and cases* (Geneva, ILO, 1999).

Bullock, S.: *Women and work* (London, Zed Books, 1994).

Bundesministerium für Bildung, Wissenschaft, Forschung und Technologie: *Total E-Quality: Chancengleichheit im Unternehmen Oaradigmenwechsel in der Personalpolitik* (Brussels, European Commission, 1997).

Burke, R. J.; Mckeen, C. A.: "Career development among managerial and professional women", in Davidson and Burke (eds.): *Women in management: Current research issues* (London, Paul Chapman, 1994), pp. 65-79.

Byrne, E. M.: *Investing in women: Technical and scientific training for economic development*, Training Discussion Paper No. 62, Training Policies Branch (Geneva, ILO, 1991).

Canadian Human Rights Commission (CHRC): *Annual Report 1999* (Ottawa, 2000).

Carnevale, P.; Stone, S. C.: "Diversity beyond the golden rule", in *Training and Development*, Oct. 1994, pp. 22-39.

Chan, A.; Lee, J.: "Women executives in a newly industrialized economy: The Singapore scenario", in N. J. Adler, and D. N. Izraeli (eds.): *Competitive frontiers: Women managers in a global economy* (Cambridge, Mass., Basil Blackwell, 1994), pp. 127-142.

Chari, U. A.: *Positive action measures to promote the equality of women in employment in Zimbabwe*, Working Paper No. 16, Equality for Women in Employment Interdepartmental Project (Geneva, ILO, 1993).

Charlesworth, K.: *A question of balance? A survey of managers' changing professional and personal roles* (London, Institute of Management, 1997).

Collinson, M.: "It's only Dick: The sexual harassment of women managers in insurance sales", in *Work, Employment and Society* (London), Vol. 10, No. 1, 1996, pp. 29-56.

Davidson, M. J.; Burke, R. J. (eds.): *Women in management: Current research issues* (London, Paul Chapman, 1994).

Dulude, L.: *Seniority and employment equity for women* (Kingston, Ontario, IRC Press, 1995).

—: *Participation and leadership in Latin America and the Caribbean: Gender indicators* (Santiago, Chile, 1999).

Edwards, C.; Woodall, J.; Welchman, R.: "Organizational change and women managers' careers: The restructuring of disadvantage?", in *Employee Relations* (Manchester), Vol. 18, No. 5, 1996, pp. 22-45.

Fagenson, E. A. (ed.): *Women and work, Vol. 4: Women in management – Trends, issues and challenges in managerial diversity* (Newbury Park, Ca., Sage Publications, 1993).

Ferreira, S.; Corbo, R.: *Situación actual del empleo de las mujeres en el Uruguay* (Montevideo, Ministry of Labour and Social Security, National Employment Office, 1996).

Fletcher, J. F.: *Men and women working together: The KOM programme* (Uppsala, Ord & Form AB, 1994).

Furchtgott-Roth, D.; Stolba, C.: *Women's figures: An illustrated guide to the economic progress of women in America* (Washington, DC, AEI Press, 1999).

Gershenberg, I.: "Gender, training, and the creation of a managerial elite: Multinationals and other firms in Jamaica", in *Journal of Developing Areas* (Macomb), Vol. 28, No. 3, 1994, pp. 313-325.

Glezer, H.; Wolcott, I.: *Work and family life: Reciprocal effects*, Paper presented at the Sixth Australian Institute of Family Studies Conference on Changing Families, Challenging Futures, Melbourne, Nov. 1998. Published by Australian Institute of Family Studies. http://www.aifs.org.au/institute/afrc6papers/glezer.html.

González, R. B.: *Participación de la mujer ejecutiva en Colombia*, Working paper commissioned by the ILO (Bogotá, ILO, 1996).

Heller, L.: *Porqué llegan las que llegan?* (Buenos Aires, Feminaria Editoria, 1996).

Horrell, S.; Rubery, J.; Burchell, B.: "Gender and skills", in *Work, Employment and Society* (Cambridge), Vol. 4, No. 2, 1990, pp. 189-216.

Horowitz, F. M.; Bowmaker-Falconer, A.; Searll, P.: "Human resource development and managing diversity in South Africa", in *International Journal of Manpower* (Bradford), Vol. 17, 1996, No. 4/5, pp. 134-151.

Institute of Management: *Labour market trends* (London, 1998).

International Labour Organization (ILO): *Action plan on gender mainstreaming and gender equality* (Geneva, 1999).

—: *Conditions of Work Digest: Combating sexual harassment at work*, Vol. 11, No. 1 (Geneva, 1992).

—: *Economically active population*, 1950-2010, Vols. II-V (Geneva, 1996).

—: *Equal remuneration*, General Survey by the Committee of Experts on the Application of Conventions and Recommendations, Report III (Part 4B), International Labour Conference, 72nd Session, Geneva, 1986.

—: *Equality in employment and occupation*, General Survey of the Committee of Experts on the Application of Conventions and Recommendations, Report III, (Part 4B), International Labour Conference, 75th Session, Geneva, 1988.

—: *Equality in employment and occupation*, Special Survey by the Committee of Experts on the Application of Conventions and Recommendations, Report III (Part 4B), International Labour Conference, 83rd Session, Geneva, 1996.

—: *Gender issues in employers' activities* (Geneva, 1998).

—: *Gender! Partnership of equals* (Geneva, 2000).

—: *Key Indicators of the Labour Market 1999* (Geneva, 1999).

—: SEGREGAT database.

—: *Women in technical trades* (Geneva, 1990).

—: *World Employment Report 1998-99: Employability in the global economy – How training matters* (Geneva, 1999).

—: *Yearbook of Labour Statistics* (Geneva, 1996; 1999; 2000).

—: Bureau of Employers' Activities (ACT/EMP): *National workshops on women and gender issues through employers' organizations*. http://ILO.org/public/english/dialogue/actemp/conf/1998/recent.htm#r20.

Imada, S.: "Female labor force after the enforcement of the equal employment opportunity law", in *Japan Labor Bulletin* (Tokyo), Vol. 36, No. 8, 1996, pp. 5-8.

Inter-American Development Bank: *Women in the Americas: Bridging the gender gap* (Washington, DC, 1995).

Jacobsen, J. P.; Levin, L. M.: "Effects of intermittent labour force attachment on women's earnings", in *Monthly Labor Review* (Washington, DC), Vol. 118, No. 9, 1995, pp. 14-19.

Japan Institute of Labour, Ministry of Labour: *White Paper on labour 1991: Present state and problems of females and young workers – Outline of the analysis* (Tokyo, 1992).

Kandola, R.; Fullerton, J.: "Diversity: More than just an empty slogan", in *Personnel Management* (London), Vol. 26, No. 4, 1994, pp. 46-50.

Koch, U.: "Equality issue lands on the manager's desk", in *Nordic Labour Journal*, Vol. 2, 1998, pp. 9-11.

Lam, A.: "Equal employment opportunities for Japanese women: Changing company practice", in J. Hunter (ed.): *Japanese women working* (London and New York, Routledge, 1993), pp. 197-223.

Larwood, L.: "Career paths of successful executives: Do they differ by sex?" in D. M. Saunders (ed.): *Fairness in employee selection Vol. 1: New approaches to employment management* (Greenwich, Ct., Jai Press, 1992), pp. 87-104.

Lie, S. S.; Malik, L.; Harris, D.: *World Yearbook of Education 1994: The gender gap in higher education* (London and Philadelphia, Kogan Page, 1994).

Lim, L. L.: *More and better jobs for women: An action guide* (Geneva, ILO, 1996).

Masanja, V. G.: *Girls, mathematics and science: Problems and strategies to overcome them*, Paper presented to the Seminar on Girls' Education in Anglophone Africa, Nairobi, 16-20 May 1994, organized by the Forum for African Women Educationalists (FAWE) and Higher Education for Development and Cooperation of Ireland (HEDCO).

Mass, M. et al.: *Rompiendo el techo de cristal: Las mujeres en el management en Argentina*, ILO working paper (Geneva, ILO, 1998).

Mattis, M. C.: "Organizational initiatives in the USA for advancing managerial women", in M. J. Davidson and R. J. Burke (eds.): *Women in management: Current research issues* (London, Paul Chapman, 1994), pp. 261-276.

McDougall, M.: "Equal opportunities versus managing diversity: Another challenge for public sector management?", in *International Journal of Public Management* (Glasgow), Vol. 9, No. 5/6, 1996, pp. 62-72.

Ministry of Social Affairs and Health, Finland: *Equal rights, equal responsibilities, equal opportunities* (Helsinki, 1994).

Moskos, C.: "Affirmative action: The army's success....", cited in A. M. Joseph and H. A. Coleman: *Affirmative action and economics: A framework for analysis*, in *Public Productivity and Management Review* (Thousand Oaks, New Delhi and London), Vol. 20, No. 3, 1997, pp. 258-271.

National Foundation for Women Business Owners (NFWBO): *Characteristics of women entrepreneurs worldwide*, Research Summary, released 5 Mar. 1999 (Washington, DC).

National Partnership for Women and Families: "Affirmative action programs help women shatter the glass ceiling". http://www.nationalpartnership.org/workand family/affirmact/aa_glass.htm.

Norton, B.; Tivey, J.: *Management directions, Vol. 8: Mentoring* (Corby, United Kingdom, Institute of Management, 1995).

Odaga, A.; Heneveld, W.: *Girls and schools in sub-Saharan Africa: From analysis to action*, World Bank Technical Paper No. 298, African Technical Department Series (Washington, DC, World Bank, 1995).

Pardo, P.: "La mujer en las decisiones económicas", in M. E. Valenzuela (ed.): *Igualdad de oportunidades para la mujer en el trabajo* (Santiago, Servicio Nacional de la Mujer, 1996).

Pollack, E. M.: "Mujeres y mercado de trabajo: Desafíos para una participación con equidad", in Valenzuela (ed.), 1996.

Posadskaya, A.; Zakharova, N.: *To be a manager: Changes for women in the USSR*, Discussion Paper No. 65, Training Policies Branch (Geneva, ILO, 1990).

Quack, S.; Hancké, B.: *Women in decision-making in finance*, Report prepared for the use of the European Commission, Directorate General V, Industrial Relations, Employment and Social Affairs (Berlin, Wissenschaftszentrum Berlin für Sozialforschung, 1997).

Ramirez, S.: "En las altas esferas", in *Fempress*, No. 206, 1998.

Roosevelt, R. T.: "Managing diversity: A conceptual framework", in S. Jackson et al.: *Diversity in the workplace: Human resource initiatives* (New York, Blackwell, 1992).

Rosener, J.: "Ways women lead", in *Harvard Business Review*, Nov./Dec. 1990, pp. 119-125.

Royal Bank of Canada: *The Diversity Factor*, Vol. 4, No. 1, 1995.

Sieh Lei, M. L.: *Strategies to reach the top for women in management: Perspectives from ASEAN*, Working Paper No. 114, Salaried Employees and Professional Workers Branch (Geneva, ILO, 1998).

Siengthai, S.: *Women and economic decision-making in international financial institutions and transnational corporations in Thailand*, Paper prepared for the Expert Group Meeting on Women and Economic Decision-Making in International Financial Institutions and Transnational Corporations, United Nations Division for the Advancement of Women, Boston, Mass., Nov. 1996.

Singh, J.: *Women graduates and the labour market: The Commonwealth experience*, Working paper of the Commonwealth Secretariat for the 5th UNESCO/NGO Collective Consultation on Higher Education: The Consequences of Change for Graduate Employment, Paris, Feb. 1996.

Snyder, M. M.; Osland J.; Hauter, L.: "Personnel practice in careers of women at the top in government and business in Nicaragua and Costa Rica", in *Public Administration and Development* (Chichester), Vol. 15, No. 4, 1995, pp. 397-416.

Teicher, T.; Speritt, K.: "From equal opportunity to diversity management: The Australian experience", in *International Journal of Manpower* (Bradford), Vol. 17, No. 4/5, 1996, pp. 109-133.

Thomas, C.; Taylor, R.: *Enforcement of equality provisions for women workers*, Working Paper No. 20, Equality for Women in Employment Interdepartmental Project (Geneva, ILO, 1994).

Timmerman, G.; Bajema, C.: "Sexual harassment in the European workforce", research project commissioned by the European Commission and conducted by the University of Groningen, Netherlands, Oslo, Apr. 1997. http://www.nikk.uio.no/publikationer/nyhetsblad_e.html.

Trades Union Congress (TUC), United Kingdom: *Professional and managerial staffs – trends and prospects*, Report prepared by the Labour Research Branch Department for the TUC Professional and Managerial Staffs Symposium, London, Feb. 1997.

Traves, J.; Brockbank, A.; Tomlinson, F.: "Careers of women managers in the retail industry", in *Service Industries Journal* (London), Vol. 17, No. 1, 1997, pp. 133-154.

United Nations Development Programme (UNDP): *Human Development Report 1999* (New York and Oxford, Oxford University Press, 1999).

United Nations Economic Commission for Latin America and the Caribbean (ECLAC): *Access to power and participation in decision-making in Latin America and the Caribbean: Policies for gender equity looking to the year 2000*, Seventh Session of the Regional Conference on the Integration of Women into the Economic and Social Development of Latin America and the Caribbean, Chile, Nov. 1997. http://www.eclac.org/English/Meetings/confwomen/l-1063-i.htm.

United Nations Educational, Scientific and Cultural Organization (UNESCO): *World Education Report 1995* (Paris, 1995).

—: *Statistical Yearbook* (Paris), various years.

—: *World Science Report* (Paris, 1996).

Universidad de Chile: *Las mujeres en la toma de decisiones económicas* (Santiago, 1995).

Venkata Ratman, C. S.; Chandra, V.: "Sources of diversity and the challenge before human resource management in India", in *International Journal of Manpower* (Bradford), Vol. 17, No. 4/5, 1996, pp. 76-108.

Vinnicombe, S.; Colwill, N. L.: *The essence of women in management* (London, Prentice Hall, 1995).

Welbourne, T. M.: *Wall Street likes its women: An examination of women in the top management teams of initial public offerings*, Working Paper 99-07, Centre for Advanced Human Resource Studies (CAHRS), Cornell University. http://www.ilr. cornell.edu/depts/cahrs/PDFs/WorkingPapers/WP99-07.pdf.

Wiig, M: *Women in the bank group: A review of progress, issues and future actions* (Washington DC, World Bank, 1994).

Wilson, P. (ed.): *Salaried and professional women: Relevant statistics* (Washington, DC, AFL-CIO, 1999).

Women Watch: "Beijing+5: What and when". http://www.un.org/womenwatch/ followup/ beijing5/index.html; UN News: "5 Year Review: Beijing+5". http:// www.un.org/ womenwatch/followup.

Gender disparity: HDI, GDI and GEM rankings by country

HDI ranking	Country or territory	GDI ranking	HDI minus GDI ranking[1]	GEM ranking
1	Canada	1	0	4
2	Norway	2	0	1
3	United States	3	0	8
4	Japan	8	−4	38
5	Belgium	6	−1	17
6	Sweden	5	1	2
7	Australia	4	3	9
8	Netherlands	9	−1	10
9	Iceland	7	2	7
10	United Kingdom	11	−1	16
11	France	10	1	36
12	Switzerland	12	0	14
13	Finland	13	0	6
14	Germany	15	−1	5
15	Denmark	14	1	3
16	Austria	17	−1	12
17	Luxembourg	19	−2	15
18	New Zealand	16	2	11
19	Italy	18	1	26
20	Ireland	20	0	20
21	Spain	21	0	22
22	Singapore	22	0	32
23	Israel	23	0	37
24	Hong Kong, China	24	0	...
25	Brunei Darussalam	25	0	...
26	Cyprus	...	...	68
27	Greece	26	0	66
28	Portugal	28	−1	19
29	Barbados	27	1	...
30	Korea, Rep. of	30	−1	78
31	Bahamas	29	1	13
32	Malta	32	−1	...
33	Slovenia	31	1	42
34	Chile	33	0	54
35	Kuwait	35	−1	72
36	Czech Rep.	34	1	27
37	Bahrain	38	−2	...

Breaking through the glass ceiling

HDI ranking	Country or territory	GDI ranking	HDI minus GDI ranking[1]	GEM ranking
38	Antigua and Barbuda	...	...	...
39	Argentina	37	0	...
40	Uruguay	36	2	56
41	Qatar	41	−2	...
42	Slovakia	39	1	34
43	United Arab Emirates	45	−4	96
44	Poland	40	2	35
45	Costa Rica	42	1	23
46	Trinidad and Tobago	44	0	24
47	Hungary	43	2	48
48	Venezuela	46	0	43
49	Panama	47	0	47
50	Mexico	48	0	33
51	St. Kitts and Nevis	...	...	...
52	Grenada	...	...	...
53	Dominica	...	...	...
54	Estonia	49	0	46
55	Croatia	50	0	...
56	Malaysia	52	−1	52
57	Colombia	51	1	31
58	Cuba	53	0	21
59	Mauritius	57	−3	61
60	Belarus	54	1	...
61	Fiji	60	−4	79
62	Lithuania	55	2	28
63	Bulgaria	56	2	49
64	Suriname	...	...	60
65	Libyan Arab Jamahiriya	68	−9	...
66	Seychelles	...	...	...
67	Thailand	58	2	64
68	Romania	59	2	67
69	Lebanon	66	−4	...
70	Western Samoa	...	...	...
71	Russian Federation	61	2	...
72	Ecuador	70	−6	29
73	Former Yugoslav Rep. of Macedonia	63	2	...
74	Latvia	62	4	30
75	St. Vincent and the Grenadines	...	...	...
76	Kazakhstan	64	3	...
77	Philippines	65	3	45
78	Saudi Arabia	78	−9	...
79	Brazil	67	3	70
80	Peru	71	0	63
81	St. Lucia	...	...	...
82	Jamaica	69	3	...
83	Belize	...	...	39
84	Paraguay	74	−1	65

HDI ranking	Country or territory	GDI ranking	HDI minus GDI ranking[1]	GEM ranking
85	Georgia	...	...	73
86	Turkey	73	1	85
87	Armenia	72	3	...
88	Dominican Rep.	75	1	25
89	Oman	85	–8	...
90	Sri Lanka	76	2	80
91	Ukraine	...	...	...
92	Uzbekistan	...	...	...
93	Maldives	77	2	76
94	Jordan	...	...	98
95	Iran, Islamic Rep. of	81	–1	88
96	Turkmenistan	...	...	...
97	Kyrgyzstan	...	...	...
98	China	79	2	40
99	Guyana	83	–1	57
100	Albania	80	3	...
101	South Africa	84	0	18
102	Tunisia	87	–2	75
103	Azerbaijan	82	4	...
104	Moldova, Rep. of	86	1	...
105	Indonesia	88	0	71
106	Cape Verde	90	–1	62
107	El Salvador	89	1	41
108	Tajikistan	92	–1	...
109	Algeria	93	–1	92
110	Viet Nam	91	2	...
111	Syrian Arab Rep.	95	–1	81
112	Bolivia	94	1	...
113	Swaziland	96	0	69
114	Honduras	98	–1	53
115	Namibia	97	1	...
116	Vanuatu	...	...	...
117	Guatemala	101	–2	44
118	Solomon Islands	...	...	...
119	Mongolia	99	1	...
120	Egypt	103	–2	86
121	Nicaragua	100	2	...
122	Botswana	102	1	51
123	Sao Tome and Principe	...	...	...
124	Gabon	...	...	...
125	Iraq	...	...	...
126	Morocco	106	–2	84
127	Lesotho	105	0	55
128	Myanmar	104	2	...
129	Papua New Guinea	107	0	91
130	Zimbabwe	108	0	58
131	Equatorial Guinea	...	...	89

Breaking through the glass ceiling

HDI ranking	Country or territory	GDI ranking	HDI minus GDI ranking[1]	GEM ranking
132	India	112	−3	95
133	Ghana	109	1	...
134	Cameroon	110	1	87
135	Congo	111	1	...
136	Kenya	113	0	...
137	Cambodia	...	...	...
138	Pakistan	116	−2	101
139	Comoros	114	1	...
140	Lao People's Dem. Rep.	115	1	...
141	Dem. Rep. of Congo	...	...	...
142	Sudan	117	0	97
143	Togo	118	0	100
144	Nepal	121	−2	...
145	Bhutan	119	1	...
146	Nigeria	120	1	...
147	Madagascar	...	...	...
148	Yemen	128	−6	...
149	Mauritania	122	1	99
150	Bangladesh	123	1	83
151	Zambia	125	0	82
152	Haiti	124	2	...
153	Senegal	127	0	...
154	Côte d'Ivoire	130	−2	...
155	Benin	129	0	...
156	Tanzania, United. Rep. of	126	4	...
157	Djibouti	...	...	...
158	Uganda	131	0	...
159	Malawi	132	0	90
160	Angola	...	...	...
161	Guinea	134	−1	...
162	Chad	135	−1	...
163	Gambia	133	2	93
164	Rwanda	...	...	...
165	Central African Rep.	137	−1	94
166	Mali	136	1	74
167	Eritrea	...	...	50
168	Guinea-Bissau	139	−1	...
169	Mozambique	138	1	59
170	Burundi	140	0	...
171	Burkina Faso	141	0	77
172	Ethiopia	142	0	...
173	Niger	143	0	102
174	Sierra Leone	...	...	...

... = data not available. GDI: Gender-related Development Index; HDI Human Development Index; GEM: Gender Empowerment Measure.

[1] The HDI minus GDI rankings used in this column are those recalculated for the universe of 143 countries. A positive figure indicates that the GDI ranking is better than the HDI ranking, a negative figure the opposite.

Source: UNDP: *Human Development Report 1999* (New York, 1999), pp. 138-145.